THE QUESTION AND ANSWER BOOK OF

MONEY

AND

INVESTING

THE QUESTION AND ANSWER BOOK OF
MONEY
AND
INVESTING

VICTOR L. HARPER • **ARTHUR S. BRINKLEY**
WITH SARAH E. DALE

ADAMS MEDIA CORPORATION
Holbrook, Massachusetts

Published by Adams Media Corporation
260 Center Street, Holbrook, MA 02343

ISBN: 1-55850-438-9

Printed in the United States of America.

J   I   H   G   F   E   D   C

Library of Congress Cataloging-in-Publication Data
Harper, Victor L.
    The question and answer book of money and investing : with over 1000 answers
to the most commonly asked questions about money, investing, and personal finance / Victor
L. Harper, Arthur S. Brinkley, with Sarah E. Dale
    p.   cm.
    Includes index.
    ISBN 1-55850-438-9
    1. Investments—Handbooks, manuals, etc. 2. Finance, Personal—Handbooks,
manuals, etc. I. Brinkley, Arthur S. II. Dale, Sarah E. III. Title.
HG4527.H333   1995
?32.6'78—dc20   95-9329
                                                                    CIP

This book is available at quantity discounts for bulk purchases.
For information, call 1-800-872-5627
(in Massachusetts, call 617-767-8100).

Visit our home page at http://www.adamsmedia.com

To my blue chips . . .
Anne
Kathryn
Landon
Frances
—VLH

To Stacy, Maguire, and Archer
—ASB

To Mum, Dad, Jamie, Rob, Al, and Ben
—SED

TABLE OF CONTENTS

ACKNOWLEDGMENTS

This book arose from others' ideas and input. Richard J. Staron, senior editor with Adams Publishing, created the idea of an investment book with a question-and-answer format and offered us the opportunity to write it. We discussed the project over several months, and we became convinced of the validity of the idea that people learn by asking questions and getting good answers.

After almost two years of diligent work, the idea has become a reality. We thank Dick for his inspiration, support, . . . and pushing at times.

We would be remiss in not thanking Alice Manning, who spent many hours editing the questions and answers and improving the way many of them were expressed.

We must thank the clients we have had during our many years of investment experience as it is from them that we have learned the questions that need to be answered. We also thank the many people who have helped us get the answers. It would be impossible to personally thank all of the clients, research analysts, mutual fund personnel, associates, and friends who have taught us, allowed us to tap their knowledge, reviewed our work, and guided us so as to make this book a reality. Nevertheless, special thanks go to: Adrian L. Banky, Management Consultant and former Executive Vice President and General Manager of the Securities Industry Association; J. Alfred Broaddus, President, Federal Reserve Bank of Richmond; Eliott T. Cooper, Former Business Editor, *Richmond Times Dispatch*; Richardson A. Dickson, Registered Option's Principal, Scott & Stringfellow, Inc.; Richard B. Fisher, Chairman, Federated Securities Corp.; Franklin B. Heiner, First Vice President, Retirement and Estate Services, Scott & Stringfellow, Inc.; Michael D. Johnston, CPA, Vice President, Finance and Tax, Scott &

Stringfellow, Inc.; Harold T. Lipscomb, Assistant Vice President, Federal Reserve Bank of Richmond; Richard J. Malek, CLU ChFU, I.M.A., Inc.; Upton S. Martin, Vice President, Signet Bank; Laura Carey Miller, CLU, I.M.A, Inc.; Peter F. Muratore, President, Quest for Value Distributors, C. Wayne Penick, Executive Vice President, Signet Bank; C. Eddie Williams, Graphic Designer, Scott & Stringfellow, Inc.

We do want to thank our associates at Scott & Stringfellow, Inc. Its leadership—S. Buford Scott, Chairman; Frederic Scott Bocock, Vice Chairman; and William P. Schubmehl, President and Chief Executive Officer—has developed an outstanding brokerage firm, and one that gives people like us the opportunity to expand our horizons and write. Many other investment brokers and associates have also been very helpful, answering our questions and reviewing the way we answered many of them.

The most important thanks go to our families, who gave us the encouragement and support we needed to spend those long hours researching, outlining, writing, and editing. Without their support, this book would have continued to be a dream.

Chapter 1

Why a Question and Answer Book?

Q: Why a question and answer book?

A: When individuals want more information on subjects of interest, they ask questions. The Q & A format is the clearest, most straightforward method of presenting information. The Q & A format is one of the easiest ways to teach and to learn.

Q: Why a Q & A money book?

A: Individuals have become increasingly more interested in money and investments. They insist on *understanding* more about their investments and investment alternatives. This interest is demonstrated by the increasing demand for financial books, financial magazines, financial news programs on radio and television, and expanded business sections of newspapers.

Q: What are the forces driving the increasing interest in money and investing?

A: The forces driving this increased interest in money and investing include:

Demographics: An increasing percentage of the population is entering the peak saving and investing years.

Greater uncertainty of returns: The performance of all savings and investments has become less predictable in recent years. The returns on even "safe" investments like bank deposits have changed radically as a result of wide swings in interest rates, converting millions of savers to investors. Individuals have thus demanded a better understanding of their money and investment alternatives so they can improve their returns.

Uncertain financial outlook: Many individuals are perhaps less confident that their future financial security will be assured by sources such as Social Security and employer retirement plans. Because of this uncertainty, many individuals believe they must provide for their own financial security.

More involvement in investment decisions: Individuals appear to be less willing to simply deposit their money with banks or brokers and turn their attention elsewhere. They demand to *understand* and *participate* more actively in the management of their money.

Q: Why not write a conventional book?

A: No matter how hard their authors try to remain clear, many informational books intimidate readers with page after page and chapter after chapter of dry, involved explanations. What individuals really want is to have their questions answered, not to read lengthy explanations. In this book, we have attempted to organize the information individuals seek about their money and investing in a simple, approachable format.

Q: Who should read this book?

A: The market for this book is any individual who is seeking answers to questions about money and investments. Also, professional advisors who are attempting to give answers to savers and investors will find this book very helpful as a resource.

CHAPTER 2

HOW TO USE THIS BOOK

An overview on how to approach this book and how it is organized may help you to make productive use of it. It is appropriate that there be a how-to-use chapter in a "how-to" book. Generally, the way you can best use this book will depend on your circumstances.

Savers and investors include individuals with a wide variety of different financial needs. If you are just beginning your financial life cycle, you will need one level of information, whereas if your investment plans are more developed, you will need another. The differences in readers' financial status will influence their best approach to this book.

The structure of this book can facilitate either an overall reading or the accurate location of specific topics. The material is presented in a manner that allows you to read the book from cover to cover if you are seeking a complete overview of financial subjects. You should get ideas that will be helpful to you in using your money, making investments, and planning. The material is also indexed and cross-referenced so that you can use the book as a reference source to answer specific questions that arise.

The following chapters give readers a vast amount of basic information on various money, saving, investment, and planning opportunities. For some people, this may be the only financial reference book they will need. For others, it will only scratch the surface and give them a desire for more in-depth inquiry. Once you understand the basics discussed in these pages, you may wish to seek additional information from your advisors or other sources.

Q: What types of savers and investors may find this book helpful?

A: Your particular financial needs will influence how you can best make use of this book on your path to financial security. Your best approach would vary depending on whether you are

- Young and just beginning your financial life cycle
- Ready to begin accumulating a portfolio of investments
- An existing investor seeking a deeper understanding of areas of investment in which you are currently participating
- Concerned about better understanding your retirement plans and how they fit into your overall financial security goals
- Seeking information concerning opportunities to plan for the distribution of your wealth when you die
- A professional advisor using this book as a resource when working with clients

Q: How could young people who are just beginning their financial life cycle use this book?

A: If you are young and just beginning your financial life cycle, you will probably want to read this book from cover to cover. This will give you a financial overview so that you can begin developing a savings and investment plan that will help you achieve your short-term and long-term goals.

As a starter, you will probably want to concentrate on the chapter on personal money as you establish checking, savings, and borrowing relationships with one or more financial institutions. If you are still in college or graduate school, you may be interested in the student loan information.

As you move through your financial life cycle and begin to explore investments, you will want to turn to the investment sections and other material in this book.

Q: How could investors who are beginning to accumulate a portfolio of investments use this book?

A: If you are ready to begin accumulating a portfolio of investments, you will want to study the chapters covering the specific investments in which you have the most interest. Investment topics include stocks, bonds, mutual funds, and life insurance and annuities.

Not only will you begin to more fully understand the investments to which you may commit your hard-earned money, you will also have a resource that will help you to better understand the types of investments your advisors may recommend and the investment terms they may use.

As a beginning investor, you may also want to study such longer-term opportunities as retirement plans, retirement planning, or estate planning. The more information you have about your money and how it is working for you, or not working for you, the better able you will be to seek opportunities that can assist you in achieving your financial goals.

Q: How could investors who already have a portfolio of investments and are seeking other opportunities use this book?

A: If you already have a portfolio of investments and are seeking other investment opportunities, you can use this book to make certain you understand your current investments. Fully understanding the risks you are assuming is as important as understanding your investment opportunities.

The material in this book will also give you information on investment opportunities that you may be unaware of. It will allow you to study possible investment opportunities *before* you talk to your advisors, who may be attempting to sell you an investment, and help you evaluate your advisors' recommendations. Having this basic knowledge will help you decide whether a proposed investment is suitable for you.

You may also want to know how your current investments and other opportunities you may be considering can fit together as part of a plan to achieve financial security. Tying together your retirement plans, life insurance, trusts, and other opportunities should help you in your investment, retirement, and estate planning.

Q: How may individuals who are concerned about their retirement plans find this book useful?

A: Your employers' retirement plans and those you establish on your own will be a very important factor in obtaining a secure financial future. The more you understand about your employer's retirement plans and other retirement plan opportunities you may have, the better you can plan to achieve your financial goals.

This book will give you basic information on retirement plans and many of the investments in those plans. Many people, including coworkers, friends, neighbors, and advisors, will be giving you advice on your retirement plans—what you should have and how you may want to reposition the plans or assets in the plans. Reviewing the material in this book should put you in a better position to understand the information provided by others.

Q: How could individuals who are seeking information concerning planning opportunities use this book?

A: If you are seeking information concerning planning opportunities, you should read the chapters on retirement planning and estate planning. In addition, many of the other chapters will help you to understand your investments, retirement plans, and life insurance and give you basic information on how each may fit into your retirement and estate plans.

As with every aspect of successful investing, the more you know about planning, the better you will understand the information you receive from your advisors. Also, the more you know, the better you will be able to develop planning ideas on your own that will benefit you and help you accomplish your financial goals.

This book will be helpful to you in working with your advisors. How many times have you talked with or received information from one of your advisors and later not been able to fully remember what you were told? The information in this book should refresh your memory and help you to avoid playing catch-up in accomplishing your objectives.

Q: How could this book be helpful to professional advisors?

A: If you are a professional advisor, this book could be helpful to you in serving your clients. Often, after you have given a client advice on a relatively complex subject (even if it seems simple to you), it is helpful to give your client some reading material. Clients sometimes have selective memories and may forget some of the information you have given them.

Also, if you specialize in one area, it is not unusual for your clients to ask you questions about some topic that is outside your area of expertise. This book can serve as a reference source that will enable you to answer such questions. You can also use it as a reference when you are asked to review recommendations from a client's other advisors.

Q: How is this book organized?

A: This book is organized so that it both can be read cover to cover, providing a progression of information, and can be used as a reference source, with each chapter being able to stand alone. Often, the same basic information will be applicable to more than one investment or subject. In such cases, we have made cross-references to other sections of the same chapter or other chapters where the information is covered.

HOW TO USE THIS BOOK

Q: If I have a specific question about an investment or something to do with developing a plan, how can I find the answer?

A: If you have a specific question about an investment or something to do with developing a plan, you can read and study the chapter or chapters that discuss the general subject about which you have a question. You can also look up the key words in your question in the index and turn to the pages referred to there.

When you are using this book as a reference source, the index will be very helpful in guiding you to the appropriate material.

Q: Is this the only book about money and investing I will ever need to buy?

A: This may be your first book on money and investing, but it probably will not be the last one you will ever buy. As you become more sophisticated in your investments and planning, you will probably want material that is more advanced than the material included in these pages.

Our goal is to give you the answers to most of the basic questions you should have about your money, investment opportunities, and planning for retirement. After you finish reading, you should keep this book as a reference. As you become more comfortable with investing and planning, you should be able to make more use of the material and refer back to it to refresh your memory.

Chapter 3

The Basics

To better understand your investment opportunities and your current savings programs and investments, you need an understanding of basic terms, investment math, and risks. This chapter will address the basics that will help you develop your investment program. A better understanding of the basics will make you more effective in working with your advisors.

If you already have a good understanding of the information and concepts included in this chapter, you may just want to scan the material. If you are not confident about this basic knowledge, you may want to study this chapter closely so that you can deal more easily with the information in later chapters.

Much of the material in this chapter is also covered in other chapters. Each section and chapter is written to be inclusive. Therefore, information introduced in this chapter will be discussed further in other chapters.

Q: Why should I save?

A: You should save a portion of your current income in order to have money for emergencies and to provide for future financial needs, such as educating your children, buying a new automobile, buying a new home, or securing retirement income.

Part of your total income, or *gross income* (see box), is required to pay fixed expenses—mortgage, taxes, utilities. The portion of your income remaining after you have paid your fixed expenses is your *discretionary income*; it is available for you to spend or save. You should save as much of your discretionary income as possible to build wealth for future financial needs.

Terms About Your Income

Gross income — Your total income from all sources.

After-tax income — Your income after you pay all income taxes and Social Security taxes.

Discretionary income — Your income after the payment of all taxes plus your fixed expenses such as mortgage, rent, utilities, insurance, automobile payments, and so forth. You should save or invest a portion of your discretionary income so that you have an emergency fund and money for future use.

THE BASICS

Q: What is an investment?

A: An investment is an asset acquired with the expectation of receiving a future benefit. The future benefit may be increased income or increased wealth.

Save versus Invest

Save: To accumulate money for emergencies and future investments. Usually, most people place their savings in very safe accounts such as insured bank deposits, money funds, or very short maturity U.S. Treasury securities.

Invest: To commit money, usually from your savings, in order to gain a profit on higher interest than paid on your savings. When you decide to invest you generally assume more risk to potentially earn greater profits.

Q: Why should I invest my savings?

A: The primary reason you should invest your savings is to make more money. By making more money, you can accumulate more wealth and increase your spendable income in the future. As you go from earning wages to retirement, your sources of income will shift from *earned income* to *unearned income* (investment income) (see box). Therefore, the larger the amount of money you are able to accumulate during your working years and the more successful you are at investing your savings, the larger your retirement (unearned) income will be, and the more secure your retirement years will be.

Earned Income — Income you earn from your labors. Earned income is paid to you by an employer or is earned by a business you own or free-lance or contract work you perform.
Unearned Income — The income earned by your savings and investments. Unearned income is also referred to as investment income.

Illustration 3-1 shows how fast your money will increase at different rates of growth or earnings. However, the greater the returns you seek, the more risk you will assume; this is discussed later in this chapter.

Illustration 3-1
Annual Investment Required to Reach $100,000 at Various After-Tax Rates of Return

Years to Retirement	Rates of Return				
	6%	8%	10%	12%	14%
5	$16,736	$15,783	$14,891	$14,054	$13,270
10	7,157	6,392	5,704	5,088	4,536
15	4,053	3,410	2,861	2,395	2,000
20	2,565	2,023	1,587	1,239	964

Q: What has driven more and more people to start investing?

A: Several major economic trends have encouraged many people to invest for the first time. These changes include:

- Wider variations in interest rates
- Changes in financial institutions such as banks and insurance companies
- Less certainty that others will provide long-term security

Q: How have interest-rate changes created more investors?

A: In the 1970s and early 1980s, interest rates and inflation were high, and this had a negative effect on many people—in particular, those living on fixed incomes, whose incomes did not increase, or at best did not increase as fast as their cost of living. Subsequently, in the early years of this decade, interest

THE BASICS

rates declined substantially. Accustomed to higher rates, people were very unhappy earning 2 percent to 4 percent on their savings accounts. In some cases, these low rates reduced their income from savings accounts by over 50 percent. Therefore, they turned to stocks and bonds in order to increase the earnings on their savings.

Q: How have changes in financial institutions created more investors?

A: Another factor that has caused many people to start investing their savings is that banks and insurance companies have begun offering investment products to their customers. Many banks now offer investments that are not guaranteed, but offer higher yields, and many insurance agents now offer noninsurance investment products. This evolution in what is called the financial services industry, has changed many people from savers to investors. The larger number of institutions offering investment products has created more opportunities, but the changes have also created confusion and increased risk. Therefore, it is more important than ever that you understand the alternative uses of your money.

Q: How has a more uncertain world created more investors?

A: In the past, individuals believed that Social Security and employer retirement plans would provide for their future financial security. Increasingly, they are coming to believe that they might not be able to depend on those sources in the future. Also, education and medical costs have become a greater financial concern. In this more uncertain environment, individuals are saving more and investing more of their savings because they realize they must take more responsibility for their own future financial security.

Q: What are the ways in which I can invest?

A: There are two basic ways to invest. You may:

- Lend your money
- Buy an asset

Q: What happens when I lend my money?

A: When you lend your money, you are turning it over to someone who promises to pay you a certain income and return your money to you at some time in the future. The organization (bank, business, or government) that is borrowing your money anticipates being able to use that money to earn more than it is paying you in interest.

When you lend money, the loan or the security evidencing that loan, is also an asset.

 Example: When you deposit money in a bank or savings institution, it pays you a stated rate of interest and tells you when you can get your money back. The bank will lend your money to others with the intent of earning more on its loans than it is paying you. When you lend money to a business (by buying a bond, for example), the business will invest your money in its operations with the intent of earning more than it is paying you in interest.

Note: When you lend your money, your returns are generally limited to the stated rate of interest. You are giving up growth opportunities.

Q: When I buy an asset, what can I expect?

A: When you buy an asset, you can expect to earn at least part of the profits generated by the asset. The profits may be in the form of rents, dividends, capital gains, or capital appreciation (growth). During the late 1980s, banks were paying their depositors (people who made loans to the bank) 2 percent to 3 percent while investors in many mutual funds and common stocks were earning 10 percent, 12 percent, or more. However, investors in mutual funds or stocks assume more risk in order to increase their returns. There are times when lenders can earn double-digit interest while stock investors actually lose money. This is why a well-balanced approach to investing is very important.

THE BASICS

Q: What are some of the terms I need to know in order to understand the returns I can earn on my invested money?

A: To understand the returns you are earning on your money, you should understand the following terms:

- Current return
- Total return
- Average annual return
- Compound annual return
- After-tax return
- Real return

Q: What is current return?

A: Your *current return* is the amount of money you earn on an annualized basis (that is, the amount you would earn in a full year), divided by the amount of money you have on deposit or have invested.

Example: If you earn $5 in a year and you have invested $100, your current return is 5 percent ($5 divided by $100). If your annual earnings on the $100 invested are $10, your current return is 10 percent ($10 divided by $100).

Q: What is total return?

A: Your *total return* is your current return plus or minus any appreciation or decline in the value of your investment.

Example: Your current return as shown above is 5 percent, *and* at the end of a year, your $100 investment has grown in value to $110. The appreciation is $10, or 10 percent ($10 divided by $100, the beginning value). Your total return is thus 15 percent (5 percent current return plus 10 percent appreciation). If the value of your investment declined by $2.50, or $2\frac{1}{2}$ percent, your total return would be $2\frac{1}{2}$ percent (5 percent current return minus the $2\frac{1}{2}$ percent decline in value).

Q: What is average annual return?

A: To properly compare the returns on different investments held for different periods of time, you need to know the annual return. The *average annual return* is the total return for a period of more than one year divided by the number of years involved. This may be the number of years you have owned the investment, or an arbitrary number, such as five or ten years, that enables you to compare the returns on a variety of potential investments. A 100 percent increase in your money over ten years provides an average annual return of 10 percent.

Q: What is compound annual return?

A: The *compound annual return* is the growth in value each year as a percentage of the value at the beginning of the year plus the accumulated earnings. If your investment doubles in 10 years, your compound annual return is 7.18 percent. Compound annual return assumes you reinvest the income, so that you earn income on both your original money *and* the accumulated earnings. See Illustration 3-2. Since you earn income on a larger and larger pool of money each year, your money will grow at a faster pace. This in turn shows the importance of saving and reinvesting your earnings.

THE BASICS

Q: What is after-tax return?

A: Your *after-tax return* is the amount of money you have earned minus any income tax payable on the earnings.

 Example: Your annual earnings on an investment of $1,000 are $60, or 6 percent. Assuming your income tax amounts to one-third of your earnings, you will pay $20 of the $60 earnings in income taxes and have $40 remaining. Your after-tax return will thus be $40, or 4 percent. As you review different investments, it is important to keep after-tax returns in mind.

Q: What is real return?

A: Your *real return* is your after-tax return minus the rate of inflation. In the example above, if your after-tax return is 4 percent and the inflation rate is 3 percent, your real return is 1 percent. In other words, your money (your investment plus

Illustration 3-2
Comparison of Average Annual Return and Compound Annual Return

A 100 percent increase over ten years provides an *average annual return* of 10 percent per year. This can also be expressed as a *compound annual return* of 7.18 percent per year. If the value of a stock you purchased at $30 a share increased by 7.18 percent each year, the value at the end of ten years would be $60.

Beginning Value	Add 7.18 %	Interest	End Value
30.00	7.18%	2.15	32.15
32.15	7.18%	2.31	34.46
34.46	7.18%	2.47	36.93
36.93	7.18%	2.65	39.58
39.58	7.18%	2.84	42.42
42.42	7.18%	3.05	45.47
45.47	7.18%	3.26	48.73
48.73	7.18%	3.50	52.23
52.23	7.18%	3.75	55.98
55.98	7.18%	4.02	60.00

the earnings) will buy only 1 percent more. If the inflation rate were 6 percent, your real return would be a *negative* 2 percent. Your money would buy 2 percent less than it would the year before.

Q: What is risk?

A: *Risk* is the possibility that a situation will have a negative outcome. Risk appears in many different forms that are not always obvious and affects every activity in your life. In many situations you run risks no matter which choices you make. If you do not save and invest, for example, you risk falling short of your financial goals. On the other hand, when you do invest, you run risks that are specific to the type of investment you select.

In general, the primary risk in investing is that your investment will become less valuable. Your investment may become less valuable by:

- Actually losing money
- Losing purchasing power (inflation)

The various types of investment risk discussed below could make your money less valuable by leading to one or both of these outcomes.

Q: I hear risk and return discussed together. How are they related?

A: The relationship between risk and return is at the very heart of understanding investments. Since risk is the possibility of a negative outcome, if you are going to assume a higher risk, you logically expect the investment to make this risk worthwhile. To do this, the investment should offer a higher potential return. This leads to the general rule that in investing, risk and return are intertwined. If you are offered a high potential return, you should expect the investment to have a correspondingly high risk.

 Note: Any investment that appears to be too good to be true, usually is! Stay away!

Q: What types of risks are involved when I invest my money?

A: The risk you may be assuming can generally be categorized as one or more of the following:

- Inflation risk (purchasing-power risk)
- Market (price) risk
- Interest-rate risk
- Liquidity risk
- Economic risk
- Political risk

Q: What is inflation risk?

A: *Inflation risk* is the risk of loss of purchasing power as a result of inflation, which increases the cost of just about everything we buy, from food to a car to clothes. If your spendable income does not increase at least as fast as the rate of inflation, it will buy less and less of what you need.

Example: If you currently need $50,000 a year to cover your expenses and the average rate of inflation over the next 10 years is 5 percent a year, you will need about $81,500 ten years from now just to maintain your current standard of living.

Inflation is a greater problem at some times than at others, but it almost never goes away completely. Inflation is commonly measured by the Consumer Price Index (CPI), an index published by the U.S. Department of Labor indicating the increase in consumer prices. In the 1950s and 1960s, the CPI increased at an annual rate of 2 to 3 percent. In contrast, in 1979 and 1980, the CPI increased at a rate of 11.3 percent and 13.5 percent, respectively, before returning to lower levels.

During periods of high inflation, it is especially damaging if your total return (your income plus the increase in value of your investments) is not greater than the inflation rate. If this happens, as the value of your money erodes, either your standard of living declines or you are forced to dip into your principal to pay your expenses. The people who truly suffer are those living on a fixed income, whose expenses increase but whose income does not. Investing may allow you to avoid living on a fixed income.

Q: What is market risk?

A: *Market risk* is the risk that the value of your investment will decline. This may happen for several reasons:

- The market in which you are investing may decline.
- The area of investment you selected may be out of favor.
- The price of your investment may decline for reasons specific to your investment.

Example: If you have invested in stocks and the stock market declines, as it did in 1987, the prices of the majority of your stocks will decline regardless of how well the particular companies in which you have invested are performing. Also, if you have invested in real estate and the entire real estate market is under price pressure, your particular investment will probably be affected.

Market risk will be discussed in more detail in the common stock chapter.

Q: What is interest-rate risk?

A: *Interest-rate risk* is the risk of a decline in the value of your investments when interest rates increase. Most of your fixed-income investments will decline in value when interest rates increase, and the value of common stocks will generally also decline.

Conversely, when interest rates decline, the value of most of your fixed-income investments will increase, and the value of common stocks will generally increase.

 Note: For a discussion of how interest rates may affect your fixed-income investments, refer to the questions in Chapter 8, "Bonds: Lending Your Money."

Q: What is liquidity risk?

A: *Liquidity risk* is the risk that you will be unable to convert your investments to cash. Stated another way, liquidity is the ability to sell your investment at a fair price.

Liquidity risk can occur in any type of investment that does not have a well-established market. Some stocks have very few shares outstanding, and buying or selling a large amount will cause a large price movement. You may even find instances where there are virtually no buyers for a stock or bond you own, so you just have to hold your investment.

During the late 1980s, many people who wanted to sell their homes or other real estate holdings could not find buyers at a price they believed was adequate. Some found that their real estate was hard to sell even if they lowered the price. In such cases, their real estate lacked liquidity.

Many investors who in the 1970s and early 1980s purchased limited partnerships that invested in oil and gas, real

THE BASICS

estate, or other such assets found later that they could not sell their holdings at any price.

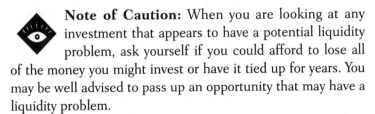 **Note of Caution:** When you are looking at any investment that appears to have a potential liquidity problem, ask yourself if you could afford to lose all of the money you might invest or have it tied up for years. You may be well advised to pass up an opportunity that may have a liquidity problem.

Q: What is economic risk?

A: *Economic risk* refers to how your investments perform over the course of economic cycles. During a recession (a temporary decline in economic activity), the prices of your common stocks and many of your other investments probably will decline. Some investments will decline more than others; for example, stocks of industrial companies will decline because the companies will generally not be earning as much as when the economy is in an up cycle. Other investments, such as government bonds, are less sensitive to economic cycles, or not sensitive at all.

Conversely, when the economy is performing well and corporations are earning better than expected profits, your common stocks and similar investments generally will perform well.

Note: Most investors would be well advised to hold their good investments through recessions. A classic investment mistake is to follow the crowd and sell at a low point. Most companies will continue to pay their dividends, and their stock prices will recover. However, you should always monitor your investments and be willing to reposition your holdings based on risk.

Q: What is political risk?

A: *Political risk*, sometimes referred to as legislative risk, is the effect a political or legislative action can have on your income and the value of your investments.

Tax changes are the most significant political risk that affect you, whether you invest or not. Every time income, sales, or Social Security taxes are increased, your spendable income decreases. Conversely, if taxes are decreased, your after-tax income increases.

If you do not invest, increases in total tax costs may erode the buying power of your income and decrease your standard of living in the same way that inflation does. Investing wisely will allow you to increase your income and the capital on which to earn more income. Within your portfolio, tax changes will affect some types of investments positively and others negatively.

In general, an increase in taxes is bad for the economy because more money is sent to the government and the public has less money to spend or save. On the other hand, a decline in taxes is good for the economy because the public has more money to spend or save. The other side to this thought, the effects of national debt and of government spending, will not be addressed in this book.

Note: Even though tax planning is important, you should not allow taxes or potential tax liability to dominate your investment decisions. You should make investment decisions primarily on the basis of profit opportunities, not fear of income tax liability.

Political risk can take other forms as well. The Arab oil embargo in the early 1970s caused the price of oil to increase by almost six times. Many companies that used oil in the manufacture of their products had a sharp increase in their cost of goods, affecting their profits and, in turn, their stock prices.

Regulatory changes are another political risk. An increase in regulation may create more red tape, reduce profitability, and hurt your investment. Deregulation can help or hurt. If it promotes efficiency, profits and stock value could rise. But if it causes more competition at lower prices, companies' profits and, in turn, their stock prices will decline.

Q: How can I position my investments so as to avoid risk?

A: The short answer is that you cannot avoid risk. Leaving your money under the mattress subjects you to the risk of not earning any returns on your money. If you place your money only in very safe guaranteed accounts, your investments are subject to inflation and tax risks.

You can manage or control risk by diversifying your investments over many types of risks (see below). Also, it is important for you to understand the types of risk you are willing to assume in order to potentially increase your returns. You will want to assume or avoid certain risks, depending on your investment objectives.

Q: What is diversification?

A: *Diversification* means placing your money in a variety of investments with different types and degrees of risk. You will still be exposed to risks in these investments, but they will react differently to any particular risk.

You should diversify among types of investments, including keeping a portion of your money in a safe reserve for emergencies. You should also diversify within each type of investment. For example, if you decide that common stocks are suitable for you, you should diversify by owning stocks of companies in different industries.

Example: Some investors have relied very heavily on electric utility stocks. They believed that the prices of utility stocks would always perform well and that the companies would pay good dividends and regularly increase these dividends. However, because of increasing interest rates, the prices of most utility stocks peaked in the third quarter of 1993 and declined by 25 percent over the following year, and some utilities reduced their dividends. In addition, new competitive pressures have arisen that may make these stocks even less predictable in the future.

In stock investing, you should also diversify among stocks that support different objectives, such as conservation, growth, emerging growth, income, or speculation. For further discussion of stock diversification, see Chapter 5.

If you are going to invest in bonds, do not invest all of your money in one bond. Invest in several bonds from different issuers and with different maturities.

By overly concentrating your investments in one stock or industry, you are subjecting your investments to a magnification of any unexpected problems that may arise. Diversifying your investments allows you to control your risk. Generally it will result in more stable returns within your investment objectives.

SUMMARY

The purpose of this chapter is to give you a better understanding of the basic concepts of investing. Understanding these basic concepts is essential for any discussion of investments.

After reviewing the material in this chapter, you should be better able to use this book to develop an investment program suitable for your needs.

THE BASICS

Chapter 4

Personal Money

One of the first things you must learn is what to do with money when you first receive it. You must learn to manage immediate money matters such as bank deposits, credit cards, and loans before you can consider longer-term matters such as investing or retirement planning.

When you were young and you received money from an allowance or part-time work, what did you do with it? Did you hide it under the mattress or did you deposit it in a checking or savings account at your local bank? Now that you are gainfully employed and thinking about investing, you still face decisions about what to do with your paycheck. This chapter will discuss checking accounts, savings accounts, and other bank services, such as loans and mortgages.

This chapter will help you lay the foundation before you begin investing. It will give you the information you need if you are just beginning your financial life cycle—if you are just starting to save, to use credit cards and obtain loans, and to think of buying a house.

Once you have these financial foundations in place, you can turn to longer-term matters, such as using life insurance to protect your family and starting to invest. Life insurance and investment opportunities are discussed in later chapters.

Q: What should I do with the money I get from my employer?

A: When you receive your earnings from your employer or from a business in which you are involved, you should deposit the money in a checking or savings account at a financial institution.

Q: How much money should I have for emergencies?

A: As one of your most immediate financial priorities, you should have a savings account for emergencies. It used to be said that you should have the equivalent of at least six months' income in a savings account in case of sudden expenses or unemployment. However, the requirement is lower if you have lines of credit, credit card balances, or equity lines of credit on your home available to you. All of these emergency sources will be discussed in this chapter.

Q: What types of accounts should I have at my financial institution?

A: Many years ago, banks and savings and loan associations had only two types of accounts: checking and savings. Now, investigating the types of checking and savings accounts may be like trying to read a very long restaurant menu.

Not only are there now many more types of checking and savings accounts, but the distinction between the two major types has blurred. You may now earn interest on a checking account, whereas formerly only savings accounts paid interest. On the other hand, you may now have checkbook access to your savings account, whereas formerly this was impossible because of restrictions on withdrawals from savings accounts.

You should talk to an officer of the financial institution with which you want to establish a relationship and ask about the different types of accounts. You should ask questions such as:

- What are the fees on various accounts?
- What minimum balances are you required to maintain to avoid having to pay fees?
- What rate of interest does the institution pay on each account?

Q: How can I avoid having to pay fees on checking or savings accounts?

A: At most financial institutions, you can avoid paying fees on checking and savings accounts by either maintaining minimum account balances or maintaining average balances at a certain level. Sometimes balances in more than one account can be combined in calculating the minimum. The money saved by not paying these fees represents a return on the money held as a minimum balance. Unless you are confident that you can earn a higher return elsewhere, it is a good idea to keep the minimum balance in the account.

Example: If your checking account fee would be $120 a year and you can avoid the fee by maintaining a minimum balance of $1,500, this is equivalent to earning 8 percent on your $1,500 balance.

Q: Can I sometimes avoid other bank fees by maintaining deposit balances and loans?

A: Yes. Many financial institutions will waive many of their other fees, such as those on credit cards, issuance of traveler's checks, and, in some cases, safe deposit boxes, if you maintain certain deposit balances and outstanding loans.

Note: You should always ask what fees and charges your financial institution will waive if you maintain the required deposits and/or loans.

Q: Will I be paid interest on my checking and savings deposits?

A: In some cases, you will. However, your checking and savings account balances are freely available to you. In exchange for giving you that freedom, the financial institution pays low rates of interest or, in the case of some checking accounts, no interest at all. In addition, you may be required to maintain a minimum level of deposits, say $1,500, for an account to qualify for interest.

PERSONAL MONEY

Q: Are my deposits at a financial institution insured?

A: Generally, most deposit accounts at banks or savings banks are insured by the Federal Deposit Insurance Corporation (FDIC), an agency of the U.S. government, for up to $100,000 for all accounts in one name. However, if you have both a personal account and a joint account with your spouse or child, generally each of these accounts will be insured for $100,000.

Note of Caution: With the changing rules of financial institutions and of the FDIC, you should always inquire about the amount of deposit insurance on the various accounts you have at a financial institution. If there is any question about whether or not your deposits are insured, you should request a letter from an officer of the institution detailing the coverage. If you cannot get such a letter, you should consider moving some of your deposits.

 Additional Note of Caution: As discussed in other sections of this book, your financial institution may now offer some nondeposit accounts and investments that are not covered by FDIC insurance.

Q: How can I make certain that I do not overdraw my checking account?

A: To protect yourself from overdrafts in case your math is not as accurate as it should be or you forget to make a deposit, you can establish one of the following automatic transfer arrangements with your financial institution:

- From your credit card to your checking account (see page 34)
- From a line of credit to your checking account (see page 37)
- From another of your deposit accounts to your checking account

The above arrangements are referred to as *overdraft protection*. You can also establish overdraft protection from your credit card or deposit account for the checking account of a child.

Q: How can I deposit money?

A: To deposit money, you can:

- Take the money to the financial institution and deposit it to your checking or savings account.
- Instruct your employer or the entity paying you to make an automatic deposit to your account.
- Deposit the check in the financial institution through one of its automatic teller machines (ATMs) (see page 31).

- Mail it to the bank, using a special form supplied by the bank for the purpose.

Q: Some people receive checks for their Social Security payments, retirement plan distributions, and investments like mutual funds or annuities. How should these types of checks be deposited?

A: If you are receiving checks from Social Security, retirement plan distributions, or investments like mutual funds, you should always inquire if the payments can be made directly to your checking or savings account. Social Security definitely offers a direct deposit alternative. Many retirement plan administrators provide the same service, and so do many mutual funds and insurance companies.

Q: Why should I use direct deposit of distributions whenever possible rather than just receiving a check and depositing it?

A: Rather than having a check mailed to you, direct deposit may be advantageous to you for several reasons:

- You do not have to worry about checks being lost in the mail.
- You do not have to take the time to go to the financial institution to make deposits.
- Your money becomes available to you (see below) once it is direct deposited (wired) to your account.

Q: When I deposit checks into a financial institution, the institution sometimes will not allow me to withdraw all of the deposit immediately. Why?

A: Technically, you cannot withdraw money from a financial institution until that institution has collected the money from the financial institution on which the check is drawn. This is often referred to as having *good funds*. Generally, a financial institution will place a *hold* on at least a portion of the amount you deposited by check until it can collect the funds. Usually, it takes two days to collect funds from another local financial institution and five days or more from a nonlocal financial institution. However, the length of time banks may hold funds is limited by federal law.

PERSONAL MONEY

Q: How can I avoid having a hold placed on deposits I make to financial institutions?

A: To avoid having a hold placed on money deposited to one of your accounts at a financial institution, you can:

- Make certain that the check you deposit was written on the institution in which you are depositing it.
- Have the deposit made by electronic transfer.
- Have your deposit wired from the financial institution sending your deposit to the institution receiving the deposit.

In addition, if you have an overdraft line of credit sufficient to cover the amount of the deposit (see page 31), many financial institutions will allow a check deposited to your account to be available immediately.

Q: What is an electronic transfer of money?

A: An *electronic transfer* of money is a direct transaction from one financial institution to another. The institution sending the money is responsible for making certain that the money is withdrawn from the correct account, and the institution receiving the money is responsible for making certain that it is deposited into the correct account. There are many different ways to transfer money electronically. Some involve the Federal Reserve system and others do not. For a discussion of the various methods, consult your banker or advisor.

Most financial institutions will charge you a fee of $25 to $50 to transfer money out of your account electronically. Sometimes you may be charged a fee to *receive* an electronic transfer of money as well. Wired money can often be transferred from one institution to another in one day and is considered to be good funds on the day it is received.

 Note: If you ever need to have money transferred in a hurry, you should inquire if your financial institution or brokerage firm can do so and what its particular rules and fees are.

Q: How can I withdraw cash from my checking and savings accounts?

A: You can make withdrawals from your checking or savings accounts in the following ways:

- You can write a check.
- You can go to the branch location and make a withdrawal.
- You can make a withdrawal at an ATM.
- You can use a debit card or credit card, both of which will be discussed later in this chapter.
- At some financial institutions, you can pay bills by using a computer that is tied into your checking or savings account.
- At some financial institutions, you can pay bills by using a special telephone service.

Note: Financial institutions that offer bill-paying by computer or telephone generally charge a fee for these services. If you are interested in either, you should ask your institution if it provides the service and what its fees are. Also, you should inquire about the possibility of having the fees waived.

Q: What is an automatic teller machine (ATM)?

A: An *automatic teller machine* (ATM) is a machine operated by a financial institution that is linked to the institution's computer. ATMs allow customers to make deposits, withdrawals, and transfer money from one account to another using a special card called an *ATM card*. ATMs will also allow you to use other types of cards for certain transactions.

Q: What are the types of cards that I may be able to get from my financial institution?

A: The types of cards that you may be able to get from your financial institution are:

- ATM cards
- Debit cards
- Credit cards

Q: What is an ATM card?

A: An *ATM card* is a small plastic card that will allow you to withdraw cash or transfer money from one account to another. A magnetic strip on the back of the card contains your account information; the ATM reads and relays this information through the network to your bank's computer, which makes the requested transactions to your accounts. To use an ATM card, you will need a PIN (personal identification number).

Q: What is a PIN?

A: A *PIN* is a personal security code or identification number. It is usually a four-digit number. It may be assigned to you by the financial institution that issues you the card or, in some cases, you may be able to request a PIN of your choice. Once you have inserted your card into the ATM, entering your correct PIN authorizes the transactions you request.

Q: Should I get a PIN even if I do not plan to use an ATM card?

A: Yes. Increasingly, financial institutions expect you to use ATMs and telephone access to obtain information about your checking accounts, savings accounts, credit cards, and loans, and you will need a PIN in either case. If you do not have a PIN, you may have difficulty getting information in the future.

Q: How do I get a PIN to access my current accounts?

A: If you do not have PINs on your existing accounts, you can contact the financial institutions where you have accounts, credit cards, or loans. They will be happy to send you ATM cards and/or PINs.

Q: Could I have a security problem with my PIN?

A: Yes. You should protect your PINs just as you protect cash. Someone who has your PIN and your ATM card would have full access to your account information and could get cash from your account.

Q: Are the only ATMs I can use those of the financial institutions where I have accounts?

A: No. Most financial institutions are also members of networks such as MOST, CIRRUS, or PLUS, through which you can make withdrawals. There is often a $1 to $2 charge to your account if you use an ATM from another member of a network to which your institution belongs, whereas a financial institution in which you have an account usually will not charge you for withdrawals or transactions through its own ATMs. ATMs of some financial institutions that are members of these networks will not accept deposits to or transfers within other financial institutions.

 Note: Even if you are traveling abroad, you can often find an ATM that will allow you to make withdrawals in the local currency and debit your account. The currency conversion is made by the ATM network before your account is debited for the withdrawal.

Q: What is a debit card?

A: A *debit card* is a small plastic card like an ATM card. It is issued by a financial institution. It can be used with a PIN at ATMs to withdraw cash or transfer money from one account to another, and you can use it to pay merchants for goods or services just as you would write a check. The amount of the purchases or withdrawals for which you use your debit card will be immediately deducted from the checking or savings account you have previously designated. Generally, there are no charges for using a debit card, and you pay no interest, since you are not borrowing any money.

Q: What is a credit card?

A: A *credit card* is a small plastic card that allows you to make purchases on credit. When you use a credit card, you are borrowing money. Most financial institutions will issue their customers a Visa or MasterCard if the customers are approved for credit. If you are issued a credit card, you will have an assigned credit limit, which is the maximum amount you will be allowed to charge on the credit card. With "gold," or premium credit cards, the limit may be $5,000 or more.

Q: How do credit card payments work?

A: Once you use a credit card to make purchases or get cash advances, you will have to repay the amount you have borrowed. You may pay the balance in full each month or make installment-type minimum payments, which are usually between 2 and 5 percent of the outstanding balance on the date your statement is issued.

Travel and entertainment cards like American Express and Diners' Club generally require the balance to be paid in full every month.

Q: What is the rate of interest that I may be charged on credit card balances?

A: You will be charged interest on the outstanding balance. Most credit card issuers charge interest of 14 to 21 percent. Some charge a floating rate, where the rate charged is a fixed number of percentage points above a specified benchmark.

Note: During the last few years, many credit card issuers and financial institutions have offered special lower rates of interest on credit card balances. You should monitor the rate of interest charged on the credit cards you have and any special offerings by other credit card issuers. The savings may be substantial.

Q: Do most credit cards charge an annual fee?

A: Most credit card holders are charged an annual fee of $15 to $50 for the privilege of having the card. As previously discussed, you should see if the financial institution where you have accounts will waive the fee if you maintain a minimum balance in another account or in all your accounts combined.

Q: Can I get a cash advance on my credit card?

A: Generally, yes. You can get cash from your credit card from many ATMs if you have a PIN. If you think you may want to withdraw cash from your credit card at an ATM, you should ask the issuer to give you a PIN. When you use your credit card to make withdrawals from an ATM, you are increasing the amount you have borrowed on that credit card by the amount of the withdrawal plus any fees that may be charged.

Also, you can often establish an agreement whereby overdrafts from checking accounts will become an automatic loan against your credit card.

 Note: Some parents have found that using a credit card is an efficient means of getting money to children who are studying or traveling outside of the United States. The parents make payments on the credit card, and the child uses the card with his or her PIN to make withdrawals in the foreign currency.

Q: If I pay my credit card balance in full each month, will I be charged interest?

A: Most credit cards allow a *grace period* on purchases until the next bill is due. If you pay your balance in full during this grace period, you will avoid paying interest on purchases. However, if you get cash advances on your credit card, you will have to pay interest from the day you receive the cash until you repay it. You should inquire about a credit card's grace period before accepting the card. You should also pay your balance each month if possible to avoid paying high interest rates.

Q: What are certificates of deposit?

A: *Certificates of deposit*, also referred to as *CDs*, are long-term savings instruments issued by many financial institutions. They usually pay a fixed rate of interest for a fixed period of time, usually between three months and five years. Generally, the longer the maturity, the higher the interest rate paid to the depositor.

Q: Are certificates of deposit insured?

A: If the financial institution can offer deposits that are insured by the FDIC, your CDs *may be* insured.

Note of Caution: When acquiring a CD, you should always ask about FDIC insurance. This is especially true if you have other large deposits at the institution or if you are not familiar with the institution issuing the CD. Many financial institutions now offer investments that are *not* insured by the FDIC, so you should always ask.

PERSONAL MONEY

Q: If I want to surrender a CD for cash, will I have to pay a penalty?

A: If you surrender a CD for cash before its maturity date, you may be charged a substantial penalty for early withdrawal. In many instances, the penalty could be the loss of three months' interest. Some financial institutions allow a one-time withdrawal with no penalty.

 Note: If you are about to buy a CD from a financial institution, you should always inquire about the possible withdrawal penalties.

Q: If a CD owner dies, does the withdrawal penalty apply?

A: The estate or heirs of a decedent can usually make withdrawals from or surrender a CD without the penalty being charged.

Q: Can I invest in CDs through brokerage firms?

A: Yes. Many brokerage firms will offer investors insured CDs.

Q: What types of loans can I get from depository financial institutions?

A: The following types of loans are usually available to customers of depository financial institutions:

- Credit cards (see page 33)
- Installment loans (secured or unsecured)
- Lines of credit
- Equity loans with your home as collateral
- Home mortgages
- Education loans

Q: What is an installment loan?

A: An *installment loan* is a loan repaid through regular payments over a fixed period, or term. Loans of this type are frequently used to purchase a car, boat, or other item. Most commonly, you will make fixed monthly payments over the term of the loan, which could be from 12 to 60 months. You will probably be given a payment coupon book that contains a coupon for you to include with each payment.

 Note: The interest on most installment loans is heavier in the early years of the loan because you are using more of the bank's money at that time. If you decide to repay the loan ahead of schedule, do not expect the interest to be allocated equally to each period over the term of the loan.

How to Save Money on Some of Your Loan Payments
Many financial institutions will allow a small reduction in the interest charged on loans if you will permit the institution to deduct the payment from one of your checking or savings accounts on the due date.

Q: What is a secured loan?

A: A *secured loan* is a loan that is supported by collateral—that is, something of value that the lender can claim if the borrower does not repay the loan. Examples of collateral for secured loans would be a stock, a bond, or an automobile.

Q: What is an unsecured loan?

A: An *unsecured loan* is a loan that is guaranteed only by the borrower's promise to repay the amount borrowed plus interest. Generally, the interest charged on unsecured loans is higher than that charged on secured loans.

Q: What is a line of credit?

A: A *line of credit* is an agreement that you establish with a financial institution to supply you with credit up to a specified limit. You may use all or a portion of the line of credit by calling the institution and requesting that a deposit be made to your checking account from your line. Sometimes, you can use a line of credit by writing a check for more than you have in your checking account. In this case, when your account balance is insufficient to cover a check, the excess amount will be provided in the form of a loan from your line of credit.

PERSONAL MONEY

Q: What rate of interest do most financial institutions charge on a line of credit?

A: Most institutions charge a variable rate of interest on a line of credit. The rate of interest will usually be based on some benchmark rate. For example, the interest rate might be 1 percent over the *prime rate*. In this case, if the prime rate increases, so will the rate you pay, and vice versa. Generally, you will pay interest only on the amount of the line that you borrow.

Some financial institutions may charge you an annual fee to establish and maintain a line of credit. The fee may be $^1/_2$ to 1 percent of the amount of the line. The reason for the fee is that the financial institution has an obligation to lend you money up to the limit of your line of credit.

> *Prime rate*: A commonly used interest rate benchmark. The prime rate is the rate banks charge on loans to their most favored ("prime") customers.

PERSONAL MONEY

Q: When must most lines of credit be repaid?

A: Most lines of credit have a maturity date by which any outstanding loan balance must be repaid or refinanced with a new line of credit or another loan. Obviously, any time you can repay money borrowed, you should do so, in order to reduce the amount of interest. Many lines of credit have regular minimum payment requirements.

Q: Is the interest I pay to a financial institution tax-deductible?

A: Generally, the interest you pay to a financial institution on installment loans, credit card debt, or lines of credit is not tax-deductible. If the loan proceeds are used for investment purposes, you may be able to deduct the interest up to the amount of your investment income. The interest on most loans secured by your primary residence, like a mortgage or equity line, which are discussed later in this chapter, is deductible within limits.

Note of Caution: You should check with your tax advisor about the deductibility of interest.

Q: What is an equity line?

A: An *equity line* is a secured loan that uses the value of your home as security. An equity line may have a fixed rate or a variable rate. One advantage of an equity line is that it is revolving credit. Once it is established, you can borrow the unused portion at any time. As you make payments, the funds become available again; you do not have to reapply.

Q: When must I repay an equity loan?

A: Most financial institutions require a monthly payment of $1\frac{1}{2}$ percent of the outstanding balance. Usually, the payments will be sufficient to pay the current interest due and repay a portion of the loan balance. You should always repay as much of the loan balance as you can so as to reduce your interest payments.

Q: What are the risks in establishing an equity line?

A: The primary risk of an equity line is that your home is pledged as security. It can be quite easy to borrow money from an equity line, and you could build up the loan balance to a level at which it would be difficult for you to meet the payment schedule. Some financial institutions will even give you what appears to be a credit card that you can use to borrow against your equity line. If you start charging clothes, trips, meals, and so on, you may be surprised at how fast the balance can increase.

PERSONAL MONEY

Q: How much may I be able to borrow from an equity line?

A: Most financial institutions will allow you to establish an equity line for up to 80 percent of the value of your home less your mortgage balance, depending on your income and credit history. Illustration 4-1 is a simple schedule showing how to determine the approximate amount of equity line you may be able to establish.

Illustration 4-1
How to Estimate the Amount of Equity Line Available

Estimated value of your home	$100,000
(80 percent)	X 0.80
The maximum credit line/loan available	80,000
Subtract the balance on your existing mortgage	(50,000)
The amount you may be able to borrow on an equity line	30,000

Q: Can I deduct the interest on an equity line?

A: Generally, you can deduct interest paid on equity line balances of up to $100,000. As in any tax situation, you should always consult your tax advisors.

Q: What is a mortgage?

A: A *mortgage* is a loan secured by your home. When you buy or build a home, you will usually obtain a mortgage (loan) so that you can pay for your home over a number of years. A mortgage is a secured loan, and your home is the security for the loan. Your original mortgage is usually referred to as a *first mortgage*. Sometimes people obtain an additional mortgage, referred to as a *second mortgage*. In case of a foreclosure, or forfeiture of your home because you did not make the required payments, the first mortgage must be repaid before any of the sales proceeds can be applied to the second mortgage. Generally, an equity line is a second mortgage. There are many different types of mortgages, which will be discussed in later questions.

Q: How do I obtain a mortgage?

A: Most financial institutions have what are usually referred to as *mortgage originators* to help you obtain the best type of mortgage for you, given the type of home you are purchasing. Many mortgage originators do not work for a financial institution. Such independent originators should give you advice not only on the type of mortgage that is best suited to you, but on which mortgage lender you should use.

Q: How is a mortgage originator paid?

A: A mortgage originator will usually be paid a fee based on the amount of the mortgage. Fees can be from 1 point (1 percent) to 3 points (3 percent). If you are obtaining a loan for $50,000, your origination fee would thus be $500 to $1,500. You may also have to pay a fee to the mortgage lender.

Q: What is the percentage of value down payment required to obtain a mortgage?

A: Generally, most mortgage lenders will require a purchaser to make a down payment of 20 percent of the value. This means that you can usually obtain a conventional mortgage for 80 percent of the value of a home. A lower down payment is required if you can qualify for a FHA or VA loan, both of are described later in this chapter.

Q: What types of mortgages may I be able to obtain?

A: The types of mortgages you may be able to obtain include:

- Fixed-rate mortgage
- Adjustable-rate mortgage (ARM)
- Balloon mortgage
- Jumbo mortgage
- FHA (Federal Housing Administration) loan
- VA (Veterans Administration) loan

PERSONAL MONEY

Q: What is a fixed-rate mortgage?

A: A *fixed-rate mortgage* is a long-term loan secured by your home with a rate of interest that is fixed for the term of the mortgage. The length of the mortgage can range from 10 to 30 years. Each payment includes the payment of current interest and part of the principal.

If you want your home to be mortgage-free in a certain number of years or at a certain point in time, such as at your target retirement date, you may be looking for a shorter term mortgage. Obviously, the shorter the term, the higher the monthly payments, but the sooner the mortgage will be repaid and the less total interest you will pay. If you are young and need lower payments, a longer-term mortgage may be more suitable for you.

Q: What is an adjustable-rate mortgage (ARM)?

A: An *adjustable-rate mortgage (ARM)* is a loan secured by your home with an interest rate that will increase or decrease along with some benchmark rate, such as the interest on U.S. Treasury securities. Usually, the monthly payments on an adjustable-rate mortgage are lower, at least initially, and you can often qualify for a larger loan amount.

Q: If I have an ARM, how often will my payments change as the benchmark increases and decreases?

A: On some ARMs, monthly payments are adjusted when and if the benchmark rate increases or decreases. On others, payments are fixed payments for some term, such as six months or a year, even if the benchmark rate increases or decreases during that period. Most ARMs provide for both a maximum and a minimum interest rate regardless of the behavior of the benchmark rate, and many limit the amount by which the interest rate may change in a specified period, such as a year.

 Note: Before agreeing to an ARM, you should carefully review all of its terms and possible adjustments to see what might happen in a worst-case situation. Many people decide to take a fixed-rate mortgage because they want to know with certainty what their payments will be. They do not want to have to fit higher payments into their budgets.

Q: What is a balloon mortgage?

A: A *balloon mortgage* is a relatively short-term loan secured by your home in which the principal is not reduced to zero over the term of the loan. Therefore, a large portion of the mortgage becomes due and must be paid at the end of the term, which is often five to ten years. Generally, a balloon mortgage will have a lower rate of interest and lower fixed monthly payments than a fixed-rate mortgage because the lender knows that it will be repaid in a relatively short period of time.

Q: Who should consider a balloon mortgage?

A: If you are planning to move or pay off your mortgage within a relatively short period of time, you may want to consider a balloon mortgage.

Q: What is the risk in obtaining a balloon mortgage?

A: The obvious risk in obtaining a balloon mortgage is that if your financial situation or your plans change, you may have difficulty refinancing the amount that comes due when your mortgage matures (balloons). Also, as people learned in the late 1980s and early 1990s, your home may not be as easy to sell as you had thought, and the value may not be what you expected.

Q: What is a jumbo mortgage?

A: Most mortgage loans are for amounts of up to about $200,000. The threshold amount for jumbo mortgages varies from region to region and will be indexed. Your mortgage originator should be able to tell you the jumbo mortgage limit for your area. If you are trying to obtain a mortgage for a larger amount, you are attempting to get what is called a *jumbo mortgage*. Generally, if you are seeking a jumbo mortgage, mortgage lenders will lend a lower percentage of your purchase price, and so you will have to make a larger percentage down payment than with other types of mortgages. Also, the rate of interest is usually higher on jumbo mortgages.

Q: What is an FHA loan?

A: An *FHA loan* is a loan secured by your home that is issued by the Federal Housing Administration, an agency of the federal government. People who have a limited amount of money for a down payment and up-front expenses may qualify. If you qualify, the FHA loan program will allow you to buy a home with a minimal down payment, borrow a higher percentage of the purchase price, and include closing costs in the amount of the loan.

PERSONAL MONEY

Note: If you have a limited amount of money for a down payment, you should ask a mortgage originator whether you qualify for the FHA program.

Q: What is a VA loan?

A: A *VA loan* is a loan that is secured by your home that is issued by the Veterans Administration, an agency of the federal government. Qualified veterans or their widowed spouses may qualify for a VA loan with no down payment and higher debt-to-equity-ratio allowances.

 Note: If you are a veteran or the widowed spouse of a veteran with a limited amount of money to make a down payment on a home, you should ask a mortgage originator whether you qualify for a VA loan.

Q: What are closing costs?

A: *Closing costs* are the expenses that must be paid when you close on your mortgage and receive the loan proceeds from your mortgage lender. Some items included as closing costs may be:

- Origination points and loan points
- Appraisal cost
- Cost of a credit check
- Attorney's fees
- Fees to file the home title

The loan proceeds are usually paid to the seller of the house. Mortgage fees are usually deducted from the proceeds of the loan before settlement and will therefore increase your down payment. Most closing costs are paid by the buyer. However, some of the closing costs may be paid by the seller; this can be part of the negotiations for the purchase of the property.

Q: How can I determine what my closing costs will be?

A: The mortgage originator is obligated to give you an estimate of your closing costs when you apply for your loan. If this is not offered, you should always ask for it.

Q: What are student loans?

A: *Student loans* are usually government-sponsored unsecured loans made by financial institutions to students engaged in higher education, or their parents. If they qualify, students or their parents can go to a financial institution and obtain a conventional loan to help them pay for college or higher education. Some parents take out an equity line on their homes to pay part of the cost of college for their children. However, because the cost of college has increased so much over the years, the federal government has created several programs to help students and/or their parents pay their college expenses. Some of the government loan arrangements are

- Federal Stafford—subsidized
- Federal Stafford—unsubsidized
- Federal PLUS
- Federal consolidation loan

Q: Are student loans guaranteed by the federal government?

A: Yes. The federal government guarantees 98 percent of the principal and interest on qualified student loans.

Q: What is a subsidized federal Stafford student loan?

A: A *subsidized federal Stafford loan* is an unsecured loan that is available to any undergraduate or graduate student who can show financial need.

PERSONAL MONEY

Q: What is the maximum amount that can be borrowed each year under the subsidized federal Stafford loan program?

A: The maximum amount that can be borrowed each year under the subsidized federal Stafford loan program is

Undergraduate:
- $2,625 for the first year
- $3,500 for the second year
- $5,500 for the third through fifth years

Graduate:
- $8,500 per year

Q: When must the loan be repaid?

A: Payments on subsidized federal Stafford loans are deferred until six months after the student graduates or drops below half-time attendance. At that time, the student must begin repayment. While the student is in school at least half-time, the federal government pays the interest on the loan.

Q: What is the interest rate on subsidized federal Stafford loans?

A: The rate of interest charged on student loans is variable. The maximum rate established by the government is a little over 3 percent above the 91-day Treasury bill rate (see Chapter 8, page 158). Because of the low risk of these guaranteed loans, lenders can charge lower interest rates than they would charge on comparable conventional loans.

Q: What are unsubsidized federal Stafford student loans?

A: *Unsubsidized federal Stafford student loans* are unsecured loans that are available to *all* undergraduate and graduate students while they are in school at least half-time. Parents of students of any income or asset level are eligible, depending on their credit eligibility. These loans are not based on need.

PERSONAL MONEY

Q: What is the maximum amount that can be borrowed each year under the unsubsidized federal Stafford student loan program?

A: The maximum annual loan limits under the unsubsidized federal Stafford student loan program are

Dependent undergraduate:
- $2,625 for the first year
- $3,500 for the second year
- $5,500 for the third through fifth years

Independent undergraduate:
- $6,625 for the first year
- $7,500 for the second year
- $10,500 for the third through fifth years

Graduate:
- $18,500 per year

Note: The term *dependent* refers to the student's still being dependent on his or her parents or guardians for financial support. *Independent* refers to the student's not being a dependent.

Q: When must unsubsidized federal Stafford student loans be repaid?

A: Under the federal unsubsidized Stafford student loan program, the borrower is responsible for interest payments while the student is in school. Principal payments will begin six months after the student graduates or drops below half-time attendance.

Q: What is the rate of interest on the unsubsidized federal Stafford student loan program?

A: As with the subsidized program, the rate of interest on the unsubsidized program is variable. The maximum rate established by the government is a little over 3 percent above the 91-day Treasury bill rate (see Chapter 8, page 158).

Q: What are federal PLUS student loans?

A: A *federal PLUS* (Parental Loans for Undergraduate Students) student loan is an unsecured loan to a parent or legal guardian of a dependent student who is enrolled at least half-time.

Q: What is the maximum loan amount per year under the federal PLUS student loan program?

A: The maximum loan amount per year under the federal PLUS student loan program is the cost of the education minus any other financial aid.

Q: When must federal PLUS student loans be repaid?

A: Under the federal PLUS student loan program, principal and interest payments must begin sixty days after the loan is made.

Q: What is the rate of interest on the federal PLUS student loan program?

A: The rate of interest on federal PLUS student loans is usually a little higher than the interest on Stafford loans. The rate of interest is variable, and the maximum rate established by the government is somewhat over 3 percent above the 91-day Treasury bill rate (see Chapter 8, page 158).

Q: What are federal consolidation student loans?

A: *Federal consolidation student loans* are loans that are available to students who have completed college and find their student loan repayment schedule difficult. This program allows a student to combine all his or her student loans so that there is only one monthly payment. The borrower must have at least $5,000 of federally guaranteed loans outstanding and must be current on all payments.

Q: What are the repayment requirements on federal consolidated loans?

A: The borrower will usually lock in a low fixed rate and a specific monthly repayment schedule. Graduated repayment alternatives may also be available.

Q: How do I or my children apply for federally insured student loans?

A: If you need a student loan, you should check with your local financial institutions to see if you can qualify for one or more of the federally insured student loan programs. If your financial institution participates in the student loan program, you probably will be given a package explaining these loans and offered assistance in applying. If you are in college or have a student in college, you should check with the college's financial aid office to find out about federally insured loans and any other student loans that may be available. The financial aid office can direct you to a financial institution that participates in the programs.

Q: Has the federal student loan program changed?

A: Yes. In 1992, the rules governing the federally insured student loan program were liberalized. Some loans are no longer need based, and the maximum loan limits were increased.

Q: If I am a graduate student with high expenses, is there a federally insured loan program for me?

A: If you are a graduate student in any field and need financial aid, you may be able to qualify for loans under the HEAL (Health Education Assistance Loan) program. The financial aid office at your graduate school can tell you how to apply. Repayment schedules can often be stretched out to 10 to 20 years.

SUMMARY

This chapter has addressed questions that will help you lay the foundation for handling your personal money.

What you do with your money once you receive it and pay your current expenses is a very important first step in planning for your financial security. The more you concentrate on using the various depository accounts and loan arrangements, the better prepared you will be to begin your longer-term plans, such as investing.

CHAPTER 5

STOCKS: TAKING OWNERSHIP

Common stocks have been the backbone of American economic development. Ownership of common stocks by individuals, directly or indirectly, has built individual wealth and aided the expansion of many American businesses, such as AT&T, Exxon, Apple Computer, Walt Disney, Ford, Kellogg, and Dupont.

When you invest in a corporation's common stock, you become a part *owner* of that corporation.

If you own stock in a corporation, you are a *direct owner* of a portion of that corporation. You may also be an *indirect owner* of common stock if you:

- Own shares in a mutual fund
- Participate in a retirement plan
- Own life insurance policies
- Deposit money with certain financial institutions

In this chapter we discuss the features and benefits of common stock ownership and methods of buying stock. The first few questions provide basic information on common stocks. The remainder of the chapter discusses how to buy and sell common stocks.

Q: What are my rights as a shareholder, or part owner, of a corporation?

A: As a shareholder, you have the following rights:

1. *Voting.* You have the right to vote for members of the board of directors, for auditors, and on other routine matters at the corporation's annual meeting. The directors

elect the corporation's officers. You also have the right to vote on certain essential matters affecting the corporation, such as mergers, reorganizations, or recapitalizations.

2. *Dividends.* You have the right to receive dividends when they are declared by the board of directors.
3. *Limited liability.* Your potential loss is limited to the amount you invested in the common stock.
4. *Liquidation rights.* You will receive a share proportional to your ownership of any assets remaining after all debts are paid if the corporation liquidates its operations. If the corporation splits itself into separate businesses, you will receive a proportional share of each.

Q: Why should I buy (invest in) common stocks?

A: The short answer is that you can often make more money than you can make from other savings and investment alternatives. You make money owning common stocks by:

1. Receiving dividends
2. Making a profit through capital appreciation

The *payment of dividends* is a way for a corporation to share part of its profits with its owners. Many corporations have a history of regularly *increasing the dividends* they pay their owners (stockholders). By increasing dividends, the corporation increases the return to owners as its profits increase. Increasing dividends serves as an *inflation hedge* for the corporation's stock owners. (Refer to page 62 for an explanation of dividends.)

Another way of making a profit on common stocks is through *capital appreciation*, an increase in the price of the stock over a period of time. If you bought a common stock at $30 a share ten years ago and it is now selling at $60 a share, you would have capital appreciation of $30 a share, or a 100 percent increase in the value of your invested money over the ten years.

To properly compare the returns on different investments held for different periods of time, you need to know the annual return. A 100 percent increase over ten years provides an average annual return of 10 percent per year. It also provides a compound annual return of 7.18 percent per year. If the value of a stock you purchased at $30 a share increased by 7.18 percent each year, the value at the end of ten years would be $60. (Refer to Chapter 3, pages 15-16.)

Illustration 5-1 compares the long-term record of returns on common stock to the returns on short-term savings accounts, CDs, and long-term Treasury bonds.

Note: Short-term savings accounts often guarantee your deposits, whereas the dividends and prices of common stocks fluctuate and are not guaranteed.

Illustration 5-1

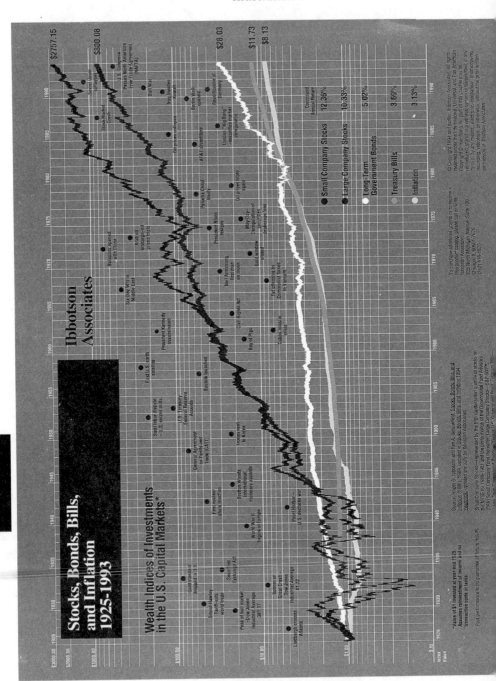

Q: What are the earnings of a corporation?

A: The *earnings* of a corporation are the money it has remaining after paying all expenses and income taxes.

A corporation's earnings are similar to your spendable income after taxes and regular expenses. From your gross earnings, you must pay your expenses and income taxes. The amount remaining is your net spendable income, which you can use for major purchases, savings, or investments.

A corporation can use after-tax income either to pay dividends or reinvest the income in its business to provide future growth.

Q: What is a corporation's earnings per share?

A: *Earnings per share* is the after-tax income available to common shareholders (after preferred stock dividends are paid) divided by the number of common shares outstanding. (See Chapter 6.)

 Example: If a corporation has earnings of $10 million, 1 million shares outstanding, and no preferred stock, the earnings per share would be $10 ($10 million divided by 1 million). The corporation may pay part of its earnings in a dividend or invest the earnings for future growth.

Q: What does earnings per share mean to me? How will earnings per share make me money?

A: Earnings per share shows that the corporation in which you own stock is making a profit. More importantly, the regular *growth* in earnings per share shows that your company is making more money each year.

If a corporation's earnings and earnings per share are steadily and regularly increasing, its dividends and ultimately the stock price should also increase. Stock prices are dependent on investors' expectations, and increasing dividends should lead to rising expectations and positively influence the stock price.

STOCKS

Illustration 5-2

Ten-Year History of Earnings per Share of PepsiCo

Year	Earnings per Share
1984	$0.38
1985	$0.50
1986	$0.58
1987	$0.74
1988	$0.97
1989	$1.12
1990	$1.31
1991	$1.50
1992	$1.61
1993	$2.05

Note: Illustration 5-3 shows a ten-year price chart of PepsiCo common stock. From 1984 to 1993, PepsiCo's earnings per share increased at a compound annual rate of 20.59 percent. (These earnings per share figures are adjusted for 3-for-1 stock splits in 1986 and 1990. See page 102 for a discussion of stock splits.)

Illustration 5-3

Ten-Year Price Chart of PepsiCo Common Stock

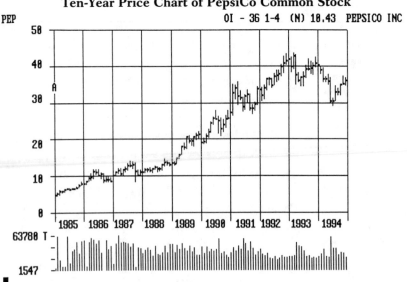

STOCKS

Q: What is the price-earnings ratio?

A: The *price-earnings ratio*, often referred to as the *P/E ratio*, is the price of a stock divided by the company's earnings per share.

 Example: If a stock's price is $60 and the earnings per share are $4.00, the price-earnings ratio is 15 (60 divided by 4 = 15). If the price is $40, the P/E ratio is 10 (40 divided by 4 = 10).

Q: Why is the price-earnings ratio important to me?

A: The price-earnings ratio can be a good measure of whether a stock is a bargain or overvalued.

1. If the P/E ratio of the corporation you are reviewing is lower than that of similar corporations, you may want to investigate why it is lower. The stock may be a bargain.
2. Conversely, if the P/E ratio of the corporation you are reviewing is higher than that of similar corporations, you may want to investigate why it is higher. The stock may be overvalued.

Illustration 5-4

Ten-Year History of the Average Annual P/E Ratio of PepsiCo Common Stock

Year	Average Annual P/E Ratio
1984	11.8
1985	12.6
1986	16.3
1987	15.5
1988	12.6
1989	15.7
1990	17.8
1991	20.4
1992	22.8
1993	20.0

STOCKS

Q: What is a corporation's cash flow?

A: *Cash flow* is the total amount of cash, including earnings, a corporation has available to invest in its business or to pay dividends. Cash flow from operations is the corporation's after-tax earnings plus noncash deductions that reduce earnings, but do not use any cash. Cash flow from operations is always larger than after-tax earnings.

Such noncash deductions include *depreciation* of real estate or equipment, *depletion* for corporations that produce natural resources like oil and gas, and *amortization of intangibles*. Many corporations show very little in earnings because of noncash deductions, but generate large cash flows. Examples include real estate and natural resource corporations, and corporations that are capital-intensive (businesses that have large amounts of depreciable equipment).

Q: What are some of the cash flow terms that I should be aware of?

A: Some of the cash flow terms you should be familiar with are:

- amortization
- depreciation
- depletion
- intangibles

Q: What is amortization?

A: *Amortization* is a method of spreading the cost of an asset over the period in which it is used. For accounting and income tax purposes, part of the cost of the asset is subtracted from gross income (written off or amortized) each year for a number of years to reflect the asset's theoretical decline in value. The value of the asset on the corporation's balance sheet is also reduced by the same amount. The amount written off should be added to earnings in determining cash flow because it is a noncash expense.

Q: What is depreciation?

A: *Depreciation* is a type of amortization expense, reflecting the theoretical loss of value of buildings or equipment because of use or obsolescence. In the case of buildings, the

STOCKS

income tax laws and accounting principles provide for the writing off of part of the cost each year, even though the market value may be increasing. Whether the asset loses or gains actual value, the annual write-off is allowed. Depreciation is a noncash charge deducted from earnings before computing income taxes.

Q: What is depletion?

A: *Depletion* is a type of amortization expense that represents the theoretical consumption of a natural asset such as oil, gas, timber, or ore. Because the asset is consumed to generate revenues for the corporation, the depletion is calculated in relation to those revenues. Depletion is also a noncash charge deducted from earnings before computing income taxes.

Q: What are intangibles?

A: *Intangibles* are nonphysical assets that income tax laws and/or accounting principles allow corporations to amortize. Deductions for amortization of intangibles are noncash expense items. The best-known intangible is "goodwill," the amount by which the price one corporation pays to acquire another exceeds the acquired corporation's *book value*. Generally, goodwill is amortized over fifteen years and is deducted from earnings before calculating income taxes. (Note: Tax laws are constantly changing, which may change the schedules of deductibility.)

 Example: If corporation A acquires corporation B for $150 million, which is $50 million over its $100 million book value, the $50 million is written off over 15 years, or $3,333,333 per year.

Book value is also referred to as *net worth*. The book value of a corporation is the total assets minus all liabilities.

Most investors do not need to fully understand all components of cash flow. What is important is understanding that cash flow provides the cash available for the payment of dividends or to reinvest for future growth. Positive cash flow also may enhance the returns on your invested money.

STOCKS

Q: What is cash flow per share?

A: *Cash flow per share* is the after-tax earnings plus noncash deductions divided by the number of shares outstanding.

 Example: In 1993, PepsiCo had earnings per share of $2.05 and cash flow per share of $3.70. The $1.65 by which cash flow per share exceeds earnings per share times the number of shares outstanding is additional money that Pepsi could use to pay dividends or reinvest in the company for future growth and expansion.

Illustration 5-5

Ten-Year History of PepsiCo's Cash Flow per Share

Year	Cash Flow per Share
1984	$0.69
1985	$0.90
1986	$1.10
1987	$1.47
1988	$1.76
1989	$2.10
1990	$2.45
1991	$2.83
1992	$3.15
1993	$3.70

 Note: From 1984 to 1993, PepsiCo's cash flow per share increased at a compound annual rate of 20.51 percent.

Q: What are primary earnings per share?

A: *Primary earnings per share* are a corporation's earnings per share on current shares outstanding.

Q: What is fully diluted earnings per share?

A: *Dilution* occurs when a corporation's earnings are spread over more shares, or "diluted," to allow for the possible future issuance of additional common shares in connection with existing warrants, convertible securities, or options. If issued, the additional shares would increase the number of common shares outstanding and therefore decrease the corporation's earnings per share.

Q: What are warrants?

A: *Warrants* are rights to buy shares of a corporation's securities, usually common stock, at a specified price for a limited period of time. Warrants are primarily issued as a marketing technique to help make other securities of a corporation more attractive to investors. Many warrants have a market value and a trading market for buying and selling. If warrants are exercised, they are a potential source of additional shares of common stock.

Q: What are convertible securities?

A: *Convertible securities* are securities, usually debt securities (bonds) or preferred stock (which will be discussed later), that can be converted until some future date into a fixed number of shares of other securities (usually common stock of the same corporation). Convertible securities are a potential source of additional shares of common stock.

Q: What are options?

A: *Options*, in a discussion of potential dilution, are rights to buy a fixed number of shares at a fixed price for a fixed period of time. Options are issued to a corporation's officers based on the company's performance or for other reasons. The options usually require that an officer remain employed for a certain period of time. Options are a potential source of additional shares of common stock.

When you see a corporation report primary earnings per share, this means earnings per share based on current shares outstanding.

When you see a corporation report *fully diluted earnings per share*, this means the earnings per share if all possible shares were issued. It does not mean that all the potential additional shares will be issued. The warrants, convertible securities, or options are only possible sources of additional shares.

STOCKS

61

Q: What is a dividend?

A: A *dividend* is the portion of earnings the directors of a corporation pay to the corporation's owners (shareholders). In addition to or in lieu of cash dividends, some corporations may pay *stock dividends* (see page 97). Most corporations pay dividends quarterly, or every three months.

Thus, if a corporation pays a dividend on December 31, you should also receive a dividend check around the end of March, June, and September.

Dividend cycles for quarterly payments are usually:

Cycle 1	Cycle 2	Cycle 3
January	February	March
April	May	June
July	August	September
October	November	December

If you own stocks in one dividend cycle, you will receive dividends every three months. If you own stocks in all three cycles, you will receive dividends every month.

Q: Why do some corporations with earnings not pay a dividend or pay a very small dividend?

A: Corporations that pay no dividend, or a very small dividend, are usually growth companies that need to reinvest all or most of their earnings if they are to continue to grow. These companies are usually relatively new or are corporations whose products or markets are rapidly expanding and that need cash for continued growth.

Q: Where can I find dividend news on the corporations of interest to me?

A: Dividend news on most large corporations is carried in major financial publications, such as the *Wall Street Journal*, *Investor's Business Daily*, and *Barron's*. Local newspapers and media generally carry dividend news on local and regional corporations. Your local library may also be a good resource. It should carry publications such as *Value Line*, *Standard & Poor's*, and *Moody's*, which are all good sources for key dividend dates and financial data. Your broker should also be able to provide you with key dividend information.

Q: What is meant by growth of dividends?

A: *Growth of dividends* means increases in dividends. Many corporations raise their dividends each year. See Illustration 5-6, Pepsi dividends.

Illustration 5-6
Ten-Year History of Dividends per Share Paid by PepsiCo

Year	Dividends per Share
1984	$0.19
1985	$0.20
1986	$0.21
1987	$0.22
1988	$0.27
1989	$0.32
1990	$0.38
1991	$0.46
1992	$0.51
1993	$0.58

Note: From 1984 to 1993, PepsiCo's dividends per share increased at a compound annual rate of 13.2 percent.

Q: What does growth of dividends mean to me?

A: Increasing the dividends it pays is a way for a corporation to share its increasing earnings with you and its other owners. Growth of dividends (or increasing dividends) is an inflation hedge: As the cost of the items you purchase increases, it is important that your income increase also. Owning common stocks may provide you with increasing income as well as potential growth of your invested assets.

Illustration 5-7 shows how growth of earnings and cash flow leads to dividend growth.

STOCKS

Illustration 5-7

Ten-Year History of Earnings per Share, Cash Flow, and Dividends of PepsiCo

Year	Earnings per Share	Cash Flow per Share	Dividends per Share
1984	$0.38	$0.69	$0.19
1985	$0.50	$0.90	$0.20
1986	$0.58	$1.10	$0.21
1987	$0.74	$1.47	$0.22
1988	$0.97	$1.76	$0.27
1989	$1.12	$2.10	$0.32
1990	$1.31	$2.45	$0.38
1991	$1.50	$2.83	$0.46
1992	$1.61	$3.15	$0.51
1993	$2.05	$3.70	$0.58

Q: What are the key dividend dates? I keep seeing the news of a dividend being declared on one date, paid on another, and so forth. What are these dates?

A: The key dividend dates you should be aware of include:

● declaration date
● ex-dividend date
● record date
● payment date

Q: What is a declaration date?

A: The *declaration date* is the day a corporation's board of directors meets and declares the amount of the dividend. A public announcement will usually be made.

Q: What is the ex-dividend date?

A: The *ex-dividend date* is the first day on which a seller of a stock is no longer entitled to the dividend and a purchaser is entitled to the dividend.

A good rule to remember is: If the date of a buy/sell transaction is any day *up to* the ex-dividend date, the seller is entitled to the dividend. If the transaction occurs on or *after* the ex-dividend date, the dividend belongs to the buyer.

Q: What is the record date?

A: The *record date* is the day the corporation closes its corporate books to determine the stockholders who are entitled to the dividend. The record date is established by the board of directors when the dividend is declared.

Q: What is the payment date?

A: The *payment date* is the day the corporation's dividend-paying agent (usually a bank) mails dividend checks to the corporation's stockholders.

For an example of the key dividend dates, the calendar that follows uses PepsiCo's dividend of 16 cents per share paid on September 30, 1993.

Declaration date:	July 22, 1993
Ex-dividend date:	August 3, 1993
Record date:	August 10, 1993
Payment date:	September 30, 1993

Illustration 5-9

July

Sunday	Monday	Tuesday	Wednesday	Thursday	Friday	Saturday
				1	2	3
6	7	8	9	10		
13	14	15	16	17		
20	21	22 Declaration Date	23	24		
			30	31		

August

Sunday	Monday	Tuesday	Wednesday	Thursday	Friday	Saturday
1	2	3 Ex-Dividend Date	4	5	6	7
8	9	10 Record Date	11	12	13	14
15	16	17	18	19	20	21
22	23	24				
29	30	31				

September

Sunday	Monday	Tuesday	Wednesday	Thursday	Friday	Saturday
			1	2	3	4
5	6	7	8	9	10	11
12	13	14	15	16	17	18
19	20	21	22	23	24	25
26	27	28	29	30 Payment Date		

STOCKS

Q: What happens if I buy a stock before the ex-dividend date, but the records of the corporation cannot be updated in time for proper dividend credit?

A: If the buyer is entitled to a dividend, but the ownership has not been transferred on the corporation's books in time for the dividend to be paid to the buyer, the brokerage firm executing the transaction is responsible for claiming the dividend from the seller and making certain that the payment is made to the buyer. This is referred to as a *dividend claim*.

Q: What is the current yield on a stock?

A: The *current yield* is the anticipated annual dividend divided by the current price of the stock.

 Example: If you purchase a share of PepsiCo at $40 and the anticipated annual dividend is $0.64 per share, your current yield is 1.6 percent ($0.64 divided by $40 = 1.6 percent).

Q: Why can *my* yield on a stock be different from the current yield I see in the paper?

A: If you invested in PepsiCo ten years ago and your cost was $4 per share, the yield on your cost is 16 percent ($0.64 divided by $4 = 16 percent). The current yield of 1.6 percent is based on today's price of $40 ($0.64 divided by $40). The reason your yield is higher than the current yield is that your cost is much less than the current price.

Q: Why do stock prices go up and down?

A: The current price of a stock is the price investors will pay for that stock at that moment. The price represents the present value of the expected future cash to be received from that stock, either from dividends or through capital appreciation. When you buy a stock for its appreciation potential, you believe that expectations about the corporation will improve and investors will pay higher prices for the stock. Since the price depends on investors' expectations, the price will rise or fall as new developments occur, such as:

- *Company developments.* The corporation's own operations will sometimes exceed or fall short of investors' expectations. For example, IBM's internal troubles from 1991 to 1993 caused its stock to fall even as the stocks of other computer companies continued to rise.
- *Industry/group developments.* The industry of which the corporation is a part will experience better or worse prospects from time to time, such as the banking industry during the credit crisis in the 1989–1991 period.
- *Market developments.* The entire stock market environment can change, pulling a stock's price along with it regardless of how well the corporation is doing. The bull market that began in 1982 elevated the price level for stocks in general, and the market crash of October 1987 pulled most down temporarily.

Q: What is a bull market?
A: A bull market is a period during which the general level of stock prices is rising.

Q: What is a bear market?
A: A bear market is a period during which the general level of stock prices is falling.

- *Economic/political developments.* Good or bad reports on the economy and political events such as elections or new laws can affect expectations about a corporation, an industry, or the entire stock market. As a historic example, the Arab oil embargo of 1973–1974 affected not just oil stocks, but the stock market and the economy as a whole.

STOCKS

Q: What is the total return on my stock?

A: *Total return* is dividend yield plus appreciation.

 Example: You bought a stock paying a 50 cents per share dividend one year ago for $10 a share (5 percent yield). Today, the stock is worth $12 a share

($2 per share appreciation or 20 percent). Your total return is 25 percent: the dividend yield of 5 percent plus appreciation of 20 percent.

If you had owned the stock for five years, your total dividends would be $2.50 (50 cents per year for five years), or 25 percent ($2.50 divided by 10). Add the appreciation of 20 percent and your total return is 45 percent over five years. This translates into an average annual return of 9 percent, or a compound annual return of 7.7 percent (see Chapter 3, pages 15-16).

Q: What is my stock portfolio?

A: Your *stock portfolio* is your entire holdings of stocks. As your investment strategy develops and changes, you should regularly review your portfolio to make sure it continues to meet your objectives and requirements.

Q: How do I diversify my stock portfolio?

A: You diversify your stock portfolio by owning several different types of stocks. You should not put all your eggs in one basket by investing all your money in one security. Diversification into different types of stock will reduce risk. Often a difficult period for one type of corporation or industry will be offset by good relative performance of the rest of the portfolio. You may diversify in several different ways, including:

- Company size
- Industry group
- Market behavior
- Investment objective

Q: How do I diversify by company size?

A: Stocks are available from companies of a wide variety of sizes. A corporation's size is often referred to as its *market capitalization*, or the total value of all of its outstanding stock.

The three classifications of company size are:

- large-capitalization
- mid-capitalization
- small-capitalization

STOCKS

68

Q: What are large-capitalization stocks?

A: *Large-capitalization* stocks are issued by the largest and most established companies in the nation. Such stocks are often called *blue chip* because the companies are leaders in their industry and have a history of profits and dividend payments. They also have a large number of shares outstanding and the total market value of their stock is large. Large-capitalization stocks include such very recognizable companies as Exxon, AT&T, and Walt Disney.

> The name *"blue chip"* comes from games of chance. The blue chip has the highest value.

Q: What are mid-capitalization stocks?

A: *Mid-capitalization* stocks are issued by companies smaller than the world leaders and the market value of their outstanding stock is much less than that of large-capitalization stocks. These include many well-established and familiar companies, such as Liz Claiborne, Shoney's, and Armor All Products.

Q: What are small-capitalization stocks?

A: The great majority of stocks in the public marketplace are *small-capitalization* stocks. Their market capitalization may be small because the corporation is young and has yet to grow into the mid-capitalization range and beyond, or because the corporation operates only in a narrow region or business line. These companies may be well known to investors who know the business or region. They may be corporations such as your local bank, a retailer in your area, or a rising manufacturer in a regional industry.

If you are seeking a diversified stock portfolio, you should consider spreading your investments among the capitalization classifications, since the market may favor large-capitalization stocks at some times and small-capitalization stocks at other times. For instance, large-capitalization stocks did very well during the 1980s, whereas in earlier decades, small-capitalization stocks performed better.

STOCKS

Q: How do I diversify by industry groups or sectors?

A: Companies operate in many different industries, and those industries are grouped into industry sectors. The major *industry sectors* and some industries within those sectors are the following:

- *Basic Industry*
  Chemicals
  Metals
  Paper

- *Capital Goods*
  Machinery
  Computers
  Electrical Equipment
  Telephone-Long Distance
  Pollution Control
  Aerospace/Defense

- *Consumer Durables*
  Appliances
  Autos
  Building
  Photography

- *Consumer*
  Nondurables/Services
  Foods and Beverages
  Drugs/Health
  Retail
  Publishing

- Tobacco
  Household
  Entertainment/Leisure

- *Energy*
  Oil Service/Drilling
  Oils—Domestic
  Oils—International

- *Financial*
  Banks
  Other Finance
  Insurance

- *Transportation*
  Air
  Rail
  Truck

- *Utilities*
  Electric
  Gas
  Telephone

- *Miscellaneous*

Investing in a broad variety of industry groups usually allows you, the investor, representation in the different sectors of the economy. Companies in an industry sector will be affected by the same industry developments, but companies in other sectors often will be affected by different factors and circumstances. Diversifying a portfolio among industry sectors usually reduces the risk from down cycles in any one sector.

Q: How do I diversify by market behavior?

A: Classifying stocks by their historic price behavior in various market environments is another way of seeking diversification. In addition to size and industry groupings, stocks also may be

STOCKS

classified by how their price reacts to various cycles within the stock market and the economy. At the start of an economic upturn, for instance, *cyclical stocks* (those tied most closely to the economy's health, like steel or machinery stocks) will usually perform well. The reverse is also true; as the economy turns down, *defensive stocks* (those of companies making staple goods, such as foods and beverages) will resist the downturn better than others.

Q: How do I diversify by investment objective?

A. Stocks may also be classified by which investment objective, such as *growth* or *income*, they most closely fulfill.

Q: What are growth stocks?

A: *Growth stocks* are those of corporations, such as computer makers, that are growing rapidly and that reinvest the majority of their earnings in this growth rather than paying them out as dividends. Growth stocks have a long-term record of superior appreciation tied to growth of the company's earnings. Since the shareholder's total return and accumulation of wealth often depends on this growth, the stocks tend to be more volatile than stocks with higher dividends.

Q: What are income-oriented stocks?

A: *Income-oriented* stocks generally provide a high income and often a steady growth of income, but do not hold as much promise for growth and appreciation. Examples include utility stocks or real estate investment trusts. Such stocks are usually steadier in price behavior because investors are not demanding dynamic appreciation potential. Generally, the higher the yield of a stock, the less opportunity there is for capital appreciation. The prices of income stocks will decline if interest rates increase. Their prices will rise if interest rates decrease.

 Note of Caution: If a stock is yielding a great deal more than similar stocks, you may want to investigate whether its dividend is in jeopardy.

STOCKS

Q: Can I diversify by investing in foreign stocks?

A: As the world becomes smaller and stock markets develop abroad, many investors are seeking opportunities in foreign stocks. You can invest in foreign stocks either directly or through *American Depositary Receipts (ADRs)*. Generally, an American investor will not purchase the stock of foreign corporations directly. He or she will invest in American Depository Receipts.

Shares of many of the larger foreign corporations, such as British Petroleum, Sony, and Honda, are traded in U.S. markets via ADRs. Even though ADR certificates look like stock certificates, they actually represent shares of a foreign corporation that are held by an American bank, which issues the ADR. ADRs are a popular way for Americans to invest in foreign corporations because of the ease of transfer and sale.

Q: What are some of the risks of investing in foreign securities?

A: If you invest in foreign stocks, your investments may be subject to currency adjustments, special taxes, or transfer difficulties. Currency adjustments mean that the dollar value of your foreign stocks *may* fluctuate because of a change in the value of the foreign currency relative to the U.S. dollar rather than because of any corporate event or news. Rules and regulations and reporting requirements for foreign markets are often different from those for domestic corporations. Foreign stocks that are traded in U.S. markets must conform to U.S. reporting requirements.

 Note of Caution: Before investing in ADRs or foreign securities, you should look into potential problems and see if you are willing to assume the additional risk.

Q: Is there a possible tax consequence in owning foreign securities?

A: When you own ADRs or own shares of a foreign corporation directly, the country in which the foreign corporation is located will often withhold income tax from the dividends you receive. Generally, you may credit such withholdings against your U.S. income taxes. For precise information on the taxation of the dividends or distributions from foreign corporations, you should consult your broker or tax advisor.

Q: Every day I hear quotes for the Dow Jones Industrial Average and the S&P 500. What do these quotes mean to me?

A: Indexes reflect the general direction of the stock market or specific segments of the stock market. When news commentators want to indicate the direction of stock prices, they quote the movements of one or more stock indexes.

Indexes are published daily to give investors the general direction of stock prices. The indexes are commonly reported by the news media as part of regular coverage. When large movements occur in stock prices, the change in the indexes often makes headlines.

Different indexes are formulated to measure different sectors of the market. The Dow Industrials includes only 30 large-capitalization stocks, whereas the S&P 500 measures the broader market, covering 500 stocks.

Q: What are some of the more popular indexes and averages?

A: Some of the most popular indexes and averages include:

- The Dow Jones Industrial Average
- The Dow Jones Transportation Average
- The Dow Jones Utility Average
- The Standard & Poor's 500 Index
- The NASDAQ Composite Index

Q: What is the Dow Jones Industrial Average?

A: The *Dow Jones Industrial Average* is a measure of the price movement of the general stock market based on thirty widely held stocks listed on the New York Stock Exchange. The average is calculated by adding the prices of the thirty stocks and dividing by an adjusted number of shares. Because of stock splits, stock dividends, and substitutions, the number of shares divided into the prices is constantly changing. (For a discussion of stock dividends and stock splits, refer to page 97.)

STOCKS

Q: What is the Dow Jones Transportation Average?

A: The *Dow Jones Transportation Average* is a measure of the general price direction of transportation stocks. The index consists of twenty transportation stocks listed on the New York Stock Exchange.

Q: What is the Dow Jones Utility Average?

A: The *Dow Jones Utility Average* is a measure of the general price direction of utility stocks. The index consists of fifteen utility stocks listed on the New York Stock Exchange.

Q: What is the Standard & Poor's 500 Index?

A: The *Standard & Poor's 500 Index*, also known as the S&P 500, is a broad measure of the price movement of stocks. This index is considered a good indication of the stock market because it includes a large number of stocks—500. The index includes common stocks of 400 industrial corporations, 20 transportation corporations, 40 financial corporations, and 40 public utility corporations. The *S&P 400 Index* includes only the 400 industrials.

Q: What is the NASDAQ Composite Index?

A: The *NASDAQ Composite Index* is among the broadest possible measures, including all issues except warrants that trade in the over-the-counter market. NASDAQ is short for National Association of Securities Dealers Automated Quotations system. There are roughly 5,000 issues trading on NASDAQ that are included in the index. This index gives the direction of price movement for over-the-counter stocks. The index is market-value-weighted, so that the weight given to each security is proportional to its last-sale price multiplied by the total shares outstanding.

Q: How do I go about buying and selling stocks?

A: Your first step is to establish your general investment objectives and the role stocks should play in your strategy to achieve those objectives. For assistance in establishing your investment objectives, you may turn to a professional at a brokerage house, bank, or other advisory firm. (See Chapter 14, "Advisors.")

Q: How do I choose stocks that meet my investment objectives?

A: The process of searching for appropriate stocks is called *investment research*. Some investors conduct their own first-hand research, which may be of two major types:

- Fundamental analysis
- Technical analysis

Q: What factors are included in fundamental analysis?

A: In *fundamental analysis*, the investor considers the fundamental operating factors of the corporation. This may include:

- Analyzing a corporation's financial reports
- Calculating performance statistics
- Studying the corporation's industry conditions
- Estimating future cash flows
- Assessing whether the corporation's stock price fairly reflects such factors

Fundamental research should lead you to select stocks whose prices, based on their past performance and your positive expectations for future results, are likely to rise.

Q: What is technical analysis?

A: *Technical analysis* involves observing how the stock's price movement and volume follow recognizable patterns. People who rely on technical analysis are sometimes called "chartists" because they study stock price charts. Their stock decisions are based on chart patterns rather than fundamental operating performance.

 Note: Many investors believe that both approaches provide worthwhile information about future stock prices and will consider both fundamental and technical factors before investing in or selling a stock. Some investors use technical analysis to confirm or contradict the indications of fundamental analysis.

STOCKS

Q: Are there published research sources that I can consult instead of doing my own research?

A: Yes. Not all investors have the time, resources, or training to carry out first-hand research. Many will use research prepared by professional analysts. Brokerage firms publish research reports on many major national and regional stocks to assist their clients in stock selection. Subscription publications such as *Value Line*, *Standard & Poor's Stock Reports*, and investment newsletters also offer company analysis. Your public library may carry such research sources, along with others such as computer databases or files of company annual reports.

Q: Are there other sources of investment information or recommendations?

A: There are many investment newsletters that publish at various intervals. The cost of these newsletters can vary greatly. A subscription may cost under $100 or several hundred dollars a year. Most newsletters will advertise in major financial publications like the *Wall Street Journal*, *Investor's Business Daily*, or *Barron's*. Often you may subscribe for a short "trial period" for a price lower than that of an annual subscription. A trial subscription allows you to review a particular newsletter to see if it meets your needs and objectives.

Q: What are some of the most popular newsletters?

A: Listed below are several newsletters and their addresses. This list is not intended to be complete, nor is it an endorsement of any of the newsletters.

Dick Davis Digest
P.O. Box 9547
Fort Lauderdale, FL 33310-9547

The Dines Letter
P.O. Box 22
Belvedere, CA 94920

Dow Theory Forecasts
7412 Calumet Avenue
Hammond, IN 46324

STOCKS

Growth Stock Outlook
P.O. Box 15381
Chevy Chase, MD 20825

Personal Finance
P.O. Box 1467
Alexandria, VA 22313

The Zweig Forecast
P.O. Box 2900
Wantagh, NY 11793

Q: Where can I get stocks from?

A: Stocks can be acquired from several sources:

- Initial public offerings (IPOs)
- Secondary offerings
- Open-market purchases (existing shares)
- Dividend reinvestment plans

Q: Where do stocks come from originally?

A: Originally, shares are purchased directly from the corporation. If you are among the original public investors, your shares are issued by way of an *initial public offering (IPO)*. In such an offering, the corporation provides a *prospectus* describing the corporation's operations and past financial performance. The corporation works through a brokerage firm as *underwriter*, and during the period leading up to the offering date, you give the underwriter an *indication of interest*—how many shares you are interested in buying within the stated price range. Once the terms of the offering are finalized on the *offering date*, your order is executed and the corporation issues the shares to you and the other investors.

You may also buy stock directly from a corporation whose stock is already publicly traded when it issues additional shares in a *secondary offering*. In a secondary offering, you may also be buying existing shares from a selling shareholder.

STOCKS

Q: What are some of the terms I need to understand relating to public offerings of stock?

A: Some terms you should be familiar with in relation to public offerings include:

- initial public offering
- prospectus
- underwriter
- syndicate
- indication of interest
- offering date
- secondary offering

Q: What is an initial public offering?

A: An *initial public offering (IPO)* is the first sale of a company's stock to the public. Conducting an IPO for a company is also referred to as "taking it public."

Q: What is a prospectus?

A: A *prospectus* is the official document describing the company and the details of the offering. The prospectus is designed to reveal every significant factor that an investor should know about before buying the stock.

Q: What is an underwriter?

A: An *underwriter* is the brokerage firm that conducts an offering. It usually enters into a financial commitment to pay the company in full for the shares it is selling in a public offering. By committing its financial resources, the brokerage firm is *underwriting* the corporation's shares and assumes the risk of immediately selling the shares to the public. Another type of underwriting (rarely used) is the *best efforts* underwriting. In this case, the underwriter makes no commitment to the corporation other than to use its best efforts to sell the securities. Generally, securities issued in a best efforts underwriting are those of smaller and/or unproven companies.

Q: What is a syndicate?

A: A *syndicate* is a group of brokerage firms formed to underwrite a public offering, thus spreading the underwriting risk and efforts.

STOCKS

Q: What is an indication of interest?

A: An *indication of interest* is an investor's request for a certain number of shares in the offering.

Q: What is the offering date?

A: The *offering date* is the date on which the offering's selling period ends. On this date, the price and size of the offering are made final and the shares are fully committed.

Q: What is a secondary offering?

A: A *secondary offering* is a public offering by a company that has already had an IPO. The underwriting method is the same as that for an IPO.

Q: Other than through public offerings, how do I buy shares of stock?

A: In most cases, an investor will buy existing shares that another investor is selling. Such transactions take place either on a stock exchange or between dealers in the *over-the-counter (OTC)* market.

When the stock is listed on an *exchange,* such as the New York Stock Exchange, your broker's representative will take your order or electronically transmit it to a stock *specialist.* The specialist will match your buy order with someone else's sell order, executing thousands of such trades every day. This method of trading is referred to as an *auction market,* since the bidding occurs in a fixed place, with the specialist acting as auctioneer. In addition, specialists may buy and sell for their own account to stabilize the trading market in their stocks. Once your order is executed, it will be confirmed back to you. All such trades are recorded in the exchange's reports for the day.

Daily trading on each exchange-listed stock is reported in major newspapers. The following illustration shows the standard format for this information.

STOCKS

Illustration 5-9

A Newspaper Quote for PepsiCo

52 Weeks		Stock	Sym	Div	Yld %	PE	Vol 100s	Hi	Lo	Close	Net Chg
Hi	Lo										
46⅛	29¼	PepsiCo	PEP	.80	1.7	21	35354	47	45½	47	+1½
(1)	(2)	(3)	(4)	(5)	(6)	(7)	(8)	(9)	(10)	(11)	(12)

(1), (2). *52-week high and low stock price for PepsiCo:* 46⅛, 29¼
(3). *Name of the corporation:* PepsiCo
(4). *The trading symbol for the stock:* PEP
(5). *The estimated dividend for the next 12 months:* $0.80 per share
(6). *The yield in percent:* 1.7%
(7). *The price-earnings ratio:* PepsiCo's current price is 21 times the last 12 months' earnings
(8). *Number of shares traded, in hundreds:* On this day, 3,535,400 shares of PepsiCo were traded
(9). *The highest price at which the stock traded during the day:* 47
(10). *The lowest price at which the stock traded during the day:* 45½
(11): *The closing price for the day:* 47
(12). *The net change from the prior trading day's closing price:* +1½

Each newspaper will have its own special codes for such items as:

- Stock splits
- Stock dividends
- New issues
- Stocks trading ex-dividend or ex-rights
- Stocks not being delivered until distributed
- Stocks being delivered when issued
- Stocks trading with warrants
- Stocks trading without warrants

Q: What are the major U.S. stock exchanges?

A: The major U.S. stock exchanges include:

- New York Stock Exchange
- American Stock Exchange
- Pacific Stock Exchange
- Philadelphia Stock Exchange
- Midwest Stock Exchange

There are also stock exchanges in many foreign countries.

When you buy or sell a stock that trades *over-the-counter* (*OTC*), your order is not sent to New York or Philadelphia or any other exchange location. Your broker's own trading desk makes direct contact with another firm's traders. They negotiate price and execute the transaction themselves, reporting the trade to you and to the networks of OTC trading firms around the country. The major OTC reporting network is called the *National Association of Securities Dealers Automated Quotations (NASDAQ)* system. Another OTC reporting service called the "Pink Sheets" is published by the National Quotation Bureau Inc. and reports trading in smaller stocks. Daily trading in many OTC stocks is reported in major newspapers. The format is the same as that used for exchange-listed stocks. Refer to the example on page 80.

Q: What are some of the over-the-counter market terms I should know?

A: Some over-the-counter market terms you should understand are:

- bid price
- asked price
- spread

Q: What is the bid price?

A: The *bid price* is the price a dealer would pay a seller for shares.

Q: What is the asked price?

A: The *asked price* is the price a dealer would charge a buyer for shares.

Q: What is the spread?

A: The *spread* is the difference between the bid and asked prices, which the dealer keeps as compensation for the trader who executed the transaction. Your broker may also charge you a commission.

STOCKS

Note: Bid and asked prices for major stocks are no longer reported in the newspaper.

 Note of Caution: If your broker says your transaction was executed on a *net basis* and there was no commission, he or she is generally still being compensated. On a net trade, the broker's compensation is part of the spread.

Q: Is there a way to buy stock directly from a corporation without going through a brokerage firm?

A: Yes. You may be able to buy additional stock in a corporation through a *dividend reinvestment plan*, or *DRIP*. A DRIP allows you, as a shareholder, to have the corporation invest your dividends directly in additional shares of the corporation's stock, rather than paying them to you in cash. Some corporations' DRIPs will absorb all the costs of the plan, including commissions and fees. Some corporations issue new shares to participants in their DRIP, whereas others buy existing shares in the open market for the plan. A few corporations allow stockholders to reinvest their dividends at a discount to the market price. The discount, if allowed, is usually 5 percent.

Q: How do I sign up for a dividend reinvestment plan?

A: In order for you to establish a dividend reinvestment plan, your shares must be registered in your name. The certificate can be held by your brokerage firm or kept in your possession. After the certificate has been issued to you, the corporation will send you information on its DRIP, including the rules of the DRIP and how to sign up for the plan. You should read the information carefully and keep all of the key addresses and telephone numbers with your investment records.

Q: Can I invest additional cash in a DRIP?

A: Yes. Many DRIPs also allow shareholders to make direct investments of $25 to $3,000 a quarter. The investments will be made according to the rules of the plan. The rules of DRIPs for different corporations vary, so you need to review the rules of each specific plan.

Q: What kind of records will I get on my DRIP investments?

A: Each time a dividend is invested in additional shares or cash you mail in is invested in additional shares, you will receive a confirmation of the transaction. The number of shares purchased will usually be expressed to three decimal places. It is imperative that you keep records of all purchases made in your reinvestment plan. When you sell or liquidate all or some of the shares held in the plan, you will have a gain or loss, depending on the current market price of the stock. After years of participating in DRIPs, many investors have been shocked to learn that they should have kept the records for tax purposes.

Q: What happens to my certificates in a DRIP?

A: Generally, all shares acquired in a DRIP are held by the reinvestment agent, usually a bank, as unissued shares. The reinvestment agent is holding the shares as your agent. You are the owner. If you want a certificate for the shares issued to you, write to the reinvestment agent, whose name and address, and often a telephone number, are printed on the confirmation statement.

Q: How can I sell my shares in a DRIP?

A: There are two ways to sell:

1. You can request that a certificate be issued to you and then, after you receive the certificate, sell the shares at the current market price through a broker.
2. You can write the reinvestment agent and request that all or some of your shares held in the plan be sold and a check for the proceeds mailed to you.

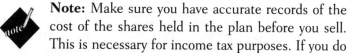

Note: Make sure you have accurate records of the cost of the shares held in the plan before you sell. This is necessary for income tax purposes. If you do not have the records, you can review previous income tax returns and determine the amount of dividends for that stock for each year. The amount of dividends reinvested each year will be your cost for DRIP shares bought that year.

STOCKS

83

Q: Do I have to pay income tax on the reinvested dividends, since I am not receiving the cash?

A: Yes. You must include all dividends reinvested each year as taxable income, even though you do not receive the cash. Also, any discounts allowed by a DRIP in which you participate will generally be taxable income. The reinvestment agent will notify you of any taxable discounts. If the dividends are reinvested at a discount, the discount may be taxable income. You should check with your tax advisor.

Q: Is there a good source of information on DRIPs?

A: Yes.

- If you own stock in a corporation, you will receive the information directly from that corporation. If you do not receive it, you can contact the corporation's investor relations department.

- For general information on DRIPs or a directory of corporations that offer DRIPs, you may want to contact:

  Evergreen Enterprises
  P.O. Box 763
  Laurel, MD 20725-0763
  (301) 953-1861

  There will be a charge for its publication and services.

Q: Now that I know what and where to buy, how do I actually make my investment?

A: To purchase stock, the first step is to contact a broker at a full-service brokerage firm, bank, or discount broker and open an account. This takes only a few minutes. The broker will ask for standard information, such as your name, address, phone number, and Social Security number. The broker will also ask specific questions to determine your investment background and the types of investments suitable for you:

- Your investment objectives
- Your occupation and employer
- Your financial resources: income, net worth, liquid assets, etc.
- The bank and brokerage firms you use

STOCKS

- Whether this is an individual or a joint account (with a spouse, etc.)
- Whether you prefer stock certificates and dividends to be held in the account or mailed to you

---

Q: What are some of the ways my stock can be registered?

A: Your stock can be registered in the following ways:

- register and ship
- held in customer name
- held in street name

Q: What does register and ship mean?

A: If your account is coded to *register and ship*, a certificate will be registered in your name and shipped to you. All dividends and corporate information will be mailed directly to you at your address of record by the company or its agent.

Q: If my account is coded to hold in customer name, what does this mean?

A: If your account is coded to *hold in customer name*, a certificate will be registered in your name but held at the brokerage firm for safekeeping. All dividends and corporate information will be mailed directly to you at your address of record.

Q: If my account is coded to hold in street name, what does this mean?

A: If your account is coded to *hold in street name*, securities are registered in the name of the broker/dealer for the benefit of you, the owner. This method facilitates transfer, collection of dividends, identification, and notification of major corporate events. All dividends and corporate information are mailed to the broker/dealer and forwarded to the investor. The investor may instruct the broker to hold dividends for future investment.

Q: What are some of the different orders I can enter?

A: Once the account is open, you may enter an order to purchase or sell stock. Again, you may state your preference on a number of factors, including *price* and *time*.

STOCKS

On *price*, you may enter either a *market order* or a *limit order*. Whether buying or selling, you have the additional options of entering a *stop* or a *stop limit* order.

On *time*, you may enter either a *day order* or a *good-until-canceled (GTC)* order, also known as an open order.

Some of the different types of orders include:

- market order
- limit order
- sell stop order
- buy stop order
- sell stop limit order
- buy stop limit order
- day order
- good-until-canceled order

Q: What is a market order?

A: A *market order* is an order to buy or sell at the current market price when the order is placed, with no restrictions specified by the investor.

Q: What is a limit order?

A: A *limit order* is an order to buy or sell only at a price equal to or below (for a purchase), or equal to or above (for a sale), a specified price.

Q: What is a sell stop order?

A: A *sell stop order* allows investors to limit their exposure to a decline in a stock's value, thus either limiting the loss or preserving a profit. A sell stop order sets a specific price below the current price. If the stock's price falls to the stop order level, the stop order becomes a market order. It will be executed as soon as possible whether or not the price at that time is at the stop price.

Note: Investors using stop orders still risk having the sale executed at a lower price.

Q. What is a buy stop order?

A: A *buy stop order*—seldom used—specifies a price above the current price. It instructs the broker to buy once the stock has reached a certain price that the buyer believes sets the stage for further advances. Buy stop orders are often used to limit the risk in short sales. (See page 93).

Q: What is a sell stop limit order?

A: A *sell stop limit order* is similar to a sell stop order, except that the order will be executed only exactly at or above the price specified. This eliminates the risk of an execution at a lower price, but the investor may miss the opportunity to sell near the desired price if the stock price continues to decline.

Q: What is a buy stop limit order?

A: A *buy stop limit order* is like a buy stock order, except that the order will be executed only at or below the limit price specified. The risk of a buy stop limit order is missing the opportunity to buy if the stock's price continues to rise.

Q: What is a day order?

A: A *day order* is an order entered for execution on a particular trading day. At day's end, the order will expire if it has not been executed.

Q: What is a good-until-canceled order?

A: A *good-until-canceled order* is an order that will remain open until either it is executed, it expires, or you cancel it.

Q: What happens if you have an open order to buy or sell a stock and a dividend is paid while your order is still on the broker's books?

A: An open order does not establish ownership until it is executed, so you are not entitled to the dividend. Any open order price to buy or sell a stock is automatically reduced by the amount of the dividend on the ex-dividend date unless the order is marked *"do not reduce"* (DNR). If a dividend is not divisible by 12.5 cents per share, the open order price will reduced by the next higher. For instance, if a dividend is cents per share, open orders will be reduced by $^3/_8$ (37.5 ce per share).

Fractions on Stock Quote Translated into Cents per Share

$$1/8 = 12.5 \text{ cents}$$
$$1/4 = 25 \text{ cents}$$
$$3/8 = 37.5 \text{ cents}$$
$$1/2 = 50 \text{ cents}$$
$$5/8 = 62.5 \text{ cents}$$
$$3/4 = 75 \text{ cents}$$
$$7/8 = 87.5 \text{ cents}$$

Q: What happens to open orders if a corporation pays a stock dividend or splits its stock?

A: The prices of open orders are adjusted as explained above for cash dividends for the approximate value of the stock dividend or the stock split on the date of distribution.

Example: A stock is selling at $60 per share and splits 2-for-1, which means that stockholders will receive one additional share for each share they own. On the date the additional shares are mailed to shareholders, the stock will begin trading at around $30 per share. The price on all open orders will be divided by 2 to reflect the split.

Q: How do I know whether how my order was executed?

A: In buying and selling securities, industry practice is generally verbal instructions from investors to brokers. When any order is executed, or when an open order is entered, you will receive a written *confirmation* from your broker specifying the terms you discussed. The confirmation contains many important items of information that you should keep for your records. Examples of confirmation statements for a purchase and a sale are illustrated below.

Illustration 5-10
Confirmation—Buy

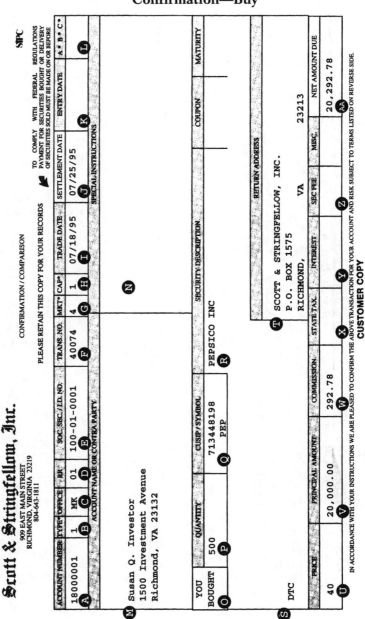

Illustration 5-11
Confirmation—Sell

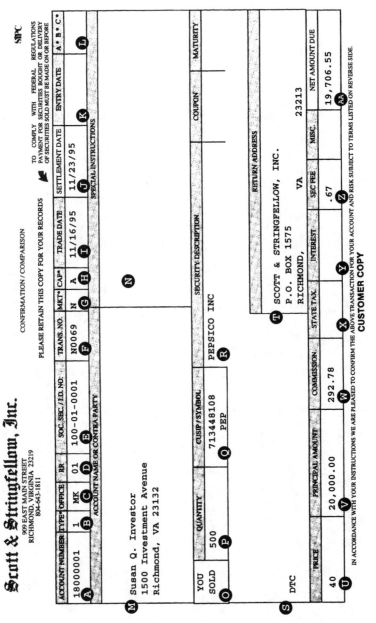

Confirmation Information Key

A. *Account number:* A number identifying the account in which you bought the shares.

B. *Account type:* The type of account you used. It may be one of the following types of accounts:

- Cash-payment account
- Margin account, in which you borrow part of the cost of the purchase
- Short sale account, in which you borrow the security because you have sold a stock you do not own

C. *Office:* The office of the brokerage firm you used.

D. *Representative number:* Your broker's identification number within the brokerage firm.

E. *Social Security or tax ID number.* A number identifying you as the buyer, whether personally (Social Security number) or through a business, estate, trust, etc. (tax ID number).

F. *Transaction number:* A number identifying your particular transaction. This facilitates tracing the transaction in case you have a question later.

G. *Market code:* The market where your transaction occurred, such as:

- New York Stock Exchange
- American Stock Exchange
- Over-the-counter market

Every brokerage firm will have its own codes for the different markets.

H. *Capacity:* The capacity in which your broker served in the transaction:

- As agent for you, simply finding shares for you to buy from another investor or broker
- As agent for both buyer and seller, matching your buy order directly with a sell order
- As principal, buying the shares and reselling them to you, either marking the price up or adding a commission

I. *Trade date:* The day your transaction is executed.

J. *Settlement date:* The day your payment is due if you are buying, or delivery of the certificate is due if you are selling.

Settlement date is currently five business days after trade date, but changed to three business days after trade date in June of 1995.

K.   *Entry date:* The day an order is entered if it is not the trade date.

L.   *A * B:* Delivery/special codes; refer to the key on the back of your confirm.

M.   *Account name:* Your name and address as recorded in the brokerage firm's records.

N.   *Special instructions:* Special conditions pertaining to the account status or the security.

O.   *Transaction type:* Whether you are buying, selling, etc.

P.   *Quantity:* Number of shares you are buying or selling.

Q.   *CUSIP/symbol:* Identification number of the security you are buying or selling. Just as you have a Social Security number to confirm your identity, so too does each security have a CUSIP (Committee on Uniform Securities Identification Procedures) number and trading symbol to pinpoint its identity.

R.   *Security description:* The formal name and description of the security.

S.   *Trailer notes:* Optional add-on notes requested by you or your broker for information purposes.

T.   *Return address:* Your broker's address for you to use in returning payment or correspondence.

U.   *Price:* The price per share that you paid.

V.   *Principal amount:* The number of shares multiplied by the price per share.

W.   *Commission:* The fee added to or subtracted from the principal amount as compensation to your broker.

X, Y.   Do not apply to stock transactions.

Z.   *SEC fee:* A nominal fee charged only on sales, calculated as 1 cent per $300 of principal amount. This fee is remitted to the Securities and Exchange Commission, the federal agency that regulates securities matters.

AA.   *Net amount due:* In a purchase, the total amount you owe the brokerage firm. In a sale, the total amount the brokerage firm owes you.

 Note: This explanation is from a sample brokerage firm confirmation. Every brokerage firm will have its own confirmation format, which may differ somewhat from the one shown.

Q: What is a short sale?

A: Sometimes investors sell a stock that they do not own with the intention of repurchasing it at a lower price. This transaction is known as a *short sale*. If the short sale is successful, the difference between the sale price and the purchase price is the investor's profit.

Example: An investor decides that IBM common stock is overvalued at $100 per share and sells the stock, which she does not own. Six months later, IBM is selling for $50 a share, and the investor purchases stock to close the position. Her profit is $50 per share.

Q: Are there any special rules when entering a short sale order?

A: Yes.

You must notify the broker that you are selling short (selling stock you do not own), and the broker must make arrangements to borrow a certificate for the number of shares you are selling to make delivery. The buyer of the stock you are selling must receive a certificate for the stock he or she is buying.

Short sales must be executed in a short account. In order to execute a short sale, you must also have a margin account (refer to Chapter 14, page 379 for an explanation of margin accounts). On most major exchanges, short sales can only be executed when the price of the order is higher than the last trade. This is referred to as the *uptick rule*.

Q: What is the risk in entering into a short sale?

A: When you invest in a stock, you are risking only the money you invested. In a short sale, in theory, your risk is unlimited—that is, the price of the stock you short could continue to rise indefinitely.

In the IBM example, if the price of IBM stock rose to $300 and the investor decided to repurchase at that price, her loss would be $200 a share ($300, the price at which she purchased the stock, less $100, the price at which she sold the stock).

STOCKS

Note of Caution: If the price of a stock you short-ed increases, you may receive a margin call for a portion of the rise in value (refer to Chapter 14, page 380 for an explanation of margin calls). In some instances, you may not be able to enter a short sale because your broker cannot borrow a certificate to make delivery.

Short sales are very speculative and should be entered into only by experienced and knowledgeable investors.

Q: I have heard of buying through dollar cost averaging. How does it work?

A: In *dollar cost averaging,* you invest a fixed amount of money each month, quarter, or year in a stock or other investment. Since the stock's price will fluctuate from period to period, you will be buying at different price levels. If you are investing $250 per period, your money will buy more shares when the stock's price is lower, and fewer shares when the price is higher. The method averages your dollar cost over time, which is why it is called dollar cost averaging.

One of the main benefits of dollar cost averaging is that the steady buying of shares lets you take advantage of temporary market declines. If there is a sudden market decline, many investors tend to shy away from a stock out of fear. If you are dollar cost averaging, you make your regular investment as always, buying a greater number of shares and lowering the average cost of your investment in the stock. The following table illustrates how the method might work:

STOCKS

Illustration 5-12
Dollar Cost Averaging

Investment Amount	Price Paid	Number of Shares Bought
$250	$25	10.00
250	27	9.26
250	30	8.33
250	25	10.00
250	20	12.50
250	18	13.89
250	21	11.90
250	23	10.87
250	25	10.00
$2,250	$23.26 (avg.)	96.75

Q: After I buy a stock, how do I follow my stock's progress?

A: It is important that you keep current on your stock's activity, the underlying company, and general market conditions. By checking your stock regularly, you can determine if there is an upward or downward trend in its price movement and if its trading volume is above or below average. Volume trends can reinforce or contradict the trend you see in price movement.

For instance, if your stock's price is rising and its trading volume is heavier than usual, this may indicate not only that investors are willing to pay higher prices, but also that there is increased demand at the higher price levels. On the other hand, if the price has been falling, but the volume is getting very light, there may not be many more sellers willing to accept the lower prices, and the price decline may be ending.

News on corporate developments will affect the price of your stock. By reviewing the company's quarterly and annual reports on sales and earnings, and any news releases the company may issue, you will notice the effect good or bad news can have on your stock's price. You should also watch general news, since broader developments in the market and the economy can also affect your stock, regardless of how well the

STOCKS

particular corporation is doing. One-time events may not have a major effect on your long-term investment. But if such events become a trend in the corporation's operations, the nature of your investment will change, and you might want to decide whether to hold, buy more, or sell your stock.

Q: How will dividend changes affect the price of my stock?

A: Dividend payments are one of the most direct contributors to your investment return. Once you know the quarterly dividend payment dates and the amount of the dividend the stock has been paying, you can record the upcoming dates in your calendar and anticipate these payments. From time to time, corporations will increase or decrease the dividend. One indication that a stock is a good investment is a record of steady increases in its dividend.

If you own a stock and the corporation announces a dividend increase, you may see the stock price appreciate as investors react to the good news. A dividend increase is a message that the board of directors has a positive expectation for the corporation's future.

The reverse is also true. If your corporation is having difficulties and announces a reduction or elimination of its dividend, this is generally a negative signal on the corporation's outlook.

Q: What do I do if I have a problem with my dividend?

A: If your dividend payment date has passed and you have not received your dividend, there could be several different explanations.

If you are working with a brokerage firm and your shares are in street name, you may rely on the broker to research the problem and resolve it for you.

You may also contact the corporation's investor relations department or dividend-paying agent directly. It can tell you whether:

- The dividend was interrupted and you missed the announcement.
- The mailing was delayed by a holiday or technical problem.

STOCKS

- Their records show you at a wrong address.
- The dividend was mailed properly and your mail service is the problem.

You can find the address and phone number of your corporation's headquarters in the annual report, in investment services in your library, or from your broker. When contacting the corporation, ask for the investor relations or stockholder relations department.

Once you have determined where the problem arose, you can work it out with the parties involved.

Q: What is a stock split?

A: A *stock split* is a proportional division of a corporation's outstanding shares. A shareholder will receive a proportional number of additional shares, and the par value and market price of the stock will decrease proportionately.

Q: What is a stock dividend?

A: A *stock dividend* is a distribution of additional shares to current shareholders in addition to or in lieu of a cash dividend. As in a stock split, your shares will increase in number, but your overall ownership and value remain the same.

Q: How do stock dividends and stock splits affect the value of my investment?

A: In theory, stock splits and stock dividends do not affect the value of your investment. In both cases, the corporation issues more shares and the stock's market price is automatically adjusted proportionately so that the value of your total investment stays the same. For instance, if you own 100 shares of a stock priced at $60 (a $6,000 value) that splits or declares a stock dividend, the math will change, but the value will not:

Pre-split	100 at $60 = $6,000 value
2-for-1 split	200 at $30 = $6,000 value
100% stock dividend	200 at $30 = $6,000 value
3-for-2 split	150 at $40 = $6,000 value
50% stock dividend	150 at $40 = $6,000 value

STOCKS

97

Like cash dividends, stock splits and stock dividends will have a declaration date, a record date, and a payment date. (See page 64, "Dividends.") If the payment date has passed and you have not received your new shares, you may follow the same procedures outlined for cash dividend payment problems.

 Note: *Par value* is a nominal dollar value per share set by the corporation's charter when the stock was originally issued. Currently, par value has little significance except for bookeeping purposes within the corporation.

Q: How do stock splits and stock dividends affect my stock's price?

A: Though the value of your holdings does not change when a split or stock dividend occurs, the market price will be adjusted proportionately. In addition, the event may have a positive effect on the stock price. Often a corporation whose stock price has climbed substantially will declare a split to reduce the stock price to a lower level that may be more attractive to many investors. If the stock price is adjusted, say, from $60 to $30 (a 2-for-1 split), many investors may perceive the stock as more affordable. Also investors often perceive such an event as a positive indication of the corporation's progress. The result is often increased demand for the shares and thus a higher price.

Q: What is a reverse split?

A: Corporations whose stocks have very low prices, say under $1 per share, may declare a *reverse split* to adjust the price upward to what investors may perceive as a more mainstream price level. For example, a holder of 1,000 shares of a $0.75 stock declaring a 1-for-10 reverse split would receive a replacement certificate for 100 shares, and the price would adjust to $7.50.

 Note of Caution: A reverse split will substantially reduce the number of shares you own. If you own a stock selling at under $1.00 per share and you suddenly see the price quoted several times higher, you should inquire whether an event such as a reverse split has affected your holdings. If you sell stock that you do not own, you may be obligated to purchase additional shares to make delivery, even if the result is a loss.

Q: When a corporation announces a corporate restructuring, how does that affect my stock's return?

A: The term *corporate restructuring* may stand for any of a wide variety of measures a corporation can undertake to improve its operating efficiency or its stock market valuation. The result of a restructuring may turn out to be:

- Layoffs and plant closings
- Redefinition of departments or divisions within the corporation
- Divestiture of a subsidiary through a spin-off to the shareholders or its sale to another company

Q: What is a spin-off?
A: A *spin-off* is the creation of a new independent corporation by a parent corporation through a distribution of stock in the new corporation to shareholders of the parent corporation. Shareholders receive new certificates in the newly created corporation, and their old shares represent ownership in the remainder of the parent corporation.

Regardless of what form it takes, restructuring is a significant event for the corporation, and it will probably affect your stock and its price. The effect on your stock's price will be negative if the restructuring is perceived as news of previously undisclosed problems. The effect on your stock's price could be positive if the restructuring is perceived as a resolution of existing problems.

STOCKS

99

Q: How do stock repurchase plans affect the price of my stock return?

A: A *stock repurchase plan* will generally have a positive effect on your stock's price. The direct effect will be a major buyer's demand for the shares, which will tend to support or raise the stock's price. Indirectly, when a corporation announces a stock repurchase plan, it is stating publicly that the management believes that the stock is a bargain. This may encourage other investors to buy as well. Fewer shares outstanding because of repurchase will mean higher earnings per share even with level earnings, which often results in a higher stock price.

Q: How do mergers affect the price of my stock return?

A: Mergers can range from minor additions by a giant corporation to the absorption of your entire corporation into another. If you own stock in a corporation that buys another corporation, and the acquisition is large relative to your corporation's size, the price of your stock may rise or fall. It will probably rise if investors perceive the combination as being particularly beneficial to your corporation. It will probably fall if investors believe that the purchase is not advantageous or that the price is too high. It may also fall simply to adjust for the effects of dilution if your corporation issues new shares to pay for the merger.

If your corporation is being bought by another, the effect on your stock's price is most often positive. Since acquirers generally pay a premium over the current market price, your shares become more valuable as soon as the announcement of an agreement is made. The new price for your shares may still be below the offer price, since investors will believe that there is some risk that the merger may not be completed, but the price will approach the full offer price as you get closer to the completion date. Generally, the greater the difference between offer price and market value, the greater the risk investors see that the merger will not be completed. Alternatively, the market price may rise *above* the offer price, indicating that investors anticipate that the merger will be completed at a higher price.

STOCKS

Q: What are some merger terms I should be aware of?

A: Some merger terms you should be familiar with include:

- a tender offer
- a friendly takeover
- a hostile takeover
- white knights

Q: What is a tender offer?

A: A *tender offer* is a public offer by an acquirer to buy shares of the target corporation at a certain price on a certain date.

Q: What is a friendly takeover?

A: As the name implies, a *friendly takeover* is a cooperative arrangement by an acquiring corporation to buy control of its target corporation, with agreement of the target corporation's management and directors.

Q: What is a hostile takeover?

A: A *hostile takeover* is an attempt by the acquiring corporation to buy control of the target corporation against the will of the target corporation's management and directors.

Q: What does the term white knight mean?

A: *White knight* refers to a corporation that arranges a friendly purchase of a target corporation after a hostile takeover attempt so that the hostile acquirer does not succeed in the takeover attempt.

Q: I have heard of corporations filing for Chapter 11 bankruptcy status. How would that affect my stock?

A: A filing for bankruptcy under *Chapter 11* is one of the most drastic events a shareholder can experience. The corporation, by making such a filing, is stating that it needs a court's protection to avoid being liquidated by creditors before it can reorganize its operations. As a shareholder, you own a share of the corporation's *net worth*, or the resources that would remain after all creditors had been paid in full. If the corporation is unsure that it can satisfy its creditors, there is not likely to be much, if any, value left for the shareholders. In such a case, your stock could become worthless. If one of your cor-

STOCKS

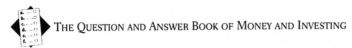

porations files for bankruptcy, consult your broker and/or tax advisor as to the actions you should consider.

SUMMARY

When you invest in the stock of a corporation, you become a part owner of that corporation and participate in all its developments—the risks and rewards. As we showed in Illustration 5-2, the rewards of a diversified portfolio of stocks have historically outweighed the risks and provided a superior return. You can begin with a modest amount of money and build a stock portfolio over time, building wealth and participating in the economic development of the nation.

This chapter should answer many of the questions you may have about common stock investing. As you gain investment experience, you will want to read further in other sources and inquire further of investment advisors.

CHAPTER 6

PREFERRED STOCKS

Preferred stocks are equity in a corporation. Like common stockholders, preferred stockholders are owners of the issuing corporation and have certain rights of ownership. Preferred stocks usually pay a higher dividend than common stocks, but their owners generally have no vote on corporate matters.

The class of equity ownership discussed in this chapter is called "preferred stock" because preferred stockholders have priority over common stockholders in the payment of dividends and the distribution of assets if the company is liquidated.

Preferred stock is similar to a bond in that the owners are generally paid a fixed amount. However, most preferred stock has no maturity date on which the issuer promises to repay the investor. Also, if the corporation is liquidated, bondholders will be paid before preferred stockholders, who will be paid before common stockholders.

Q: How does preferred stock work?

A: Issuing preferred stock is a way for corporations to raise money from the investing public. When a corporation issues preferred stock, it assigns a *par value* (see below). For many years, the par value of most preferred stocks was $100 a share. In recent years, corporations have issued preferred stocks with par values of $50 and $25.

When issuing preferred stock, the corporation will usually establish a fixed *dividend*, taking into account the general level of interest rates at the time the stock is issued. The dividend must originally be established at a level that makes the preferred stock issue attractive to investors.

Q: What is the par value of a preferred stock?

A: The *par value* of a preferred stock is the value assigned to the new offering and the price per share the original investors pay. It is also the value on which the redemption price is based. Unlike common stock par value, which has little or no significance as to the price, preferred stocks use par value as an indicator of value.

Q: How can I find the details of a preferred stock offering?

A: The details of a preferred stock offering must be given in a *prospectus*. The prospectus is the official summary of the offering. It must be filed with the Securities and Exchange Commission and given to the original purchasers of the issue. The prospectus must contain all material information about the issue, such as the dividend, when it is paid, special features, and so on.

Q: What are the dividends paid on preferred stock?

A: Dividends paid on preferred stock are distributions of cash from the company's net profits made at the discretion of the board of directors. In most cases, the amount of the dividend on preferred stock is set at the time of original issue and does not rise or fall. Generally, dividends on preferred stock must be paid before any dividends can be paid on common stock, but each payment must still be authorized by the board.

Q: Why would I want to invest in preferred stocks?

A: You might want to invest in preferred stocks for several reasons:

1. To receive a higher income than would be available from alternative investments
2. To take advantage of high interest rates, since preferred stocks, like bonds, tend to increase in value when interest rates decline
3. To take advantage of some of the special features offered by some preferred stocks (some of these features will be discussed later in this chapter)

Q: Why would a corporation issue preferred stock?

A: Corporations may issue preferred stock for many reasons, including:

1. Issuing preferred stock may be the best way to raise equity capital in a particular market environment.
2. They can include features that ultimately allow the issuer to control conversion of the preferred stock into common stock. Effectively, the issuer will potentially increase its common equity at a more favorable price later.
3. Other corporations may want to invest in the issuer, but want the higher yield and tax advantages of a preferred stock.

Q: How can preferred stock issues offer me a higher income?

A: Preferred stocks generally pay higher dividends than common stocks. Some investors prefer the higher income of preferred stocks to the potential gains offered by common stocks.

Q: How do I compute the yield on a preferred stock?

A: Since most preferred stocks pay a fixed dividend, in order to compute your annual yield you divide the dividend by the value of the preferred stock.

 Example: If your preferred stock is paying an annual dividend of $5 and the price is $100 per share, the annual yield is 5 percent. If the price is $50 per share, the annual yield is 10 percent.

Q: How are dividends on preferred stocks paid?

A: Dividends on preferred stocks are usually paid quarterly, like those on common stocks. The board of directors of the issuing corporation must declare the dividend on the preferred stock. Key dates are the same as those for dividends on common stocks. (Refer to Chapter 5, page 64.)

PREFERRED STOCKS

Q: If I sell my preferred stock between dividend dates, will I earn a portion of the next dividend?

A: No. You must buy a preferred stock before the ex-dividend date in order to receive the dividend. In this respect, the payment of preferred stock dividends is similar to the payment of common stock dividends and different from the payment of bond interest. If you miss the ex-dividend date when buying a preferred stock, you will generally have to wait until the next dividend is declared. In other words, you may have to wait more than three months after purchase to receive your first quarterly dividend.

Q: How are preferred stock dividends taxed?

A: Generally, dividends paid on preferred stocks are taxed as ordinary income, like dividends paid on common stocks.

 Note: Because preferred stock is equity capital of a corporation, preferred dividends are *not* tax-deductible to the corporation paying the dividends.

Q: What are the special income tax advantages for a corporation that receives dividends on preferred or common stocks of other companies?

A: Corporations that receive dividends on preferred and common stocks of other companies may exclude a portion of the dividends from taxable income. The rules are very complex, and if you are considering investing in preferred or common stocks through a corporate structure in order to benefit from the income tax exclusion provisions, you should consult your tax advisors.

Q: What do I get as evidence that I own my preferred stock?

A: You may have evidence of ownership of your preferred stock in one of two forms: certificate, or regular statements.

Certificate: Preferred stock issuers sometimes issue certificates to their stockholders as evidence of their ownership. The front of the certificate will show the name of the issuer, the dividend, and the CUSIP number (see page 92).

Statements: If you are not issued a certificate representing ownership, you should receive periodic statements from the financial institution (broker or bank) that holds your preferred stocks. The statement is evidence of your ownership and should include most of the information that would be on a certificate.

Q: What are the types of preferred stocks?

A: A preferred stock issue is generally classified according to the features the stock has. Some of the types are:

- Perpetual
- Cumulative
- Callable
- Convertible
- Straight
- Preferred equity redemption cumulative stock (PERCS)
- Adjustable-rate
- Participating

Any of the features indicated above may be included in a preferred stock issue.

 Note: In recent years, underwriters and corporations have been constantly issuing new types of preferred stocks with new features or combinations of features in order to raise additional equity capital. You must always fully investigate the features of any new type of preferred stock to see if the issue suits your investment needs and goals and your risk tolerance.

Q: What are perpetual preferred stocks?

A: Most preferred stocks are *perpetual*, which means that they have no stated maturity date or any other feature that obligates the issuing corporation to redeem the shares. The preferred stock will remain outstanding unless the issuing corporation buys the shares back from investors. In recent years, there have been very few preferred stocks issued with maturity dates.

Q: What are cumulative preferred stocks?

A: *Cumulative preferred stocks* are preferred stocks that give their holders a claim to any dividends that have been omitted. If the company fails to pay the dividend for one or a number of quarters, the omitted dividends accumulate and the total amount in arrears must be paid before any distributions may be made to the common stockholders.

Q: What are noncumulative preferred stocks?

A: Preferred stocks are *noncumulative* if omitted dividends do not continue to be obligations of the issuing corporation.

Q: What are callable preferred stocks?

A: *Callable preferred stocks* are preferred stocks that include a feature permitting the issuing corporation, at its option, to call (retire) the preferred stock issue by paying the shareholders a predetermined amount for their shares. The call price is usually somewhat higher than par for the first few years after issue, but in later years it is generally at par.

An issuer of a preferred stock will generally call an issue when market conditions make it feasible to replace the issue with a new issue that will entail a lower cost to the corporation.

Q: Is there a limit to the price I should pay for a callable preferred stock?

A: A call feature may limit the upside price potential of a preferred stock. If a $100 par value preferred stock with a dividend of $5 is currently selling at par and is callable at $101, the price of the preferred will not increase much, no matter how much general interest rates decline. Investors will be very hesitant to pay much over $101 per share for a stock that could be redeemed at any time for $101. This generally applies to straight preferred stocks, not convertible preferred stocks.

Q: What are convertible preferred stocks?

A: *Convertible preferred stocks* are preferred stocks whose owners are permitted to exchange the preferred stock for a predetermined number of shares of (usually) common stock at any time.

The price of the convertible preferred stock is usually related to the price of the common stock of a corporation. *Parity* is the price of the convertible preferred stock that makes its value equivalent to that of the common stock for which it could be exchanged.

 Example: If each share of a convertible preferred stock is convertible into 5 shares of common stock and the common stock is selling for $10, then the preferred stock is selling at parity when its market price is $50 (5 shares times $10 per share is $50). When the convertible stock is selling above parity, it is said to be selling at a *premium*. When the preferred is selling below parity, it is said to be selling at a *discount*.

Note: Parity should not be confused with par value, which is the value at which a preferred stock is issued.

Q: What are straight preferred stocks?

A: Straight preferred stocks are preferred stocks that are not convertible into any other security.

Q: Why do convertible preferred stocks rarely sell at a discount to parity?

A: If a convertible preferred stock were to sell at a significant discount to parity, investors would find it attractive to purchase the convertible preferred stock, convert it to common stock and immediately sell the common stock for an automatic profit. Such an investment opportunity would generally attract more investors and cause the convertible preferred stock's price to rise. This would reduce or eliminate the discount rapidly.

Q: Why do most convertible preferred stocks sell at a premium to parity?

A: Convertible preferred stocks usually sell at a premium to parity because most investors place extra value on the additional income and are willing to pay a premium to earn the higher income.

Q: When does a convertible preferred stock trade like a bond?

A: If the price of the common stock falls below a level that would provide a market yield on the convertible at parity, the chief investment attraction of the convertible preferred stock is its yield. At such times, the yield will stop the price of the convertible from falling with that of the common; instead, the convertible preferred stock's price will rise and fall with interest-rate changes like a bond's price.

Q: When does a convertible preferred stock trade with the common stock?

A: When the market price of the common stock underlying the convertible preferred stock rises above a level that would provide a market yield on the convertible at a reasonable premium, the market price of the convertible preferred will also increase. As the price of the common shares get higher, the premium at which the convertible will sell usually gets smaller. The preferred stock trades with the common stock.

Q: Why should I consider investing in convertible preferred stocks?

A: You may want to consider investing in convertible preferred stocks to earn a higher yield than that paid by the common stock and still participate in the growth of the underlying company. You may also have the downside price protection afforded by any fixed-income investment.

Q: Can a corporation call a convertible preferred stock?

A: If a preferred stock is both callable and convertible, the issuing corporation will often call the issue to force conversion. Once the call notice is sent to the convertible preferred stockholders, they must decide whether to convert or sell their stock.

 Example: A callable and convertible preferred stock with a $50 par value is convertible into common stock at $10 (5 shares). If the common stock is selling at $40 per share, the convertible preferred stock would most likely be selling at around $200 (5 shares times $40). If the convertible preferred is then called at $101, you would probably either sell your preferred or convert to the common stock to realize the $200 value, rather than accept the $101 call.

Q: What are preferred equity redemption cumulative stocks (PERCS)?

A: *Preferred equity redemption cumulative stocks (PERCS)* are a type of convertible preferred stock. They usually pay a higher dividend than the common stock of the same issuer. Many PERCS issued in the early 1990s carried a yield that was approximately twice that of the common stock. The additional income compensates investors in part for the fact that PERCS include a limit on appreciation. Whereas most convertible stocks may participate without limit in the appreciation of the underlying common stock, PERCS are designed to participate only up to a point, perhaps 20 to 30 percent appreciation.

After being outstanding for some period of time, often two to four years, the PERCS are convertible into common shares at the discretion of the issuer, not of the PERC owner.

 Note: You must be willing to own the common stock when you invest in PERCS.

Q: What are adjustable-rate preferred stocks?

A: *Adjustable-rate preferred stocks* are preferred stocks whose dividends are adjusted quarterly (sometimes annually) based on an index such as the yield on a U.S. Treasury issue. Most adjustable-rate preferred stocks have a maximum and minimum dividend, and the adjustments take place within the stipulated range. Many corporations issue adjustable-rate preferred stocks during periods of rising and volatile interest rates because investors do not want to be locked into a fixed rate.

Q: What are participating preferred stocks?

A: With *participating preferred stocks*, the owners can receive an extra dividend if one is declared by the directors of the corporation. After common stockholders of the same issuer receive dividends equal to the preferred dividends, additional distributions are shared equally by the common and participating preferred stockholders. This feature is very unusual. The only time it is likely to be included is if the issuing corporation is in very poor financial condition.

PREFERRED STOCKS

Q: Preferred stocks are often considered to be safe. Is this true?

A: Not always. Preferred stock is equity in a corporation. If the issuing corporation is having financial difficulties, the value of the preferred stock will reflect those difficulties. In addition, if you own preferred stock, it is imperative that you understand all of its features and how each feature fits with your investment and financial goals. Many investors purchase preferred stocks because of the high dividend yield without investigating the preferred's provisions and features. Such haste can lead to unpleasant surprises and dissatisfaction when the investors learn of certain features.

Q: Where can I get information on preferred stocks in which I am interested?

A: You can obtain information on most preferred stocks from your local library or your broker. Also, information on preferred stock is included in reports on companies from such research services as *Standard & Poor's*, *Moody's*, or *Value Line*. Often there will be other reports that provide information on particular preferred stocks. Many brokers will have a database service like Bloomberg that can give the features and details of most preferred stocks. The best source of complete information on any preferred stock is the prospectus; however, it may be difficult to get a prospectus on an older preferred issue.

Q: What is the language of preferred stocks?

A: Generally the language of preferred stocks includes terms about yield, dividend, and special features of a particular issue. Examples of some of the terms and their meanings are:

5% preferred: The preferred issue has a dividend rate of 5 percent based on the par value.

$5 preferred: The preferred issue has an annual dividend of $5. To compute the yield on par value, divide the $5 dividend by the par value.

$5 convertible preferred: The annual dividend rate is $5 and the preferred issue is convertible into a specific number of shares of common stock of the issuer.

$5 callable preferred: The dividend is $5, and the preferred issue is callable at the option of the issuer.

Series A: Usually refers to a class of preferred stock when several are issued. It is an easy way for traders and transfer agents to refer to a specific preferred issue.

 Note: A preferred stock issue may have many features. If a stock is described as $5 convertible preferred, this does not necessarily mean that other features, such as cumulation or a call provision, are not included.

Q: What is a sinking fund?

A: A sinking fund is a provision requiring the preferred stock issuer to set aside an amount of money, usually annually, to provide for the early retirement of a portion of a preferred stock issue. Most of the time, some of the preferred stock is retired in the year in which money is set aside. The retirement of the preferred stock may be made by:

- Calling the stock
- Making open-market purchases

Note: If the preferred stock is selling for less than the call price, the issuer may purchase shares rather than exercise the call (if allowed) as stated in the sinking fund provision.

Q: Who should typically consider investing in preferred stocks?

A: The following are types of investors who may be interested in investing in preferred stocks:

- Investors in a low income tax bracket who are seeking maximum income
- Investors who have accounts where the income or earnings are tax-deferred, such as IRAs or other qualified retirement plans
- Investors who want to take advantage of some of the provisions or features of a preferred stock issue that make it particularly attractive, such as convertibility, a call provision, or a sinking fund

- With convertible preferred stock, investors who are willing to pay a premium to earn additional income while waiting for the anticipated increase in the value of the common stock
- Corporate investors who want to take advantage of dividend exclusion provisions

Q: What are the risks of investing in preferred stocks?

A: The following are some of the risks you may assume when investing in preferred stocks (not all preferred stocks will have all of these risks):

Interest-rate risk: Since preferred stocks are a fixed-income investment, when interest rates increase, the value will decline (of course, the converse is also true). Interest rate risk is less for convertible preferred stocks than for straight preferred stocks.

Credit risk: There is a possibility that the issuing corporation will not be able to continue to pay the dividends on its preferred stock.

Call risk: Your callable preferred stock could be called away from you, resulting in your receiving cash or common stock that will probably be yielding less than the preferred.

SUMMARY

Preferred stocks have a place in many portfolios. When you invest in the preferred stock of a corporation, you become a part owner. You will receive a stipulated dividend and have other rights as outlined in the prospectus.

Generally, preferred stocks are for individuals who are seeking a higher income in exchange for giving up some growth opportunities. But it is imperative that you understand the provisions and features of preferred stocks in order to protect yourself against unexpected risks.

PREFERRED STOCKS

CHAPTER 7

OPTIONS AND FUTURES

Options and futures are not like stocks and bonds. They are synthetic securities created to give the buyer or seller rights over large blocks of the underlying commodities or securities for a small investment. Also, they have relatively short durations, which means that if you are not to lose money, the anticipated price movements in the underlying assets must take place in a short time.

Because these securities allow you to control large positions for a small investment, the potential rewards are large; however, so are the potential losses. Even professional investors have lost large sums of money in these securities. Therefore, except for some relatively conservative option strategies, the average individual investor should stay away from options and futures. Generally, only professional investors should plunge into these types of investments.

This chapter will briefly describe options and futures. It will discuss some of the conservative strategies that may be appropriate for you. If you are considering investing in options or futures, you will want to study books on the subjects and deal only with experts.

Q: What is an option?

A: An *option* is a contract giving the owner the right to either buy or sell something (in this case a security), at a specified price (the strike or exercise price), before a specified deadline (the expiration date).

For many years, investors could buy or sell options only on stocks traded on one of the exchanges. However, over the last few years, investors have become able to buy or sell options on a broad range of investments, such as stock market indexes, interest rates, U.S. Treasury securities, and foreign

OPTIONS AND FUTURES

currencies. However, in much of this chapter we will be focusing on options on common stock, as these are of most interest to the average investor.

In addition to the increasing variety of options, an increasing number of large institutions are using options as part of their investment strategy. This expansion in the use of options has greatly increased the trading volume of securities and the volatility of stock prices.

Q: Where are options traded?

A: Options are traded on the following exchanges:

- Chicago Board Options Exchange (CBOE)
- American exchange
- Philadelphia exchange
- Pacific exchange
- New York Stock Exchange

Q: What is a strike price?

A: The *strike price*, also referred to as the exercise price, of an option contract is the price at which the owner has the option, or right, to buy or sell the underlying security. Strike prices are established by the exchange on which the options are traded. For each underlying security, there will be several strike prices clustered around the price of the underlying security at the time the options are first traded. As the range within which the underlying security trades moves up or down, the exchange will establish new contracts with strike prices reflecting current prices of the underlying security.

Q: What is the exercise of an option?

A: The *exercise* of an option means that the owner of the contract exercises his or her rights. In this case, the seller of the contract must fulfill his or her obligation under the contract.

Q: What is the expiration date?

A: The *expiration date* is the date on which an option expires. If the owner of an option does not exercise or sell the option by the expiration date, it becomes worthless. Most option contracts have an expiration date of around ninety days from the time they start trading.

All listed options expire at 11:59 P.M. on the Saturday following the third Friday of the expiration month.

Q: What is an option premium?

A: An *option premium* is the amount of money paid by a buyer, or received by a seller, for an option contract. When the underlying security is common stock, in most cases one option contract covers 100 shares of the underlying stock, and the premium quoted (see box) is the premium per share of stock controlled, not the premium for the entire contract. When buying options, you must pay the premium in full plus commissions. The premium is equal to the intrinsic value of the option plus a time value (see page 127).

 Example: If the premium (price) of an option contract is 4, the amount you would have to pay to control (have the right to buy or sell) 100 shares would be $400. If you were to write or sell the option, you would receive $400.

	(a)	(b)	(c)	(d)		(e)
	IBM	Nov	60	call	@	4

(a) The underlying stock: IBM
(b) The expiration month: November
(c) The strike price: $60
(d) The type of contract (put or call): Call
(e) The premium: $4

Q: What is an option buyer?

A: An *option buyer* is an investor who pays the premium and acquires the rights that the particular option contract carries. He or she may be said to be *long* the option.

OPTIONS AND FUTURES

Q: What is an option writer?

A: An *option writer*, or seller, is an investor who receives the premium and is obligated to perform the responsibilities that the particular option contract carries. He or she may be said to be *short* the option.

Q: What does buying or selling an option really mean?

A: Buying an option gives you rights until the expiration date. Selling an option imposes obligations on you until the expiration date.

Q: What are the choices that an option buyer has?

A: Option buyers have three choices:

● Exercise the option (see page 116).
● Let the option expire worthless.
● Sell (or close) the option contract before the expiration date.

Q: If I buy an option contract and the price of the underlying security moves in a favorable direction, do I have to exercise the option?

A: No. You can sell your option contract. This is called *closing* the contract.

 Note: If you are the seller of a contract and the price of the underlying stock starts moving in a direction that puts you in a loss position, you may want to buy an option contract to close your position and cut your possible losses.

Q: What are the types of options?

A: There are two types of options: calls and puts.

● Buying a call gives you the *right* to buy the underlying security.
● Buying a put gives you the *right* to sell the underlying security.
● Selling a call gives you the *obligation* to sell the underlying security if the buyer of the option wishes to buy it.

- Selling a put gives you the *obligation* to buy the underlying security if the buyer of the option wishes to sell it.

Q: What is a call?

A: A *call* is a contract giving you the right to buy a security. In the case of an option on common stock, it is a contract giving you the right to buy 100 shares of a stock at a specified price before or on a specified date.

Q: What do I have if I buy a call?

A: If you buy a call, you have the right to buy the underlying security at the strike price at any time before the expiration date.

Q: Why would I buy a call?

A: The basic reason for buying or selling any option contract is to make a profit on the price movement of the underlying security during the life of the contract. The buyer of a call contract is usually betting that the price of the underlying security will rise. An investor may buy a call contract for several reasons:

- To make a speculative profit on the price of the underlying security
- To defer a decision to buy the underlying security

Q: What happens if the price of the underlying security increases?

A: If the price of the underlying security increases, there are two things you can do: you can exercise the option, or you can sell it. If you exercise the option, you must pay the full strike price of the underlying security plus a commission; then you can either sell the security at the higher market price (less commission). If you sell the option, you will make a profit equal to the increase in the price of the call—which, because of the time value, is not necessarily the same as the increase in the price of the underlying security.

 Note: The time value portion of the premium (see p. 127) declines to zero over the life of the contract. Therefore, if you are to make a profit, the underlying security must not only rise, but rise by the amount of the time value.

 Example: If you buy one IBM December 60 call at $4, you own the right to buy 100 shares of IBM at $60 per share, before the option expires in December. The cost of the contract is $400 ($4 times 100 shares). If the price of IBM increases to $68, you could exercise your option and buy 100 shares of IBM at $60 per share (your strike price) plus a commission. (Note: Your true cost would be $64 per share—$60 plus the premium of $4.) You could then immediately sell your IBM stock at $68, making a profit of $4 per share, less commissions. Alternatively, instead of actually buying and selling the underlying stock, you could simply sell your contract, since its value would have risen along with the value of the common stock. In this example, it should have risen to at least $8 (depending on the time value), and so you could sell it and realize approximately the same $400 profit. This method would also save you the extra commission cost of buying and selling the IBM stock, although you would pay a commission on the sale of the option.

Q: What happens if the price of the underlying security remains the same or decreases?

A: If the price of the underlying security has not increased sufficiently by the expiration date, you would not exercise your option; it would expire worthless. Your only loss would be the premium you paid for the option plus the commission.

Q: How do I go about exercising a call that I own?

A: If you own a call contract and the price of the underlying stock has increased, you can request your broker to exercise your contract. You will be buying 100 shares of the underlying stock for the strike price plus a commission.

OPTIONS AND FUTURES

Q: What happens if I write (sell) a call contract?

A: If you are the writer, or seller, of a call contract, you have the obligation to sell 100 shares of the underlying security at the strike price up to the expiration date if the buyer chooses to exercise the option.

Example: If you write (sell) one IBM November 50 call at $4, up to the expiration date of the contract in November, you have the obligation to deliver 100 shares of IBM stock if the *call buyer* exercises the option. You *receive* $400 ($4 times 100 shares) less commissions as the premium for selling this contract. If a call buyer *does* exercise the option, you have, in effect, sold 100 shares of IBM stock for $5,400 ($5000 [$50 times 100 shares] for the stock plus the $400 premium). If the call buyer *does not* exercise the option before expiration, you have earned $400.

Q: Why would I sell a call contract?

A: The basic reason for selling a call contract is to increase your return on a security whose price you expect to remain the same or decline during the life of the contract. The seller receives the premiums paid by the buyer and, in return, agrees to deliver the underlying stock if the stock price rises above the strike price and the option is exercised. If the option writer is correct and the stock price does not rise, the premium provides him or her with an increased rate of return.

Other objectives for selling calls might be:

- To hedge some of the risk on a stock position
- To speculate that a stock's price will not go up

Q: What is a covered call?

A: A writer, or seller, of call options against stocks he or she already owns is said to be writing a *covered call*. In this case, the risk of selling a call is that you may be required to sell your stock if the call owner exercises his or her option. This is referred to as having your stock *called away*.

OPTIONS AND FUTURES

Q: Can I sell a call without owning the underlying stock?

A: Yes. You may write (sell) a call without owning the underlying stock. Doing so is called writing a *naked call* (the opposite of a covered call). You run the risk that the stock price will increase sharply, leaving you in the position of having to deliver shares of a greatly appreciated stock that you do not own! Writing naked calls is not appropriate for the average investor because of this high risk.

Q: What is a put?

A: A *put* is a contract giving the buyer the right to sell a security. In the case of an option on common stock, it is a contract giving the buyer the right to sell 100 shares of the underlying stock at a specified price before or on a specified date.

Q: What do I have if I buy a put?

A: If you buy a put, you have the right to sell the specified security at the strike price at any time before the expiration date.

Q: Why would I buy a put?

A: There are several reasons why you might buy a put, but one of the most popular is to guard against a possible decline in the price of a stock that you own. This is an alternative to selling (writing) a call against the stock. By buying the put instead, you have the *right* to sell your stock, not an obligation to do so.

Q: What happens if the price of the underlying security decreases?

A: If the price of the underlying security decreases, there are two things you can do: you can exercise the option, or you can sell it. If you exercise the option, you will receive the strike price for the underlying security less a commission. If you sell the option, you will make a profit equal to the increase in the price of the put.

 Example: If you buy one IBM December 60 put at $2\frac{1}{2}$, you own the right to *sell* 100 shares of IBM at $60 per share at any time before the option expires in December. The cost of the contract is $250 ($2\frac{1}{2}$

times 100 shares).

If the price of IBM decreases to $52 by the expiration date, you could exercise your option and *sell* 100 shares at $60 per share less commission. (Note: Your true proceeds would be $57.50 per share—$60 less the premium of $2¹/₂.) Alternatively, instead of selling your shares, you could simply sell your contract, since its value would have risen as the value of the common stock fell. In this example, it should have risen to about $8 (depending on the time value), so you could sell it for $8 and realize a profit of $5.50 ($8 less $2¹/₂ cost) per share.

Q: What happens if the price of the underlying security increases or remains the same?

A: If the price of your underlying security increases or remains the same, you would not exercise your option; it would expire worthless. Your only loss would be the premium you paid for the option plus the commission.

Q: What happens if I want to exercise a put that I own?

A: If you own a put contract and the price of the underlying stock has declined, you can request your broker to exercise your contract. You will then be selling 100 shares of the underlying stock for the strike price less a commission.

Q: What happens if I write (sell) a put contract?

A: If you are the writer, or seller, of a put contract, you have the *obligation* to buy 100 shares of the underlying stock at the strike price up to the expiration date if the buyer chooses to exercise the option. You are agreeing to deliver cash and accept the stock.

Example: If you write (sell) one IBM January 60 put at $4¹/₂, at any time up to the expiration date of the contract in January, you are obligated to buy 100 shares of IBM stock at $60 per share if the *buyer* of the put exercises the option. The premium you receive for assuming this risk is $450 ($4$^{1}/_{2}$ times 100 shares). If a put owner *does* exercise the option, you must pay $6,000 for the stock ($60 times 100 shares). If the put buyer *does not* exercise the option before expiration, you have earned $450 less commission.

Q: Why would I sell a put contract?

A: The most common reason to sell a put contract is to increase your income by receiving the premium. As a seller of a put contract, you would be betting that the stock price would continue to rise and that you would keep the premium. If you were forced to buy the stock, your net cost would be lowered by the amount of the premium you received.

Q: What happens if the underlying stock splits while I own an option contract?

A: If the underlying stock splits, the number of contracts you own will increase accordingly. If the underlying stock splits 2 for 1, you will own two contracts for each contract you previously owned. If the underlying stock splits 3 for 1, you will own three contracts for each contract you previously owned.

If the split does not give you an amount that would give you an exact multiple of your contract, the number of shares controlled by your contract will still increase proportionately. For example, if the underlying stock had a 50 percent stock dividend, each of your contracts would represent 150 shares instead of 100 shares.

Q: What happens if the underlying stock has a spinoff or re-organization?

A: If the underlying stock has a spinoff or a reorganization, part of the stock's value will be separated into a new stock. However, the value of your contract will continue to reflect the total value of the original shares. If you exercise the option, you will be entitled to what is called a *due bill*.

Q: What is a due bill?

A: A *due bill* means that if you exercise a call, you will be entitled to buy all securities issued in the reorganization that were received by the owner of the 100 shares represented by the contract, including the shares of a spun-off entity. If you exercise a put, you must be willing to deliver the spun-off shares or other securities.

Q: When buying or selling option contracts, do I have to deal with the individual or organization on the other side of my trade?

A: No. On the day after a trade involving an option contract, the Options Clearing Corporation (OCC) becomes both the issuer and the guarantor of all listed options. The OCC is owned by the brokerage firms that trade on the exchanges. By becoming the issuer and guarantor of all listed option contracts, the OCC removes concern about the failure of the other party to an option contract.

Q: Will I be issued a certificate for an option contract?

A: No. Because options are very short-term instruments, the issuance of certificates would not be practical.

Q: What is the evidence of my option positions?

A: While you will not receive a certificate, you should receive a confirmation statement for each transaction and a regular account statement summarizing transactions and positions, just as for stocks and bonds.

Q: When is the settlement date for option trades?

A: Unlike stock and bond transactions, option transactions settle the day after the trade date. For this reason, an option investor should have a cash reserve or a money market fund at the brokerage firm.

Q: What are some of the terms I need to know if I am going to trade in options?

A: If you decide to invest in options, some of the terms you should know are:

- Opening transaction
- Closing transaction
- In the money
- Out of the money

- Intrinsic value
- Time value

OPTIONS AND FUTURES

Q: What is an opening transaction?

A: An *opening transaction* is one that creates a new position, whether you are buying or writing an option contract. Your broker must show on the confirmation statement whether or not the order is an opening transaction.

Q: What is a closing transaction?

A: A *closing transaction* is an order to buy or sell an option contract that you have open. For example, if you have previously purchased a specific call and you enter an order to sell that contract, this is a closing transaction. Again, this must be shown on your confirmation statement from your broker.

Q: Why are opening and closing important terms?

A: This distinction avoids confusion. For example, when you are selling a call, it is important to specify whether you are writing a new contract (opening) or selling a call you already own (closing).

Q: What does in the money mean?

A: A *call* option contract is said to be *in the money* when the market price of the underlying stock is *higher* than the strike price of the option. For example, an IBM November 70 call is in the money by 10 points when the price of IBM stock is at $80.

A *put* option contract is said to be *in the money* when the stock price is *lower* than the strike price of the option. For example, an IBM November 70 put is in the money by 10 points when the stock is selling for $60.

Q: What does out of the money mean?

A: A *call* is said to be *out of the money* when the price of the underlying stock is *lower* than the strike price of the call.

A *put* is said to be *out of the money* when the price of the underlying stock is *higher* than the strike price of the put.

Market Price of Underlying Stock	Put	Call
Above strike price	Out of the money	In the money
Below strike price	In the money	Out of the money

Q: What is an option's intrinsic value?

A: When an option is in the money, the difference between the strike price and the stock price is said to be the option's *intrinsic value*. Out-of-the-money contracts have no intrinsic value.

Q: Why do in-the-money options sell at premiums above their intrinsic value?

A: The premium for an in-the-money option will reflect a time value as well as the intrinsic value.

Q: What does the time value of an option mean?

A: The *time value* of an option contract refers to the fact that an option contract is a wasting asset. The amount of time left in an option contract has a value to the buyer of the option. As the expiration date draws nearer, the time value diminishes. A buyer is usually willing to pay more for a contract that has a longer time outstanding than for one that is about to expire.

How time value enters into the pricing of an option is a complex subject and is beyond the scope of this book. However, in general, it is safe to say that as the expiration date gets closer, option contracts tend to sell near or at their intrinsic value.

Q: When might an option contract be considered insurance?

A: Options are generally thought of as speculative investments. They are not investments that are usually suitable for novice investors. However, when an option is used in conjunction with a stock holding, it may be thought of as insurance.

If you own a stock position with a substantial profit, and you think the stock has the potential for further appreciation, you may want to pay a premium and buy a put contract to protect the profit. If the stock were to drop in price, the put's value would rise correspondingly. You could exercise the put option and sell at the strike price, or you could use your profit on the put to offset the decline in the price of your stock.

Q: What is the risk in selling calls against a stock I currently own?

A: The risk in selling calls against a stock you currently own is that if the price of the stock increases beyond a certain point, the owner of the calls will exercise the options. You will have to either deliver the stock from your portfolio or buy stock in the open market to make delivery.

If you deliver stock from your own portfolio, you will be taxed on any profit. You will have a capital gain of the difference between what you paid for the stock and the exercise price.

If you want to avoid the capital gain, you may purchase shares of the stock after you receive the call notice to make delivery. This allows you to keep your original shares.

 Note: If you want to begin a program of selling calls against your security positions, you will need a great deal more information and guidance than is included in this chapter. This chapter is not intended to give you in-depth option information.

Q: I have heard of option straddles. What are they?

A: A *straddle* is the buying or selling of both a put and a call with the same exercise price and expiration date on the underlying stock. The buyer has locked in a price at which he or she can either buy or sell the underlying stock. The buyer is betting on the stock's price volatility. All that the buyer needs in order to make a profit is a large enough movement in the price of the underlying stock in either direction.

Example: You might buy one IBM January 50 call and one IBM January 50 put.

 Note: This book will not discuss option straddle strategies or the other option strategies identified in the next two questions. Any investor who is interested in these strategies should get information from other sources and deal only with option specialists.

 Note of Caution: If you are considering trading in options, particularly the more complicated strategies, you should be well aware of the risk. You also must be willing to spend a great deal of time learning about, mo..itoring, and staying on top of your positions.

Q: I have heard of option combinations. What are they?

A: *Option combinations* are similar to straddles except that the expiration dates or strike prices will often be different.

 Example: You could buy one IBM January 50 call and one IBM February 60 put.

Q: What is an option spread?

A: An *option spread* is a strategy in which an option trader will simultaneously buy one option position on an underlying stock and sell a different option on the same stock. Usually, the two positions will have different strike prices, expiration dates, or both. Both positions may be calls, or both may be puts.

 Example: You could buy one IBM December 50 put and sell one IBM March 55 put.

Q: What are index options?

A: *Index options* are a type of instrument developed several years ago to allow investors to purchase or sell options on a "basket" of stocks, not a particular stock. The investor had to be right only on the direction of the market, not the direction of an individual stock.

The Chicago Board Options Exchange developed an index called the CBOE 100, which was later renamed the Standard & Poor's 100. The index is referred to as and trades under the symbol OEX. The 100 stocks included in the index are those that are considered to be the most popular with investors and traders. The price movement of the index tracks, or parallels, the general direction of stock prices fairly well.

There are also other index options, but they will not be discussed in this book.

Unlike individual stock options, index options always settle in cash. You cannot exercise the option and receive the stocks in the index.

Q: How can I determine the value of an OEX contract?

A: Financial tables giving the value of OEX contracts are published in most newspapers. Also, the updated values can be retrieved on the quote machines on brokers' desks.

Q: How do OEX contracts trade?

A: Just like any option contract, OEX contracts are assigned expiration dates and strike prices based on the value of the index. If the value of the OEX index is $325, each contract will control $32,500 (100 times $325).

Q: If I buy one OEX call option, what do I have?

A: If you buy one OEX call option, you have the right to buy the value of the basket of stocks at your strike price until the expiration date. If you buy one OEX November 325 call and the value of the OEX index increases to $335, the value of a call on the index will increase to about $33,500, less commissions.

Q: If I buy one OEX put option, what do I have?

A: If you buy one OEX put option, you have the right to sell the value of the basket of stocks at your strike price until the expiration date. If the value of the stocks included in the index declines, the value of your put contract will increase. If you buy an OEX put with a strike price of $325 and the index's value declines to $300, the value of your put should increase by about $2,500 ($25 times 100) less commissions.

Q: How might I use index options to protect the value of my portfolio of stocks if I think the general direction of stock prices is down?

A: If your stock portfolio has a value of about $100,000 and you believe that the market value of stocks is headed down, you may be able to protect the value of your portfolio against a decline by buying OEX puts. If the OEX index is valued at $325 ($32,500), three puts would protect about $97,500 (3 times $32,500) against a decline in the basket of stocks.

If the value of the index declines by 10 percent, the value of your put contracts should increase by about 10 percent.

If the value of the index increases by about 10 percent, the value of your put contracts would decline by about 10 percent. However, because you bought put contracts, your only loss would be the premiums you paid for the contracts, plus commissions.

Q: Can I invest in interest-rate options?

A: Yes. There are various interest-rate option contracts that trade on the American Stock Exchange and the Chicago Board Options Exchange. The contracts are based on baskets of bonds, mostly U.S. Treasury securities. There are also options on GNMA securities and certificates of deposit.

Note of Caution: Because interest rates and bond prices move in opposite directions, using interest-rate options requires a different thought process from trading in stock or index options. Interest-rate options should be avoided by most investors, particularly novice investors.

Q: Do options on foreign currencies exist?

A: Yes. Options based on the value of several foreign currencies trade on the options exchanges. The valuation of options on foreign currencies is very difficult, and so these options should be avoided by all but very experienced or professional investors.

Q: What does the term program trading mean?

A: *Program trading* refers to the practice engaged in by a few professional traders of simultaneously buying index options and selling the stocks in the index or buying the stocks in the index and selling the index options. The orders to buy or sell are automatically entered by a computer program; hence the name program trading.

Q: Why would traders want to engage in program trading?

A: Program trading is an attempt to earn (capture) a small profit based on the difference in the value of the index and the value of the underlying stocks included in the index. Though the percentage profits are small, professional traders can make money by using the strategy on very large volumes of stocks and options.

Q: Have the program traders created problems for the stock market?

A: Yes. Over the last two decades, as program trading has become more and more popular, it has resulted in a tremendous increase in both the number of shares being traded and the volatility of stock prices.

Q: Have the regulators done anything to control the volatility of stock prices created by program trading?

A: Because of the volatility of stock prices before and after the 1987 stock market crash, Congress, the Securities and Exchange Commission, and the various exchanges investigated the effects of program trading on stock prices. After the crash, many major brokerage firms suspended their program trading activities.

The New York Stock Exchange now has a rule that forbids the entering of orders by computer programs once the Dow Jones Average has had a movement up or down of 50 points. This rule is referred to as a *collar*.

Q: What documents are needed to place option trades?

A: There are three main documents required for option trading:

• Option disclosure statement

- Option agreement
- Prospectus

Q: What is an option disclosure statement?

A: An *option disclosure statement* is a document discussing the risks of trading options. It must be provided to an investor at or before the time at which the investor is approved for option trading.

Q: What is an option agreement?

A: An *option agreement* clarifies the investor's rights and obligations in option trading. Every investor must sign this agreement, affirming that he or she has read the agreement and is aware of the risks of option trading.

Q: What is the prospectus?

A: The *prospectus* contains a full description of option types and the risks involved in this type of investment. The prospectus is published by the OCC and must be made available to investors upon request.

Q: What are commodities?

A: *Commodities* are basically physical goods. They include many of the things we eat and wear, such as soybeans, cocoa, silver, gold, pork bellies, wheat, corn, sugar, cattle, wood, and potatoes.

Q: How do people invest in commodities?

A: In addition to investing in the stock of corporations that grow, process, or sell some of these commodities, investors can invest in *futures contracts* on certain actual commodities.

Q: What is a futures contract?

A: A *futures contract* is a standardized, exchange-traded contract calling for the delivery of a specified amount of a specified commodity in a specified month at a specified number of locations. Unlike in options transactions, there can be no transfer of the underlying commodity before the delivery date.

Q: Is a futures contract like an option?

A: No. The buyers and sellers of futures contracts do not actually exchange money. Each buyer and seller of a futures contract is required to deposit earnest money, referred to as *margin*, to ensure that performance of the entire contract can be completed at the completion date.

With a futures contract, unlike an option contract, delivery of the commodity cannot take place prior to the delivery month, whereas an option contract can be exercised at any time.

Q: What does the buyer of a futures contract agree to do?

A: The buyer, or owner, of a futures contract agrees to accept delivery of the specified amount of a commodity on the delivery date at a specified location unless the contract is closed by the sale of an offsetting contract before the delivery date.

Q: What does the seller of a commodity contract agree to do?

A: The seller of a commodity contract agrees to deliver a specified amount of a commodity on the delivery date at a specified location unless the contract is closed by the purchase of an offsetting contract before the delivery date.

 Note: Most futures contracts are closed before the delivery date, when delivery of the actual commodity would be required. In fact, it is said that fewer than 5 percent of commodity futures contracts actually result in delivery.

Q: How are commissions charged on futures contracts?

A: Commissions on futures contracts are charged on what is referred to as a *round-turn* basis. This means that the total commission for the opening and closing of a futures contract is charged at the same time, usually on the opening transaction.

 Note of Caution: Investors in commodity futures should realize that although the commission on a single transaction may appear to be small relative to the large amount of money controlled, commodity contracts are very short term, and a commodity trader may pay a substantial amount in commissions over a period of time.

Q: Where does trading in commodity futures take place?

A: Trading in commodity future contracts takes place on one of the commodity exchanges. The major commodity exchanges include:

- Chicago Board of Trade
- Chicago Mercantile Exchange

Q: If I enter into a commodity futures contract, must I be willing and able to settle with the other side of the trade?

A: No. As in option trading, there is a clearinghouse affiliated with each commodity exchange. The clearinghouse acts as the intermediary between buyers and sellers. By being the party between the buyers and sellers of commodity contracts, the clearinghouse guarantees the liquidity and performance of each contract. Neither buyers nor sellers have to be concerned about the other's ability to perform on the contract, as the clearinghouse is actually the other side to all trades.

Q: Can I invest in futures contracts based on commodities other than physical goods?

A: Until the early 1970s, the futures markets were basically linked with physical goods. Over the last two decades, however, the fastest-growing part of the futures business has been that of futures contracts on financial instruments, such as stock indexes, Treasury securities, currencies, foreign securities, and so on. The list of futures on financial instruments is almost endless.

Q: Has the expansion of futures on financial instruments created difficulties in the securities markets?

A: The expansion of futures on financial instruments and indexes has been a contributor to the increased volatility of stock prices. Like increased activity in the options markets, the increased activity in futures creates what could be called artificial activity in the underlying securities. Furthermore, the increased use of what have been called *derivatives* not only has increased trading volume and volatility but has resulted in substantial losses by even sophisticated, professional traders.

Q: What are derivatives?

A: *Derivatives* are usually defined as any investment vehicle other than stocks, debt (bonds), or cash. Obviously, options, warrants, rights, and futures based on stocks, bonds, or cash would be derivatives. Derivatives also include combinations of nondirect stock, bond, or cash investments. A complete list of derivatives would be more than two pages long. Some are so obscure that even some professional investors are unaware of them.

 Note: Another definition of a derivative is any investment derived from or linked to a main non-derivative investment like a stock, bond, or cash.

 Note of Caution: The tremendous losses sophisticated investors have experienced with derivatives or combinations of derivatives certainly gives credibility to the statement, "If you don't understand an investment, you should stay away from it."

SUMMARY

Options and futures are not long-term investments. They have a short life span before their expiration. Therefore, for you to profit from these investments, a quick price movement in the underlying securities is required.

This chapter has intended to discourage most investors from going into options and futures except as part of some relatively conservative strategies to increase income or to protect a profit. With other strategies, the risk is usually greater than the potential profit. Also, if you are going to invest in options or futures, you must be willing and able to spend a lot of time studying the possibilities and developing and executing your investment strategies. Finally, certain option and futures strategies engaged in by a few professional investors, such as program trading and exotic derivatives, have increased trading volume and led to increased volatility in the marketplace.

CHAPTER 8

BONDS: LENDING YOUR MONEY

A bond is a promissory note, or IOU, of an issuer. The issuer of a bond may be the U.S. government, a U.S. government agency, a corporation, or a state or local municipality (a city, a county, or an agency of a city or county).

When you invest in a bond, you become a *creditor* of the issuer:

- You are lending money to the issuer.
- You receive a stated rate of interest.
- You receive a promise to be repaid the face amount of the bond at maturity.

As a creditor, you generally will not participate in the growth or earnings of the issuer.

If you own a bond, you are a *direct creditor* of the bond's issuer. You may also be an *indirect creditor* of an issuer by:

- Owning shares of a mutual fund
- Participating in a retirement plan
- Owning life insurance policies
- Depositing money with many financial institutions

All of these institutions may invest directly in bonds.

In this chapter we discuss the features, benefits, issuers, and methods of bond ownership. The first series of questions provides basic information about bonds. The next section deals with the various bond issuers and the features and benefits of the bonds they issue. The remainder of the chapter concentrates on the buying and selling of bonds.

Q: Why should I invest in bonds?

A: Generally, you invest in bonds for three reasons:

1. To earn a stream of income in the form of interest payments
2. To preserve your principal, as you will receive the face value at maturity (see page 141)
3. To speculate (if you anticipate a dramatic change in interest rates)

 Note: For a discussion of the changing market price of bonds, refer to page 150.

Q: What do I give up when I invest in bonds?

A: When you invest in bonds, generally you are seeking a stream of income. In order to earn this stream of income, you are usually giving up the opportunity for:

- Appreciation in the value of your investment
- Having an investment that is an inflation hedge
- Increasing income being paid by the issuer while you own the bond

Q: What are my rights as a bond owner (creditor of an issuer)?

A: Basically, the general rights of a bond owner are:

1. To receive a stated amount of interest at stated times
2. To receive the principal (face value) at maturity

However, the rights of a bond owner are *limited* to the obligations of the issuer as outlined in the bond indenture (refer to the next question).

Q: What is a bond indenture?

A: A *bond indenture* is a legal contract between a bond issuer and bond owners. The indenture clearly states the bond's terms and conditions, interest payment details, and repayment terms. It will include such obligations of the issuer as:

- The rate of interest to be paid
- The time of payments
- The maturity date

- Any prepayment provisions (calls)
- The collateral, if any, securing the bond
- The priority of claims in the event that the issuer has financial difficulty
- Trustee for the bond issue
- The payment agent that will make payments of interest and principal to bond owners.

Q: What is a bond trustee?

A: A *bond trustee*, usually a bank, is responsible for ensuring that the rights of the bondholders are protected. If any of the covenants of the bond indenture are violated, the trustee will take whatever actions are necessary to protect the bondholders.

Q: What do I get as evidence that I own my bonds?

A: Evidence of ownership of your bonds may take one of two forms: a certificate or regular statements.

Certificate: Bond issuers sometimes issue certificates to their bondholders as evidence of their bond ownership. The front of the certificate will show the name of the issuer, the interest rate (coupon), and the maturity date, as well as the certificate number and *CUSIP* number (see page 205).

Note: When you receive a certificate as ownership of a bond, the bond is said to be *registered* (see page 198).

Statements: If you are not issued a certificate of ownership, you should receive periodic statements from the financial institution (broker, bank, or Federal Reserve) that holds your bonds. The statement is evidence of your ownership and should include most of the information that would be on a certificate.

Q: What is the face value of a bond?

A: The *face value*, often referred to as the *par value* or redemption value, is the value of a bond when it matures.

Generally, bonds are issued in denominations of $1,000 or multiples of $1,000. However, bonds are most often available in multiples of $5,000.

Examples: Ten bonds with a face value of $1,000 each have a total face value of $10,000. Twenty-five such bonds have a total face value of $25,000.

Note of Caution: Although most bonds are issued with face values that are multiples of $1,000, some bonds are issued with face values of $100 or $500. If you are not certain that a bond quote represents a $1,000 face value, you should ask your broker or advisor.

Q: How do I know the interest rate on a bond?

A: *Interest* (often referred to as *coupon*) is the amount that will be paid to the bond owner each period. The interest rate (coupon) is usually stated on the bond certificate, generally as a percentage of face value. If you own a bond with a face value of $1,000 that pays 8 percent, you will receive $80 a year. If you own ten bonds with a face value of $1,000 each, the face value of the bonds you own is $10,000, and you will receive $800 a year.

Bonds are often identified by *coupon rate and maturity*. For example, bonds paying 6 percent that are due in the year 2002 might be described as "6s of '02." Other bonds might require more detail, such as "$7^1/_8$s of 7/15/06" for $7^1/_8$ percent bonds due on July 15, 2006.

Q: How is the bond interest rate originally determined?

A: At the time a bond is issued, the interest rate on *that* bond is established by the issuer at a level that makes the bond competitive with outstanding bonds of similar quality and maturity.

Q: How is bond interest paid?

A: Even though the interest paid on a bond is stated as an annual rate, it is usually paid every six months. If a $1,000 bond pays 8 percent, you will usually receive two payments of

$40 each. If the first payment is made in January, the second semiannual payment will be in July, and so on, as shown in the box.

Semiannual Bond Interest Payment Schedule		
January	and	July
February	and	August
March	and	September
April	and	October
May	and	November
June	and	December

Even though most bonds pay interest semiannually, some pay interest monthly. You should be informed about the interest payment dates when you purchase or acquire a bond. Generally, one of the interest payment dates will correspond to the month and day that the bond matures.

Q: What is the maturity date of a bond?

A: The *maturity date* of a bond is the date on which the bond owner is to be paid the face value (principal) and any unpaid interest. The bond matures just like any note or debt you might owe.

 Example: If you own a bond that matures on November 30, 2006, you will be paid the face value of the bond and any unpaid interest on that date.

Q: What does the maturity date mean to me?

A: The maturity date is the stated date on which your investment and its corresponding risks end and you are repaid your principal.

The shorter the maturity, the sooner you will get your money back. Therefore, you are assuming less interest-rate risk (see Chapter 3, page 19). Generally, the shorter the maturity, the lower the interest rate earned.

The maturity date may also be important to you in terms of the time at which you wish to achieve an important investment goal. Many investors will select bonds that mature at a time when they will need cash to achieve such goals as:

- College education
- Vacation home acquisition
- Retirement
- Special gifts (a child or grandchild's birthday or a special occasion)

This planning process is sometimes referred to as *matching maturities to needs*.

 Note of Caution: It is unwise to have *too* many bonds maturing at the same time (see page 154, diversification, and page 155, laddered bond portfolios).

Q. Do all bonds remain outstanding until their maturity date?

A. No. Many bonds include *call features*.

Q. What is a call?

A. A *call* is a feature that allows a bond's issuer to redeem a bond before maturity at specified prices and specified dates. (The call price is usually above the par value.)

 Example: A bond may have a stated maturity date of August 15, 2015. Yet, the bond may have a call feature allowing the issuer to call the bond on August 15, 2005.

Q. I have heard the term *call protection*. What does that mean?

A: *Call protection* refers to the number of years after a bond's date of issue during which it cannot be called. During that period, the investor is said to be "protected" from having the bond called. Hence, the term "call protection." In the bond call example above, if the bond was issued on August 15,

1995 and its first call date is August 15, 2005, the bond has 10 years of *call protection*.

Q: What is a debenture?

A: A *debenture* is an *unsecured* bond—that is, one that is not secured by real estate, equipment, or other collateral.

Q: What is the difference between a bond and a note?

A: A *bond* is a debt security with a maturity of ten years or longer. A *note* is a debt security with a maturity of less than ten years.

Q: What is accrued interest on a bond?

A: *Accrued interest* is the amount of interest earned between the last interest payment date and some other date, such as the settlement date when buying or selling a bond.

The *buyer* of a bond pays the *seller* the agreed-upon market price plus the interest that the seller has *accrued* from the last interest payment date to the settlement date of the transaction. On the next interest payment date, the *buyer* will receive a full interest payment, including the interest earned between the last interest payment date and the settlement date.

Accrued interest is added to the purchase price and paid to the seller.

Example: On September 30, you invest in an 8 percent $1,000 bond. The bond pays interest on June 30 and December 30 ($40 on each date, $80 a year). You will have to pay the seller three months' accrued interest, or $20 (interest from June 30 to September 30, your settlement date). On the next interest payment date (December 30), you will receive a full interest payment of $40.

Illustration 8-1
Accrued Interest on Bond Buy/Sell Transaction

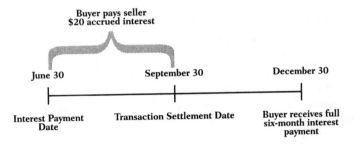

Buyer pays seller
$20 accrued interest

June 30   September 30   December 30

Interest Payment Date   Transaction Settlement Date   Buyer receives full six-month interest payment

BONDS

Q: What does trading flat mean?

A: A bond is said to be *trading flat* if it is in default and not making timely interest payments. When a bond is trading flat, the buyer does not pay accrued interest to the seller.

Q. How are bond prices quoted?

A. The price of a bond is usually stated as a percentage of the face value.

 Example: A quote of 97 for a $1000 bond is a price of $970. A quote of 103 for a $1000 bond is a price of $1,030

Q: When referring to bonds, what is a point?

A: A *point* is generally 1 percent of the value of a bond. For instance, a 1-point price change in a bond with a face value of $1,000 would be $10 per bond, $3/_4$ point would be $7.50 per bond, $1/_2$ point would be $5.00 per bond, and $1/_4$ point would be $2.50 per bond. If you owned ten such bonds, a 1-point change would make a $100 difference to you ($10 per bond times 10 bonds equals $100).

Q: What is a basis point?

A: A *basis point* is *one one-hundredth* of a point. When used in reference to bonds:

> 100 basis points equal 1 percent.
> 50 basis points equal $\frac{1}{2}$ percent.
> 200 basis points equal 2 percent.

Q: What is a premium bond?

A: A *premium bond* is a bond whose market price is higher than its face or par value.

 Example: A bond with a $1,000 face value is selling for a price of 110 ($1,100). The premium is $100.

Q: What does it mean to me if I invest in a premium bond?

A: If you invest in a bond selling at a premium, you will be paid only the face value at maturity. This means that you will get back less than you paid for the bond. You should consider that difference when you calculate your return and decide whether to invest in the bond (see page 148, yield-to-maturity).

Q: Why would I ever pay more than the face value for a bond?

A: Sometimes it may be advantageous for you to invest in a bond that is selling at a premium in order to receive a higher current income. Often a bond is priced at a premium because its interest rate is higher than the prevailing market rate for bonds of the same quality and maturity. Generally, the additional income earned over the time you own the bond should offset the premium.

Q: What are the tax consequences when I own a premium bond?

A: Income tax laws are constantly changing. You should therefore consult your tax advisor about the tax treatment of any premiums in your bond portfolio.

Q: What is a discount bond?

A: A *discount bond* is a bond whose market price is below its face or par value.

 Example: A bond with a $1,000 face value is selling for a price of 90 ($900). The discount is $100.

Q: What does it mean to me if I invest in a discount bond?

A: If you invest in a bond selling at a discount to its face or par value, you will be paid the full face value at maturity. This means that you will get back more than you paid for the bond. You should consider that discount when you calculate your return and decide whether to invest in the bond (see page 148, yield-to-maturity).

Q: Why would I consider investing in a discount bond?

A: Sometimes it may be advantageous for you to invest in a bond selling at a discount because the discount will compensate you for lower interest payments. The bond is priced at a discount because its interest rate is below the prevailing market rate for bonds of the same quality and maturity. Generally, the amount of the discount is earned over the amount of time you own the bond and will offset the lower current yield.

Q: Am I taxed on the gain when a bond I acquired at a discount matures or is redeemed?

A: Income tax laws are constantly changing. Therefore, you should consult your tax advisor about the tax treatment of any discounts in your bond portfolio. Generally, however, any gain on a bond is taxable.

Q: What is an original issue discount (OID)?

A: *Original issue discount* is an official term that the Internal Revenue Service has given to some bonds that are originally sold at less than their face value. If you own or are considering investing in a bond designated as OID, special complex tax rules may apply; therefore, you should consult a professional tax advisor.

Q: What is a sinking fund?

A: A *sinking fund* is a provision requiring the bond issuer to set aside an amount of money, usually once a year, to provide for the early retirement of a portion of a bond issue. Most of the time, bonds are retired in the year the money is set aside. However, the bond indenture may allow an alternative. The retirement of the bonds may be made by

- Open-market purchase (see page 196)
- Call provisions (see page 142)

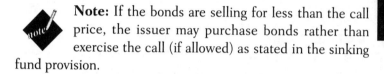 **Note:** If the bonds are selling for less than the call price, the issuer may purchase bonds rather than exercise the call (if allowed) as stated in the sinking fund provision.

If sinking funds are required in the bond indenture, they are a legal obligation of the issuer.

Q: What is pre-refunding?

A: Pre-refunding is a financing method in which an issuer borrows money by issuing another bond in order to pay off an outstanding bond. The outstanding bond issue will be retired at the earliest time possible once the new issue has been sold. The new bond will have a lower interest rate, and the cash is escrowed for redemption.

Pre-refunded bonds are generally rated AAA (see page 190, bond ratings) because the proceeds from the new bond issue are usually invested in U.S. Treasury notes or bonds that mature when the outstanding bond is to be retired. In essence, the outstanding bond is backed by U.S. Treasury securities until it is retired.

Q: How do I compute the current yield on a bond?

A: The current yield on a bond is the interest paid (coupon) as a percentage of the market price you would pay for the bond today.

Examples:

If you own a 6 percent bond that sells for $1,000 (*par*), your current yield is 6 percent ($60 yearly interest divided by $1,000 market price).

If the 6 percent bond has a market price of 90 ($900) (*discount*), the current yield would be 6.67 percent ($60 annual interest divided by $900 market price).

If the bond has a market price of 110 ($1,100) (*premium*), the current yield is 5.45 percent ($60 annual interest divided by $1,100 market price).

Q: What is yield-to-maturity?

A: *Yield-to-maturity* is the compound total return on a bond that is held to maturity. The premium or discount is amortized over the period from the time you acquire a bond to its maturity. The annual amortized amount is *subtracted* from the current yield on a premium bond and *added* to the current yield on a discount bond.

Examples:

If you pay 110 ($1,100) for a $1,000 bond that matures in ten years and pays a 6 percent interest rate, your yield-to-maturity is 4.45 percent. The current yield is 5.45 percent ($60 income divided by $1,100). Since you paid $1,100 for a bond that will pay $1,000 at maturity, the $100 premium must be amortized over ten years, or $10 per year (which is 1 percent). Thus 1 percent is deducted from the current yield, 5.45 percent, and your yield-to-maturity is 4.45 percent.

If you acquire a bond for 90 ($900) that pays $60 per year and matures in ten years, your current yield is 6.67 percent. Since you paid $900 for the bond and will receive $1,000 at maturity, the $100 discount is amortized over the time you will own the bond ($10, or 1 percent, per year). The 1 percent per year is added to the current yield of 6.67 percent for a yield-to-maturity of 7.67 percent.

Note of Caution: The above examples are oversimplified for illustration purposes. Consult your broker or advisor for precise yield-to-maturity calculations.

Q: Why is yield-to-maturity important to me?

A: Yield-to-maturity is a bond's *total annual* return to you. Since investments are compared on the basis of their total return, yield-to-maturity is valuable when you want to compare several fixed-income investments and need a "yardstick." The yield-to-maturity is also valuable when you are using a fixed-income investment to accumulate capital rather than seeking the highest possible cash income.

 Note:
- Yield-to-maturity in a premium bond is *less* than the current yield.
- Yield-to-maturity in a discount bond is *greater* than the current yield.

Q: What is yield-to-call?

A: *Yield-to-call* is similar to *yield-to-maturity* except that the *call date* instead of the maturity date is used as the redemption date. Refer to page 142 for questions on bond calls.

 Note: Yield-to-call is generally important only if the current value (*market price*) of the bond is near or above the call price.

Q: What does yield-to-call mean to me?

A: If the market price of a bond is near or above the call price, and it is likely that the bond will be called, the yield-to-call will be more pertinent than yield-to-maturity.

BONDS

Illustration 8-2
Yield-to-Maturity versus Yield-to-Call

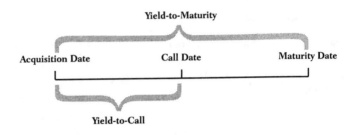

Yield-to-Maturity

Acquisition Date   Call Date   Maturity Date

Yield-to-Call

Q: Why does the price of a bond go up and down?

A: After you acquire a bond, its price will go up and down until maturity, when you are paid the face value. The price will fluctuate because of changes in:

● General interest rates
● Ratings
● Supply and demand

Q: Why will a bond's price go up and down because of changes in general interest rates?

A: Since the interest paid and the maturity of a bond cannot change, its market price (value) will change to reflect *changes in general interest rates*. One formula to remember when investing in bonds (or any fixed income investment):

● If interest rates I increase, the value P (for principal) of a bond or other fixed income investment will decline.

I P

● If interest rates I decline, the value of a bond P will increase.

You would not pay the face value ($1,000) for a ten-year bond yielding 5 percent if comparable new issues of bonds had a yield of 7 percent. The price of the bond yielding 5 percent would have to decline to 86 ($860) so that you would have a yield-to-maturity of 7 percent.

On the other hand, if you owned the 7 percent bond, you would not sell it for its face value if comparable bonds were yielding 5 percent. You would demand a price of about 115.5 ($1,155), giving the buyer a yield-to-maturity of 5 percent.

Q: Why will a bond's price go up and down because of changes in its rating?

A: Except for government and government agency bonds, the rating agencies (see page 189) assign "credit ratings" to issuers. Generally, higher-rated issuers pay their bondholders lower interest rates on newly issued bonds.

If an issuer moves down the scale in quality, the issuer will have to pay higher interest payments in order to sell bonds and the market price of its outstanding bonds will fall.

If an issuer's rating is raised, the prices of older issues should increase, reflecting the higher rating, and the issuer will not have to pay as high an interest rate on newly issued bonds. (Refer to page 189 for questions on bond ratings.)

Q: Why will a bond's price go up and down because of changes in the supply and demand for that issue?

A: Generally, *supply and demand* factors do not significantly affect the prices of most bonds. However, external circumstances can create an unusually large demand for some types of bonds, which could affect the price—for example, municipal bonds after income taxes are increased. A discussion of supply and demand factors that may affect bond prices is not within the scope of this book.

THE QUESTION AND ANSWER BOOK OF MONEY AND INVESTING

Q: What is a yield curve?

A: A *yield curve* is a graphic illustration of the relationship between interest rates and time to maturity. The illustration shows the yields on the vertical line and time to maturity on the horizontal line.

Generally, yield curves will be ascending (as illustrated below), with long-term maturities yielding more than short-term maturities. This is usually referred to as a *normal yield curve*.

BONDS

Illustration 8-3
Yield Curve: Normal-Rate Curve

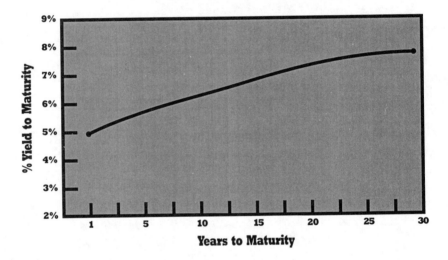

Sometimes long-term maturities have a lower yield than short-term maturities. This is referred to as an *inverted yield curve*. This usually occurs during periods of short-term economic uncertainty.

Illustration 8-4
Yield Curve: Inverted-Rate Curve

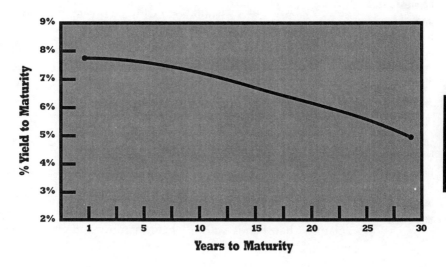

Q: What effect does time to maturity have on the volatility of a bond?

A: Generally, the shorter the time to maturity, the less risk there is in a bond investment. Therefore, the price is less volatile. The longer the time to maturity, the greater the risk. Therefore, the price is more volatile.

Q: What happens to the price of my bond if general interest rates increase from 6 percent to 7 percent?

A: If general interest rates increase from 6 percent to 7 percent:

- The price of a $1,000 bond with a ten-year maturity will decline about 7 points (say from 100 to 93).
- The price of a $1,000 bond with a thirty-year maturity will decline about $12\frac{1}{2}$ points (say from 100 to $87\frac{1}{2}$).

Q: What happens to the price of my bond if general interest rates decrease from 6 percent to 5 percent?

A: If general interest rates decrease from 6 percent to 5 percent:

- The price of a $1,000 bond with a ten-year maturity will increase about 8 points (say from 100 to 108).
- The price of a $1,000 bond with a thirty-year maturity will increase about $15\frac{1}{2}$ points (say from 100 to $115\frac{1}{2}$).

Q: Generally, what is the price effect of owning bonds with longer maturities?

A: Usually, lengthening the maturity substantially adds to the volatility of bond prices.

If you know that you will get your money back soon, you are less likely to sell your bond for less than the face value. This is why shorter-maturity bonds generally have less price volatility than bonds with a longer maturity and also pay less interest.

Q: What is my bond portfolio?

A: Your *bond portfolio* is your entire holdings of bonds.

Q: How can I diversify my bond portfolio?

A: You can diversify your bond portfolio by investing in bonds with different:

- Issuers
- Maturities (laddered portfolios; see page 155)
- Size of issues
- Ratings

Q: How can I diversify my bond portfolio by issuers?

A: You can diversify your bond portfolio by owning bonds issued by different issuers. By investing in the bonds of different issuers, you are spreading the risk of bond ownership. Also, different types of issuers—the U.S. government, U.S. government agencies, U.S. corporations, foreign governments or corporations, and municipalities—will offer you different levels of security and have different income tax consequences.

Q: How can I diversify my bond portfolio by maturities?

A: You can diversify your bond portfolio by owning bonds with various maturities; you will not have all of your bonds maturing at the same time. This should provide you with a more stable stream of income and reduce your overall interest-rate risk.

If *interest rates are low* when some of your bonds mature, you will probably be unhappy because you will have to reinvest the proceeds at a lower interest rate than you were earning on the bonds that matured.

If *interest rates are high* when some of your bonds mature, you will be happy because you will be able to reinvest the proceeds at a higher yield than you were earning on the bonds that matured.

 Note: One way to reduce the risk of bond ownership is to invest in what is often referred to as a "laddered bond portfolio."

Q: What is a laddered bond portfolio?

A: You can build a *laddered bond portfolio* by acquiring bonds of various maturities. This method of investing in bonds reduces the interest-rate risk, as explained above. Generally, you will be receiving a lower yield than you could earn from investing in long-term bonds, but you do not have the added risk to the market value incurred by long-term bonds. As with any bond investing, you will generally earn a lower yield on the short maturities and a higher yield on the long maturities.

Below is an example of a laddered bond portfolio.

Illustration 8-5
Sample Laddered Bond Portfolio

Face Value	Name	Coupon %	Maturity Date		Market Price	Yield	Months Interest Is Paid
10,000	Salomon	7.0	05-15-97	@	100	7.0	5 & 11
10,000	Shell Oil	6 5/8	07-01-99	@	99 1/8	6.83	1 & 7
10,000	Philip Morris	7 1/8	08-15-02	@	94 3/8	8.07	2 & 8
10,000	AT&T	6.75	04-01-04	@	95 1/2	7.40	4 & 10
10,000	K Mart	8.125	12-01-06	@	99 3/4	8.16	6 & 12
10,000	New England Tel	6 3/8	09-01-08	@	88 1/8	7.76	3 & 9

BONDS

- When your shorter-term bonds mature, you may want to extend your laddered portfolio by investing the proceeds in longer-term bonds (beyond your longest current bond maturity). Thus, you are spreading the interest rate and maturity risk.

Q: Since bonds generally pay interest twice a year, is there a way I can get a check every month from direct bond ownership?

A: Yes. If you decide to spread the money you are investing among six different bond issues that pay interest in different months, you can arrange a bond portfolio that will pay you every month.

Note: The laddered bond portfolio example also shows how you can select a bond portfolio that will give you a check every month. (Refer to interest payment cycles, page 141).

Q: How can I diversify my bond portfolio by size of the issue?

A: You can diversify your bond portfolio by the size of the bond issues because sometimes different size bond issues will have different interest rates and trading patterns. Often smaller issues, even when sold by high-quality issuers, will have higher yields because they are considered to be less marketable than larger issues. If you are planning to hold the bonds to maturity, it may be advantageous to invest in a few bonds of small issues to earn the extra yield. Often what you are giving up to earn the extra yield is *liquidity* (see page 19). When you are seeking diversification by size in assembling a bond port-folio, you should seek the advice of a bond professional.

Q: How can I diversify my bond portfolio by ratings?

A: You can diversify your bond portfolio by *ratings* by owning bonds which have various ratings. Other than bonds issued by the U.S. government and U.S. government agencies, which are considered the safest, bonds are generally rated as to quality of the issuer by at least one rating agency (and maybe more). (See page 189, bond ratings.) However, there are many small municipal and corporate bond issues that are not rated. If you decide to invest in a nonrated bond, you or your advisor must perform research as to the likelihood that the issuer will be able to pay interest and repay principal.

Q: How do I distinguish between the different types of bond issuers?

A: Since you are depending on an issuer's ability to pay interest and principal on your bond investment, it is important to understand the differences between the different types of bond issuers. Bonds of different types of issuers have different features, such as risk levels, exposure to taxation, etc., that may affect your investment returns. The major types of bond issuers, which we will discuss in more detail in the following pages, include:

- The U.S. government
- U.S. government-related agencies
- Corporations
- Foreign issuers: governments and corporations
- Municipal issuers (states, localities, etc.)

Q: What are U.S. government debt securities?

A: U.S. government debt securities, which include bills, notes, and bonds, are issued by the U.S. Treasury Department. They are direct obligations of the U.S. government.

Q: Why are U.S. government bonds considered so safe?

A: U.S. government bonds are called *Treasury issues* because they are issued by the Treasury Department. Treasury issues are considered the safest bonds because they are direct obligations of the U.S. government and are backed by the "full faith and credit" of the U.S. government. This means the federal government must use any and all of its resources, including its ability to raise funds through taxation, to meet its obligations to the debtholders. By buying a Treasury security, you become a creditor of the U.S. government.

Q: Does direct U.S. government debt have special tax benefits?

A: Yes. The interest paid on direct obligations of the U.S. government is not subject to state and local income taxes.

Q: Are there different types of Treasury issues?

A: Yes. The U.S. government uses debt issues with many different maturities to serve different needs. Some issues are *marketable* among investors, and some are *nonmarketable*.

Q: What are marketable Treasury securities?

A: *Marketable securities* are U.S. government bonds that can be traded and transferred among investors in the open market at the prevailing market prices.

Q: What are nonmarketable Treasury securities?

A: *Nonmarketable securities* are U.S. government bonds that can be owned only by the original investor and can be redeemed only by the U.S. treasury or its agents.

Q: What is a Treasury bill?

A: Among marketable Treasury issues, the shortest-term obligations are called *Treasury bills*. Treasury bills are issued in maturities of one year or less. Since they are outstanding for such a short time, their interest is deducted from the face value as a discount rather than being paid as with most bonds.

As an investor, you pay less than the face value for the bond when you buy it, and you receive the full face value amount at maturity. The difference is your income.

Example: You buy a 6 percent one-year Treasury bill. You pay $9,400, and in one year you get back $10,000. In reality, your true yield is 6.38 percent because you are receiving an annual income of $600 on an actual investment of $9,400. This is referred to as the *coupon yield equivalent* or *equivalent bond yield*.

Because of their unique nature, Treasury bills are quoted in the newspaper differently from other debt securities. Rather than quoting a price as a percentage of face value, such as 97, Treasury bill quotes use the discount *from* par, such as bid 5.12 and asked 5.10. A sample excerpt from a newspaper quote is shown below.

Illustration 8-6
T-Bill Newspaper Quote

TREASURY BILLS

Maturity	Days to Mat.	Bid	Asked	Chg.	Ask Yld.
May 19 '94	2	3.05	2.95	+ 0.05	2.99
May 26 '94	9	3.14	3.04	– 0.01	3.08
Jun 02 '94	16	3.58	3.48	– 0.02	3.53
Jun 09 '94	23	3.59	3.49	. . . .	3.55
Jun 16 '94	30	3.58	3.54	– 0.04	3.60
Jun 23 '94	37	3.62	3.58	– 0.02	3.64
Jun 30 '94	44	3.75	3.71	– 0.02	3.78
Jul 07 '94	51	3.83	3.79	– 0.02	3.86
Jul 14 '94	58	3.87	3.85	– 0.02	3.93
Jul 21 '94	65	3.93	3.91	– 0.02	3.99
Jul 28 '94	72	4.00	3.98	– 0.07	4.07
Aug 04 '94	79	4.08	4.06	– 0.03	4.15
Aug 11 '94	**86**	**4.12**	**4.10**	**– 0.01**	**4.20**
Aug 18 '94	93	4.18	4.16	– 0.02	4.26
Aug 25 '94	100	4.22	4.20	– 0.04	4.31
Sep 01 '94	107	4.24	4.22	– 0.05	4.33
Sep 08 '94	114	4.33	4.31	– 0.02	4.43
Sep 15 '94	121	4.37	4.35	– 0.05	4.48
Sep 22 '94	128	4.39	4.37	– 0.05	4.50
Sep 29 '94	135	4.43	4.41	– 0.05	4.55
Oct 06 '94	142	4.50	4.48	– 0.04	4.62
Oct 13 '94	149	4.56	4.54	– 0.05	4.69
Oct 20 '94	156	4.59	4.57	– 0.05	4.73
Oct 27 '94	163	4.61	4.59	– 0.05	4.75
Nov 03 '94	170	4.64	4.62	– 0.05	4.79
Nov 10 '94	**177**	**4.67**	**4.65**	**– 0.04**	**4.82**
Nov 17 '94	184	4.70	4.68	– 0.05	4.86
Dec 15 '94	212	4.77	4.75	– 0.05	4.94
Jan 12 '95	240	4.85	4.83	– 0.05	5.03
Feb 09 '95	268	4.95	4.93	– 0.05	5.15
Mar 09 '95	296	5.03	5.01	– 0.04	5.25
Apr 06 '95	324	5.10	5.08	– 0.04	5.34
May 04 '95	352	5.12	5.10	– 0.06	5.37

Example:

- If you are buying a $10,000 one-year Treasury bill with an asked quote of 5.10, you will pay $9,490 ($10,000 less $510).

- If you are selling a $10,000 one-year Treasury bill with a bid quote of 5.12, you will receive $9,488 ($10,000 less $512).

Bid: The price a buyer is willing to pay a seller for a bond.
Asked: The price at which a seller if offering the bond to buyers.

Treasury bills are issued in multiples of $1,000 with a minimum denomination of $10,000. No certificate is issued—Treasury bills are issued in book-entry form (see page 198).

Q: What are Treasury notes?

A: Treasury *notes* are U.S. debt securities issued with maturities of more than one year but not more than ten years.

Q: What are Treasury bonds?

A: Treasury *bonds* are U.S. debt securities issued with maturities longer than ten years.

Q: How are longer Treasury issues different?

A: Treasury *notes* and *bonds* are the longer classes of Treasury issues. Both notes and bonds pay a fixed rate of interest in two semiannual coupon payments. Their prices are quoted in the financial media as a percentage of the face value, as illustrated below.

Illustration 8-7
T-Note and T-Bond Newspaper Quote

TREASURY BONDS, NOTES

Monday, July 11, 1994

Representative Over-the-Counter quotations based on transactions of $1 million or more.

Treasury bond, note and bill quotes are as of mid-afternoon. Colons in bid-and-asked quotes represent 32nds; 101:01 means 101 1/32. Net changes in 32nds. n-Treasury note. Treasury bill quotes in hundredths, quoted on terms of a rate of discount. Days to maturity calculated from settlement date. All yields are to maturity and based on the asked quote. Latest 13-week and 26-week bills are boldfaced. For bonds callable prior to maturity, yields are computed to the earliest call date for issues quoted above par and to the maturity date for issues below par. *-When issued.

Source: Federal Reserve Bank of New York.

U.S. Treasury strips as of 3 p.m. Eastern time, also based on transactions of $1 million or more. Colons in bid-and-asked quotes represent 32nds; 101:01 means 101 1/32. Net changes in 32nds. Yields calculated on the asked quotation. ci-stripped coupon interest. bp-Treasury bond, stripped principal. np-Treasury note, stripped principal. For bonds callable prior to maturity, yields are computed to the earliest call date for issues quoted above par and to the maturity date for issues below par.

Source: Bear, Stearns & Co. via Street Software Technology Inc.

GOVT. BONDS & NOTES					Maturity				
	Maturity			Ask					Ask
Rate	Mo/Yr	Bid	Asked	Chg. Yld.	Rate	Mo/Yr	Bid Asked	Chg.	Yld
8	Jul 94n	100:00	100:02	− 1 0.00	6³/₄	Jan 00n	96:18 96:20	− 8	7.13
4¹/₄	Jul 94n	99:31	100:01	.... 3.55	7⁷/₈	Feb 95-00	101:09 101:13	− 3	5.43
6⁷/₈	Aug 94n	100:06	100:08	− 2 4.01	8¹/₂	Feb 00n	106:06 106:08	− 6	7.13
8⁵/₈	Aug 94n	100:12	100:14	− 1 3.68	5¹/₂	Apr 00n	92:13 92:15	− 8	7.12
8³/₄	Aug 94	100:12	100:14	.... 3.80	8⁷/₈	May 00n	108:04 108:06	− 9	7.14
12⁵/₈	Aug 94n	100:24	100:26	− 1 3.50	8³/₈	Aug 95-00	102:03 102:07	− 14	6.24
4¹/₄	Aug 94n	99:31	100:01	.... 3.95	8³/₄	Aug 00n	107:17 107:19	− 8	7.19
4	Sep 94n	99:28	99:30	− 1 4.24	8¹/₂	Nov 00n	106:11 106:13	− 10	7.22
8¹/₂	Sep 94n	100:27	100:29	− 1 4.16	7³/₄	Feb 01n	102:16 102:18	− 10	7.25
9¹/₂	Oct 94n	101:06	101:08	− 1 4.47	11³/₄	Feb 01	123:14 123:18	− 12	7.20
4¹/₄	Oct 94n	99:27	99:29	− 1 4.53	8	May 01n	103:24 103:26	− 9	7.28
6	Nov 94n	100:11	100:13	− 1 4.74	13¹/₈	May 01	131:12 131:16	− 14	7.21
8¹/₄	Nov 94n	101:03	101:05	− 1 4.73	7⁷/₈	Aug 01n	102:31 103:01	− 10	7.32
10¹/₈	Nov 94	101:24	101:26	− 1 4.63	8	Aug 96-01	102:13 102:17	− 3	6.68
11⁵/₈	Nov 94n	102:07	102:09	− 1 4.71	13³/₈	Aug 01	133:15 133:19	− 16	7.24
					7¹/₂	Nov 01n	100:25 100:27	− 9	7.35

Prices of treasury notes and bonds are quoted to the nearest thirty-second of a point ($^1/_{32}$), indicated by a colon (:) in the bid and asked quotes.

Example:

- If you are buying a $10,000, seven-year Treasury note with an asked quote of 104:21, you will pay $10,466 ($104 + ^{21}/_{32} = 104.66$).

- If you are selling the same issue with a bid quote of 104:17, you will receive $10,453 ($104 + ^{17}/_{32} = 104.53$).

Q: Are Treasury securities callable?

A: Some Treasury bonds include a call provision, allowing the Treasury to redeem them prior to maturity. The Treasury Department does not often exercise its right to call debt. In the sample newspaper quote, the call feature is indicated by what appears to be a double maturity.

Example: May 00-05

The first date is the call date (May 00; i.e., May 2000). The second date is the maturity date (May 05).

Treasury notes and bonds are no longer issued in registered form, although certificates for some older issues are still outstanding. Treasury notes and bonds are denominated in $1,000 increments and have a minimum denomination of $1,000, except for the two- and three-year notes, which have a minimum of $5,000.

Q: How do U.S. savings bonds work?

A: Savings bonds are a special class of nonmarketable U.S. government bonds. They are direct obligations of the U.S. government and are backed by the full faith and credit of the U.S. government. They are issued only to a specific buyer and are registered permanently in that buyer's name. The bonds are not transferable to another owner's name, so they may not be resold or assigned as collateral for a loan.

Savings bonds may be registered in three ways:

- Single ownership in the name of one person
- Co-ownership in the joint name of two persons
- Beneficiary form, with one person as owner and another as beneficiary

Savings bonds are currently issued in two series: *Series EE bonds* and *Series HH bonds*. Older series, including Series E and Series H savings bonds, are no longer issued but many are still outstanding and continue to earn interest.

Q: How do Series EE savings bonds work?

A: Series EE savings bonds are very popular investments, since they can be purchased in small quantities and can earn market-based interest rates.

Series EE bonds are issued at a discounted price, and the owner's interest is compounded within the bond instead of being paid out during the bond's term. Currently Series EE bonds are issued at one-half their face value and are guaranteed to reach face value in eighteen years. They are available in eight denominations:

Denomination	Purchase Price
$50	$25
$75	$37.50
$100	$50
$200	$100
$500	$250
$1,000	$500
$5,000	$2,500
$10,000	$5,000

The maximum purchase for any individual is $30,000 face value ($15,000 cost) in any one year.

The purchase price discount of 50 percent gives the bonds a guaranteed annual rate of return of 4 percent, earned and compounded within the bond. Series EE bond issues dated February 1993 or earlier may carry different guaranteed interest rates.

Q: How is the interest rate on Series EE bonds established?

A: For the first five years you own a Series EE bond, the earnings will compound at the minimum guaranteed rate of 4 percent. After five years, the bond will begin to earn market-based interest rates while keeping its minimum guaranteed rate at 4 percent. If the market-adjusted interest rate rises above 4 percent, the owner will earn extra interest, which will be paid at redemption. Such extra interest will increase the bond's value above its face value at maturity.

Q: How are Series EE bonds redeemed?

A: Series EE bonds may be redeemed at any time after six months from the issue date. They will be redeemed at the original purchase price plus any accrued interest. They may also be exchanged for Series HH savings bonds if you want to start receiving current income.

BONDS

Q: How are savings bonds taxed?

A: As is the case with all direct U.S. Treasury obligations, savings bond interest is subject to federal income taxes, but not state or local income taxes. The tax is generally not payable until you redeem the bonds, and can be deferred if you exchange Series EE bonds for Series HH bonds. However, the income tax is due when the Series HH bonds are redeemed or reach final maturity, whichever comes first.

Q: Can I avoid taxation on Series EE bonds?

A: Yes. Depending on your income level, Series EE bond interest may be tax-exempt altogether if you redeem the bonds for certain educational purposes, including college and qualified technical schools. For complete tax information, consult your tax advisor, the IRS, or request materials from your local Federal Reserve office.

Q: How would I determine the current value of my Series EE savings bonds?

A: The Treasury Department produces a table that specifies the compounded current value of Series EE bonds. To determine the value of your Series EE bonds, you should contact:

- A depository institution which acts as a paying agent
- The U.S. government printing office to request a booklet of redemption tables: Superintendent of Documents, U.S. Government Printing Office, Washington, D.C., 20424
- A federal reserve bank in your area

Q: What are Series HH bonds?

A: Series HH bonds are issued only in exchange for other savings bond series. They are issued in ten-year maturities and in denominations of $500, $1,000, $5,000, and $10,000. Series HH bonds are issued at full face value (no discount) and mature at that value. These bonds pay current interest at a set percentage rate for ten years. They pay interest semi-annually by direct deposit to your checking or savings account. After ten years, they are automatically renewed for another ten years unless you redeem them. The interest rate will be reset at the current market rate. After twenty years, the bonds will be redeemed unless you reinvest in new Series HH bonds.

Although Series HH bonds are issued with ten-year terms, the Treasury Department has extended their maturities. They may be redeemed for full par value at any time after the first six months of their term if you wish to liquidate them. If you redeem them between interest payment dates, you do *not* receive accrued interest for the interim period.

Q: What should I do if I own older Series E or Series H bonds?

A: Check with your local depository institution where you conduct banking transactions to see if interest is being accrued or paid and if the maturities have been extended.

Q: How are bonds issued by government-related agencies different from Treasury issues?

A: Unlike the Treasury Department, which issues direct U.S. government obligations to fund *general* purposes, a government-related agency issues obligations to fund that agency's *specific* mission. Each agency was created by Congress to promote a public economic goal, such as individual home ownership or family farm support. Agency bonds are generally not direct government obligations, but they carry the implied support of the government and are supported by collateral assets, such as a portfolio of individual home mortgages or farm loans.

The government promotes its economic goals by encouraging lenders to offer credit to borrowers in the agency's area, such as home loans. Lenders will be able to originate more mortgages (and earn the fees that they generate) if they can get their loan principal back quickly. The agencies facilitate this by buying loans from lenders, putting together large portfolios of such loans, and selling bonds backed by these portfolios to investors. By selling these bonds, they can recoup their money so that they can buy more mortgages and thus support more lending activity. This process is depicted in Illustration 8-8.

Illustration 8-8
Diagram of Asset-Backed Loans

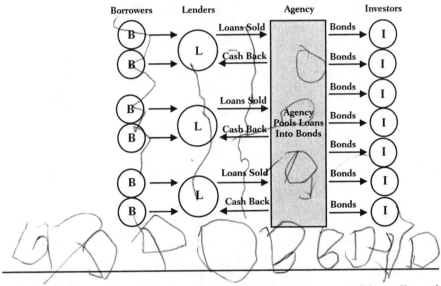

Q: What is an asset-backed bond?

A: An *asset-backed bond* is an obligation secured by collateral assets, such as a portfolio of mortgages, auto loans, and credit-card loans (see page 172).

The most common asset-backed securities are those issued by government-related agencies and secured by mortgage pools. Other asset-backed securities, not related to government agencies, include collateralized mortgage obligations (CMOs).

> **Q: What is a mortgage pool?**
> **A:** A *mortgage pool* is a term used for a group of mortgages on the same class of property that have the same interest rate and generally identical maturity dates. For example, a mortgage pool may contain mortgages with a face value of $6.45 million at a rate of 8 percent that mature in 28 years and 2 months.

When you invest in an asset-backed bond issued by a government-related agency, you generally earn a higher rate of interest than you would earn on direct Treasury obligations.

Your investment principal is also collateralized by the portfolio of underlying assets and carries the implied backing of the U.S. government.

You receive interest and principal payments over the life of the bond as the original borrowers pay their loan interest and principal. With some pools, each payment to the bondholder includes both principal and interest. On other pools, the payments to bondholders represent interest only, with occasional larger principal payments. The principal payments on such bonds are held by the trustee for the mortgage pool until there is sufficient money to issue a call on some of the outstanding bonds. As mortgages in the pool are paid, there will be more cash in the pool to call or redeem more bonds.

Q: Are asset-backed bonds risky?

A: There is not much risk to your principal or interest, but there may be risk in terms of *when* you get back your principal (*maturity risk*). How long most asset-backed obligations remain outstanding can be somewhat unpredictable. When you invest in mortgage-backed bonds, for example, they carry an *estimated life* in terms of years. But during periods of *declining interest rates*, more mortgage holders will refinance their mortgages so as to save on their monthly interest payments. This means that mortgage pools will usually have a shorter-than-expected maturity. Though one of your investment goals is to be repaid in full, getting your principal back earlier than you expected forces you to reinvest the proceeds at a time when interest rates may be unattractive.

Conversely, during periods of *rising interest rates*, mortgage holders generally do not refinance their mortgages. If they were to do so, their monthly payments would increase because of the higher interest rate they would be paying. When interest rates are rising, then, the maturity on mortgage pools is usually longer than anticipated.

Despite such uncertainties, in recent years, the high quality and liquidity of asset-backed bonds have created investor demand not only among large institutional investors, the traditional buyers of these bonds, but also among individual investors. This is particularly true for obligations of a few of the largest mortgage-oriented agencies.

 Note of Caution: Because changing interest rates may substantially change the maturities of mortgage pools, you should fully investigate the facts and risks of a particular issue in which you are considering an investment.

Q: Are there different types of government-related agency securities?

A: Yes. Several government-related agencies issue bonds; some of these are suitable for individual investors, while others are more suitable for institutions. Agency issuers include:

- Government National Mortgage Association
- Federal National Mortgage Association
- Federal Home Loan Mortgage Corp.
- Federal Land Bank
- Federal Farm Credit Bank
- Student Loan Marketing Association

Q: Which of the government-related agencies are most popular with individual investors?

A: Three of the more popular government agencies that issue bonds are:

- Government National Mortgage Association (Ginnie Mae)
- Federal National Mortgage Association (Fannie Mae)
- Federal Home Loan Mortgage Corp. (Freddie Mac)

Q: I have heard of "Ginnie Maes." What are they?

A: "Ginnie Mae" is the nickname for the *Government National Mortgage Association (GNMA)*, which is a government-owned agency. As such, GNMA is an exception among mortgage agencies in that its obligations are fully guaranteed by the U.S. government. This feature makes Ginnie Maes among the most popular of mortgage-backed bonds, since there is no significant risk of loss of principal. Each payment on a single Ginnie Mae issue will include both principal and interest.

Often several issues with different payment schedules are pooled for the convenience of investors.

BONDS

Q: What are "Fannie Maes"?

A: "Fannie Maes" are obligations of the *Federal National Mortgage Association* (*FNMA*). Like GNMA, FNMA is a government-sponsored entity charged with maintaining the liquidity of the mortgage market so that bank lenders can readily make mortgages available to individual homeowners. But unlike GNMA, it is a stock corporation owned by its investors (its shares are traded on the New York Stock Exchange). FNMA bonds, then, are *not* guaranteed by the U.S. government. Like most mortgage-backed bonds, they rely on the performance of the underlying mortgage portfolio and have only implied support from the government.

Q: What are "Freddie Macs"?

A: "Freddie Macs" are obligations of the *Federal Home Loan Mortgage Corporation* (*FHLMC*), which was originally created to work with savings banks only. Otherwise, FHLMC is similar to FNMA and is also traded on the New York Stock Exchange.

Q: I see other related agency bonds quoted in the paper. How do they differ as investments?

A: In addition to the agencies discussed above, there are a number of other issuers serving different government purposes:

The *Federal Land Bank* (*FLB*) assists lenders with farm property mortgages.

The *Federal Farm Credit Bank* (*FFCB*) assists agricultural credit corporations and grower cooperative associations.

The *Student Loan Marketing Association* (*SLMA*) assists lenders making loans to students.

Each of these agencies issues debt obligations, but not in sufficient size to create trading market liquidity suitable for the individual investor. Generally only institutional investors hold such obligations.

Q: How is the income from government-related agency obligations taxed?

	Federal Tax	State/Local Tax
GNMA	Yes	No
FNMA	Yes	Yes
FHLMC	Yes	No
FLB	Yes	No
FFCB	Yes	No
SLMA	Yes	No

Q: What are corporate bonds?

A: Bonds called *corporate bonds* are just that: bonds that are issued by corporations. They offer investors a different type of security from that offered by other issuers and different income tax treatment. Because corporations that issue corporate bonds will generally also have common stock outstanding, some of their bonds may be convertible into common stock (see page 173, convertible bonds).

Corporate bonds are issued in a variety of denominations. The prices of many of them are quoted in the financial media.

Illustration 8-9
Corporate Bond Newspaper Quote

CORPORATION BONDS
Volume, $25,317,000

Bonds	Cur Yld	Vol	Close	Net Chg.
AMR 9s16	9.7	10	93	...
ATT 4⅜96	4.6	75	95⅞ −	⅛
ATT 4⅜99	4.9	25	89½ +	½
ATT 6s00	6.3	65	95 +	¾
ATT 5⅛01	5.8	5	89 −	¼
ATT 8⅝31	8.6	519	100¼ −	⅝
ATT 7⅛02	7.3	151	97⅝ +	⅛
ATT 8⅛22	8.3	440	97½ −	½
ATT 8⅛24	8.3	255	97¾ −	¼
ATT 4½96	4.6	10	97⅛ −	⅜
ATT 6¾04	7.2	100	93¾ +	⅛
Actava 9½98	10.1	10	93¾ −	⅛
AirbF 6¾01	cv	75	99½ −	1½
AlskAr zr06	...	64	40⅜ −	⅛
Albnyint 5s02	cv	1	89½ +	¾
AlldC zr99	...	25	69⅜ +	⅞
AlldC zr05	...	10	41 −	2
AlldC zr09	...	5	29⅛ +	½
Alza zr14	...	1	35½	...
ACyan 8⅜06	8.3	42	100¾ +	½
Ametek 9¾04	9.8	70	99⅝ +	⅛
AnnTaylr 8¾00	8.9	40	98⅛ −	¼
Arvin 7½14	cv	25	99¾ −	2¼
AshO 6¾14	cv	1	95 −	1
Atchn 4s95st	4.1	5	97½ +	5/16
AubrnHl 12⅜20†	...	35	136⅜ +	1⅜
AutDt zr12	...	15	40⅞ +	⅞
Avnet 6s12	cv	15	99½ −	½
Ballys 6s98†	cv	7	84¼ +	½
Barnet 9⅞01	8.9	52	111½ +	⅛
BellPa 7⅛12	7.8	15	90⅞ +	⅛

Q: Why would I want to invest in corporate bonds?

A: Many investors choose corporate bonds because they offer an interest rate that is usually higher than that on bonds of other issuers.

Q: How is income from corporate bonds taxed?

A: Generally, income paid by corporate bonds is fully taxable by federal, state, and local authorities.

Q: Are there different types of issuers of corporate bonds?

A: Yes. Corporate bond issuers could be:

- Industrial
- Utility
- Finance
- Railroad

Q: What are industrial bonds?

A: *Industrial bonds* are usually issued by industrial corporations seeking to increase working capital or to finance expansion (research and development or building programs). As is true with all corporate bonds, the issuer anticipates earning more on the proceeds of the debt issue than it will pay in interest; the objective is to enhance earnings per share, which hopefully will increase the stock price.

Q: What are utility bonds?

A: *Utility bonds* are issued by regulated corporations that provide electricity, gas, water, sewer, or telephone services. Most utilities issue bonds in order to expand their services to customers. Generally, a utility's rate of return is regulated by a government agency and the allowed rate of return is sufficient to cover the payment of interest and repayment of bonds.

Q: What are finance bonds?

A: *Finance bonds* are issued by corporations such as banks, insurance companies, real estate investment trusts, finance or loan companies. Generally, these corporations borrow money

BONDS

at one rate and lend it at a higher rate, with the difference being a part of the issuer's profit.

Q: What are railroad bonds?

A: *Railroad bonds* are issued by railroad companies. These companies usually issue two types of bonds:

Industrial railroad bonds are often used to finance expansion (working capital, buildings, technology enhancements, and so forth).

A *railroad equipment trust* is a type of debt often used to finance the purchase of locomotives or railroad cars. As the name implies, the railroad cars, locomotives, or other equipment is the collateral for this type of debt.

Q: What is the security that supports most corporate debt?

A: In analyzing corporate bonds, you should keep in mind that the most important security is the corporation's ability to earn sufficient revenues to cover its *debt service* (see box) and earn a profit. The earning power of the corporation is the primary factor determining the corporation's ability to meet its contractual obligations. In addition to a corporation's earning power, the bond indenture may designate a specific asset, such as real estate, equipment, or buildings, as security for a corporate bond. When a bond (or debt security) is secured, or guaranteed, by such assets, it is referred to as an *asset-backed bond*.

> **Q: What is debt service?**
> **A:** *Debt service* is the issuer's required payment of principal and interest on a debt.

Sometimes, credit-card companies like Sears or Citibank will issue bonds that are secured by a portfolio of credit-card receivables (the balances due on specific credit cards are pledged to secure the bond issue). Often, in addition to pledging the loan pool, the issuing company will add its own guarantee for the timely payment of interest and repayment of principal at maturity.

BONDS

Q: What is securitization?

A: *Securitization* is a term that refers to the creation of a liquid security from an illiquid pool of assets. The securities (usually debt) are collateralized by a pool of loans, such as mortgages, credit-card balances, or loans of a finance company like Ford Motor Credit or General Electric Credit. The securitizing of loans allows the issuers to raise additional capital so they can make more loans.

Q: What is a convertible bond?

A: A convertible bond—usually a debenture, or unsecured debt—is a debt security that is convertible into a fixed number of shares of (usually) common stock of the same corporation.

 Example: A convertible bond with a face value of $1,000 has a *conversion ratio* of 25. This means that until the maturity of the bond, each $1,000 bond is convertible into twenty five shares of common stock. The owner of a convertible bond may convert at any time, but will usually wait until it is advantageous (see page 175).

Q: How do I know the value of my convertible bond?

A: A convertible bond is traded just like any other bond. Therefore, you can get a quote from a broker, a newspaper, or any other quote service. As shown in illustration 8-9 on page 170, convertible bond issues may be designated by abbreviations such as "cv."

In addition, you can determine the *conversion value* (see box) of your convertible bond by multiplying the number of shares into which each bond is convertible by the market value of the common stock.

 Example: In the example above, the conversion ratio of your bond is 25 shares for each bond. If the shares are selling for $50, the conversion value is $1,250 (25 shares times $50 market value).

Q: What is conversion value?
A: *Conversion value* is the value of your bond if you were to convert it into the underlying stock.

Q: Does the number of shares into which a bond (debenture) is convertible always remain constant?

A: The conversion ratio can be a sliding scale, so the number of shares into which the bond is convertible decreases each year or over a period of time. A conversion ratio that decreases usually is designed to encourage early conversion.

Q: What happens to my convertible bond if the stock splits or the corporation has a spin-off while I own the bond?

A: If the common stock splits while you own a convertible bond, the conversion ratio will usually increase proportionately. For example, if the conversion ratio is 25 shares and the common stock splits 2-for-1, the new conversion ratio will be 50 shares.

If a spin-off occurs, the conversion ratio will be adjusted so the owner of a convertible bond will not lose conversion value.

Q: What causes the market value of my convertible bond to rise or fall?

A: If the conversion value of a convertible bond is below the price of a nonconvertible bond with the same coupon and maturity, your bond will be valued in the market as a debt security. The price will be based on the yield, *not* on the conversion value. If the interest coupon is 6 percent, your bond will sell near the level of all other bonds with the same rating and maturity that have a 6 percent coupon.

If the market price of the common stock increases, the conversion value of your convertible bond will increase along with it. If your bond's conversion ratio is 20 and the price of the common stock increases from $40 to $80, the conversion value of your convertible bond will increase from $800 (20 times $40) to $1,600 (20 times $80). When the conversion value is greater than the price of a similar nonconvertible bond, the market price of the convertible bond will move with the price of the common stock. Generally, when the market price of the common stock is increasing in value, the market price of the convertible bond will be higher than the conversion ratio.

Q: Why would I convert my convertible bond?

A: You would exercise your conversion right under a number of circumstances, including the following:

1. Your bond is called and the conversion value is above the call price. For instance, suppose your bond is called for $1,000 and the conversion value is $1,500. If you convert, you will realize $500 more value.
2. The income from the dividend on the common stock increases to a level that is higher than the income paid on the convertible bond. If this happens, you may consider converting.

Q: What is an exchangeable bond?

A: An *exchangeable bond* is a convertible bond that is convertible into the common stock (or another security) of some corporation other than the issuer of the convertible bond.

Q: What happens if I own a convertible bond that is called?

A: A call feature, included in the indenture of a convertible bond, is generally for the benefit of the issuer. With a call feature, the issuer can force conversion of a convertible bond.

 Example: You own a convertible bond that pays 6 percent interest and is convertible into 20 shares of common stock at $50. The market price of the common stock is $75, and you receive a call at $1,050 per bond. Your choices are as follows:

- Accept the call price of $1,050.
- Convert the bond into 20 shares of common stock valued at $75 per share and realize a value of $1,500.

Obviously, you would prefer to convert in order to receive $1,500 in stock (which can be sold if you do not want to own stock) rather than $1,050 in cash.

Q: Why should I consider investing in a convertible bond?

A: By investing in a convertible security, the holder usually has the best of two worlds: security and growth opportunities.

Security: The owner has the security of owning a bond and all the rights of bond ownership. The security is sometimes referred to as "downside protection." The interest rate (coupon) limits the potential price decline of a convertible security.

Growth opportunities: If the future of the issuer continues to be bright and the common stock price increases, so will the value and market price of the convertible bond.

Q: What are the advantages to an issuer of offering convertible securities to investors?

A: An issuer would issue convertible securities because:

- The issuer was selling what is referred to as "cheap debt." Generally, the interest rate (coupon) is originally established substantially lower than the rate required to market debt that is not convertible.
- By doing so, the issuer is often able to market its common stock at a price that is greater than the price at the time the convertible security was priced. The conversion value of a convertible at the time it is issued is generally 15 to 20 percent higher than the market price of the common stock at that time.
- Interest paid to bondholders, including convertible bondholders, is deductible by the corporation before calculating income taxes. The amount paid to shareholders as dividends is not deductible by the corporation.

Q: What are floating-rate notes (FRNs)?

A: *Floating-rate notes (FRNs)* are debt securities on which the interest paid changes (floats) following some index. As previously discussed, if interest rates increase, bond prices decline because the rate of interest on outstanding bonds does not change. In the late 1970s, many issuers started selling floating-rate notes on which the interest paid would change, usually every six months, to reflect changing interest rates. The changing rate is usually tied to some benchmark, such as $\frac{1}{2}$ or 1 percent more than the six-month Treasury bill rate. Floating-rate notes were devised to help issuers sell their debt during periods of interest-rate volatility.

Q: What are foreign bonds?

A: *Foreign bonds* are obligations issued by governments and corporations in other countries. Like bonds issued in this country, foreign bonds carry a variety of maturities, features, and rates of return. Foreign bonds can be denominated in the local currency or in U.S. dollars.

Q: Why would I invest in foreign bonds?

A: Investors have increasingly accepted foreign investments, such as stocks and bonds, for a number of reasons, including diversification, superior returns, and increased availability.

Diversification: As you build an investment portfolio, the principle of asset allocation requires diversification among stocks, bonds, and other types of investments. Within your bond portfolio as well, diversification leads you to consider a variety of bond issuers and features.

Investing in foreign bonds allows you to diversify your bond portfolio into different geographic, economic, and political areas. The economies and bond markets of other countries often experience expansions and recessions at *different* times from those in the United States. Foreign bond holdings may moderate the effect that a U.S. downturn would have on your portfolio's performance or allow you to take advantage of a foreign issuer's improving economic climate.

Returns: At any one time, there are usually several foreign economies with interest rates that are much higher than those available in this country. Even among the mature industrialized countries, you may find bonds offering substantially higher coupon interest rates than similar-quality issues in this country.

Availability: Over the last ten years, investor interest and the availability of foreign bonds have risen hand in hand. As

BONDS

worldwide investor interest has risen, foreign issuers have found it increasingly advantageous to make their bonds available in other countries, and indeed to issue more bonds instead of using other forms of financing. Investment firms also have reacted to the increased demand by promoting more foreign bonds and providing research support on the bonds and their issuers. This increasing availability, in turn, has encouraged more interest by investors.

Q: Do foreign bonds carry higher risk?

A: Foreign bonds may or may not carry higher risk, but they do carry more *types* of risk. When you invest in any bond, you experience the risk that the issuer will default (*credit risk*) and the risk that interest-rate changes will affect the price of your bond (*interest-rate risk*). Foreign issuers may carry more or less credit risk than domestic issuers, and foreign bond markets may experience more or less interest-rate risk than our domestic market.

If your bond is issued in the local currency of another country, you run the *additional* risk that the foreign currency may decline in value relative to the U.S. dollar. This is called *currency risk*, and it can significantly affect your investment return either positively or negatively as the two currencies rise and fall in relation to each other. The U.S. dollar value of each of your coupon interest payments may be somewhat different during the time you hold your foreign bond investment.

Also, the principal amount you receive at maturity may be different in dollar terms from the amount you invested. Investors in foreign stocks and bonds accept this risk in anticipation of making superior returns, but it does add another type of risk to this type of investment.

Q: Can I avoid currency risk in foreign bonds?

A: Yes. Many foreign issuers offer debt that is denominated in U.S. dollars and that pays interest in U.S. dollars. Such bonds do not have a currency risk.

Q: What is a municipal bond?

A: A *municipal bond* is a debt security issued by a state, city, county, or territory of the United States, or by one of its subdivisions, such as school districts; water, sewer, or fire protection districts; or certain charter entities.

Municipal bonds are issued in a variety of denominations. Prices of some of them are quoted in the financial media (see below).

BONDS

Illustration 8-10
Municipal Bond Quote

TAX-EXEMPT BONDS

Representative prices for several active tax-exempt revenue and refunding bonds, based on institutional trades. Changes rounded to the nearest one-eighth. Yield is to maturity. n-New. Source: The Bond Buyer.

ISSUE	COUPON	MAT	PRICE	CHG	BID YLD
Anne Arundel Md Ser94	6.000	04-01-24	93⅞	– ¼	6.47
Calif Health Fac	5.550	08-15-25	85	– ½	6.70
Fla Mun Pwr Agy Ser93	5.100	10-01-25	81⅝	– ¼	6.47
Florida St Bd Ed	5.125	06-01-22	83	– ¼	6.43
Florida St Bd Ed	5.800	06-01-24	92	– ¼	6.40
Fulton Co Sch Dist Ga	5.625	01-01-21	89⅞	– ⅜	6.42
Ga Muni Elec Auth	6.500	01-01-26	99½	– ½	6.53
Hawaii Dept Budgt&Fin	5.450	11-01-23	85⅜	– ⅝	6.58
Hawaii Hsng Fin & Dev	6.000	07-01-26	91	– ⅜	6.69
humphreys idb tenn swdi	6.700	05-01-24	99⅞	– ¼	6.71
Ill Hlth Fac Auth Rev	6.000	08-15-24	91½	– ⅜	6.65
Ill Regional TA	6.250	06-01-24	96⅜	– ⅜	6.53
Kansas City Util Sys	6.375	09-01-23	99¾	– ⅛	6.39
L.A. Co. Pub Wks Fin Au	6.000	10-01-15	94⅝	– ⅝	6.47
LA Calif Wstwtr Sys	5.875	06-01-24	92	– ½	6.48
Mass Bay T A	5.900	03-01-24	92⅛	– ⅛	6.50
Metro Wash Arpt Auth	5.875	10-01-15	93⅛	– ½	6.47
Mo Hlth & Ed Facs	5.250	05-15-21	83⅛	– ¼	6.59
N.J. Econ Dev Auth PCR	6.400	05-01-32	97¼	...	6.60
NYC Indus Dev Agcy	6.000	01-01-15	93⅛	– ½	6.61
NYC Indus Dev Agcy	6.125	01-01-24	92⅞	– ⅜	6.67
NYC Lcl Govt Asst Cp	5.500	04-01-18	87⅛	– ½	6.57
NYC Muni Water Fin	5.500	06-15-23	87¼	– ⅝	6.48
NYS Environmental	5.875	06-15-14	93½	– ½	6.46
NYS Med Care Fac	6.125	02-15-14	96	– ½	6.49
NYS Med Care Facil	5.250	08-15-14	86	– ⅝	6.50
Orange Co Fla	6.000	10-01-24	95½	– ⅛	6.34
P R Elec Pwr Auth	6.375	07-01-24	97¾	– ¾	6.54
PuertoRico pub im go 94	6.450	07-01-17	99¼	– ⅝	6.51
PuertoRico pub im go 94	6.500	07-01-23	99⅛	– ⅝	6.56
Reedy Creed Fla	5.000	10-01-14	84⅛	– ⅜	6.39
S.F. Cal. Sewr Ref Rev	5.375	10-01-22	85⅜	– ⅝	6.51
Salam Co Poll Ctrl	6.250	06-01-31	97	– ⅜	6.47
Salem Co Pol Ctrl	5.450	02-01-32	83⅝	– ⅛	6.64
Salt Riv Proj Ariz	5.000	01-01-16	83⅛	– ¼	6.44
Santa Clara Wtr Calif	6.000	02-01-24	93⅞	– ⅝	6.47
TBTA NY	5.000	01-01-24	79⅝	– ¾	6.56
Univ of Calif	6.375	09-01-19	98½	– ½	6.49
Univ of Calif	6.375	09-01-24	98½	– ¼	6.49
Valdez Al Marine Term	5.650	12-01-28	85⅝	– ½	6.72

Q: How do municipal bonds differ from other bonds?

A: Municipal bonds differ in two respects:

1. The interest income paid by the issuer is exempt from federal income tax.
2. Legislation to permit the issuing unit to issue the bonds is required.

Q: Why is interest paid on municipal bonds exempt from federal income tax?

A: By reason of "reciprocal immunity," the federal government does not tax income paid by the issuers of municipal bonds. Likewise, state and local governments do not tax the income from debt issued by the federal government. Even though there is no mention of reciprocal immunity in the Constitution, the Supreme Court has recognized its legality over the years.

Q: Can municipal bond interest affect my federal income tax status?

A: Yes. Municipal bond interest may affect the taxability of your Social Security income and trigger *alternative minimum tax* (AMT). See your tax advisor for further information.

Q: Can my municipal bond interest also be free from state and local income tax?

A: Yes. States do not tax the interest paid on municipal bonds issued in that state and owned by a resident of that state. The interest paid on municipal debt securities issued in the state of which you are a resident is totally income-tax-free (sometimes referred to as "double tax-exempt," or "triple tax-exempt" if there is a local income tax).

Q: Are there different types of municipal bonds?

A: Yes. There are four general types of municipal bonds. They are:

1. General obligation bonds
2. Revenue bonds
3. Special tax bonds
4. Housing authority bonds

Q: What are general obligation bonds?

A: *General obligation bonds* are bonds for which the payment of interest and repayment of principal at maturity are backed by the full faith, credit, and taxing power of the issuer. Because of this, they are generally considered the safest type of municipal bond. This type of bond may be referred to as a "limited tax bond" if the issuer's taxing power is limited to a maximum rate. The popular abbreviation for general-obligation bonds is GO.

Q: What are Revenue Bonds?

A: *Revenue bonds* are a type of municipal security for which the payment of interest and repayment of principal at maturity are to be made from rents, charges, tolls, or other sources of income generated by the facility constructed by the proceeds of the debt issue. Revenue bonds may also be general-obligation bonds if they are also backed by the full faith, credit, and taxing power of a municipality.

Industrial revenue bonds (IRBs) are a type of revenue securities issued by an "industrial revenue or development authority" authorized by a municipality. Usually, the authority constructs a facility and leases it to a private business, which guarantees the timely payment of interest and repayment of principal at maturity. This type of obligation is generally issued to encourage businesses to locate in certain areas. The issuer, and ultimately the business, pays a lower interest rate (rent cost) because the interest paid to the bondholders is exempt from income taxes. Brokers often refer to industrial revenue bonds as IDAs (industrial development authority bonds) or IRBs (industrial revenue bonds).

 Note: Over the last few years, Congress and the IRS have started to restrict the amount and types of industrial revenue bonds that will enjoy the income tax exemption of interest.

Q: What are special tax bonds?

A: *Special tax bonds* are a type of bond for which payment of interest and repayment of principal at maturity is payable from the proceeds of a special tax. An example would be highway bonds for which interest and principal are paid from gasoline taxes. One type of special tax bond is a *special assessment bond*. Interest and repayment of principal are paid by assessments against those who benefit from the facilities built by the proceeds of the bond issue.

Q: What are housing authority bonds?

A: *Housing authority bonds* are a type of municipal bond issued by a public housing authority created by a municipality. The payment of interest and repayment of the principal at maturity are secured by the rents collected by the authority or by the Public Housing Administration of the United States. Even though the security for an issue is often a contractual obligation between the authority and the Public Housing Administration, the debt issues are *not* direct obligations of the federal government. The proceeds of housing authority bonds are used to provide low- and moderate-income housing and urban redevelopment programs. The mortgages issued by housing authorities are often guaranteed by the Veterans Administration (VA) or the Federal Housing Administration (FHA).

Q: What is taxable-equivalent yield?

A: *Taxable-equivalent yield* is the percentage of taxable yield you would have to earn in order to have the same spendable income after taxes as you would have if you bought a municipal bond.

Q: How do I calculate my taxable-equivalent yield?

A: Generally, there are two ways to determine your taxable-equivalent yield.

1. Most brokers or organizations offering tax-exempt securities will have a table that will show you the taxable-equivalent yield for certain income tax brackets and different levels of tax-exempt income. See Illustration 8-11 for an example.

Illustration 8-11
Tax-Exempt/Taxable Yield Equivalents

TAX-EXEMPT/TAXABLE YIELD EQUIVALENTS FOR 1994

The following table shows the yield before federal tax on a taxable bond to equal the yield on a tax-exempt municipal bond.

Note: These are uncompounded yields reflecting current rates and would appear greater if compounded for comparison to annual effective yields quoted for other investments.

		Taxable Income *			
Single Return	Not over $22,750	$22,751- $55,100	$55,101 - $115,000	$115,001 - $250,000	$250,001 and over
Joint Return	Not over $38,000	$38,001- $91,850	$91,851- $140,000	$140,001 - $250,000	$250,000 and over
Federal Tax Bracket	15%	28%	31% **	36% **	39.6% **
Tax Exempt Yields		Taxable	Equivalent	Yields	
2%	2.35%	2.78%	2.90%	3.12%	3.31%
2.5%	2.94%	3.47%	3.62%	3.91%	4.14%
3.0%	3.53%	4.17%	4.35%	4.69%	4.97%
3.5%	4.12%	4.86%	5.07%	5.47%	5.59%
4.0%	4.71%	5.56%	5.80%	6.25%	6.62%
4.5%	5.29%	6.25%	6.52%	7.03%	7.45%
5.0%	5.88%	6.94%	7.25%	7.81%	8.28%
5.5%	6.47%	7.64%	7.97%	8.59%	9.11%
6.0%	7.06%	8.33%	8.70%	9.37%	9.93%
6.5%	7.65%	9.03%	9.42%	10.16%	10.76%
7.0%	8.24%	9.72%	10.14%	10.94%	11.59%
7.5%	8.82%	10.42%	10.87%	11.72%	12.42%
8.0%	9.41%	11.11%	11.59%	12.50%	13.25%

*   Estimated brackets for 1994

**   The Internal Revenue code phases out the personal exemption deduction for married taxpayers filing joint returns with adjusted gross income in excess of $162,700 and for single taxpayers with adjusted gross income in excess of $108,450. In addition, certain itemized deductions are reduced for taxpayers with adjusted gross income in excess of $108,450. In general, the limit on itemized deductions will increase the effective marginal tax rate by 1% and the phase-out of personal exemption deductions will increase the effective marginal tax rate 0.7% for each exemption claimed.

BONDS

2. There is a simple formula (Illustration 8-12) that you can use to estimate your taxable-equivalent yield.

Illustration 8-12
How to Compute Your Taxable-Equivalent Yield

1. Determine your *marginal income tax bracket* (the maximum percentage applied to your highest taxable income). For example, if your federal taxable income is $50,000 and you file a joint tax return with your spouse, your marginal federal tax bracket is 28 percent.

   If you are investing in a municipal bond issued within your state of residence, you should use your *total* income tax bracket, including state and local tax percentages.

   Remember: Since state and local income taxes are deductible from federal income tax, you cannot simply add your federal, state, and local income tax brackets. For example, if your state income tax bracket is 6 percent and your federal income tax bracket is 28 percent, your state marginal bracket is 4.3 percent. Take .06, your state income tax rate, and multiply it by 28 percent, which equals 1.7 percent, and subtract the result from 6 percent to get 4.3 percent. Your total marginal income tax bracket is your federal bracket of 28 percent plus your net state bracket of 4.3 percent, for 32.3 percent.

2. Determine your after-tax margin, or what is left of a dollar after all income taxes. This is the inverse of your income tax bracket.

Starting number	1.000
Less: Marginal income tax bracket	- 0.323
After-tax margin	0.677

3. Divide the yield on the municipal bond (assume a yield of 5.6 percent) by your after-tax margin to determine your taxable-equivalent yield.

Yield on your municipal bond (5.6 percent in our example)	0.056
Divided by the inverse of your income tax bracket	0.677
Taxable-equivalent yield	8.27%

Note: For any yield above the taxable-equivalent yield, it would be advantageous to earn the taxable income and pay the income tax. Your after-tax income would be higher than the 5.6 percent tax-free yield.

 Suggestion: If you have a professional prepare your income tax, always ask for:
1. Your marginal federal income tax rate
2. Your marginal rate including your state and local income taxes

BONDS

Q: What is a bond swap?

A: A *bond swap* is a situation in which you sell a bond that is selling below the price you paid for it, and invest in another bond with similar income, maturity, and quality.

Q: Why would I want to enter into a bond swap?

A: You may want to enter into a bond swap in order to establish a loss on the bond you own that is selling for less than you paid for it. You can use the loss to offset gains from other investments or to reduce your taxable income (up to the allowable limit).

 Note of Caution: You must be certain that you are not entering into a *wash sale*, and you should ask a tax advisor about the income tax ramifications of the bond you are buying. Often, you will be buying the replacement bond at a discount, and it will mature at its face value for a gain.

Q: What is a wash sale?

A: The IRS may disallow a loss if you have merely replaced your investment with a virtually identical investment. The Internal Revenue Code states that if a loss is established from the sale of a security and the same or a similar security is purchased within thirty days before or after the sale, the resulting transaction is known as a *wash sale*. If you enter into such a transaction, you cannot use the loss from the first sale to offset capital gains or reduce taxable income. Instead, you have to add the loss to the cost basis of the second transaction (the purchase), thereby increasing its cost basis. Any time you are selling one security and buying the same or a similar security, you should seek tax advice.

Q: What are zero-coupon bonds?

A: *Zero-coupon bonds* are debt obligations on which the issuer does not pay any coupon interest—hence the term *zero-coupon*—during the life of the bond. Such bonds are issued at a discount to their face value, and the investor is paid the full face value at maturity. The interest compounds within the bond instead of being paid out over the life of the bond.

When a zero-coupon bond is issued, it is assigned a compounded rate of return designed to make it attractive relative to current market interest rates. As with regular coupon bonds, that rate may be higher or lower depending on the time to maturity, quality of the issuer, etc. Mathematically, the higher the internal compounding rate, the deeper the discount at which the bond is issued.

 Example: A twenty-year bond at various rates would be issued at the following prices:

Face Value	Rate	Original Price
$10,000	5 percent	$3,733
$10,000	6 percent	$3,074
$10,000	7 percent	$2,534
$10,000	8 percent	$2,090
$10,000	9 percent	$1,726

Over the life of the zero-coupon bond, the interest is added to the starting value, with each interest amount increasing the principal value (compounding) so that it can earn yet more interest. The interest is referred to as *accreted interest*. As it compounds, the principal value of the bond is referred to as its *accreted value*.

Q: Is the increasing value of a zero-coupon bond taxable?

A: If you own a municipal zero-coupon bond, the accreted interest is *nontaxable*. If you own a taxable zero-coupon bond (government or corporate), the annual accreted value is taxable income each year.

Q: Why would I invest in bonds that do not pay me a current income?

A: You might invest in zero-coupon bonds and willingly forgo current interest payments for reasons related to your investment goals and your view of investment alternatives during the life of your bond. Some of the reasons you may invest in zero-coupon bonds are:

- To meet a future need
- To avoid reinvestment risk
- To speculate

Q: Why would I invest in zero-coupon bonds to meet a future need?

A: Many investors invest in zero-coupon bonds to *meet a future need* or to achieve specific future investment goals. For instance, if you are seeking to fund your child's college education, your goal may be to provide a specific dollar amount in each of four future years. Based on your expectation of what the four years' costs will be, you could invest in zero-coupon bonds that will mature in those four years and provide those amounts. If you bought the bonds far enough ahead, you would be able to purchase them at considerable discounts. In any case, you would have the assurance that the specific amounts would be provided when they were needed.

Q: Why would I invest in zero-coupon bonds to avoid reinvestment risk?

A: You might invest in zero-coupon bonds in order to avoid having to reinvest interest payments over the life of the bond—i.e., to avoid reinvestment risk. Investors who do not need the current income from a bond often find it difficult to invest small interest payments at attractive rates of return. This uncertainty of being able to reinvest the interest paid by a bond at attractive rates is called *reinvestment risk*. When you invest in a zero-coupon bond, you avoid reinvestment risk by

BONDS

locking in your return at the bond's compounding rate. Over the life of the zero-coupon bond, you are assured of the return on both your original principal and the interim interest that is credited to your bond.

Q: Why would I invest in zero-coupon bonds to speculate?

A: You would invest in zero-coupon bonds *to speculate* if you believe interest rates will change significantly. You may want to invest in zero-coupon bonds for price speculation. The prices of zero-coupon bonds are generally more volatile than those of coupon bonds.

Q: Who issues zero-coupon bonds?

A: Zero-coupon bonds are issued by a variety of issuers, including the U.S. government, municipal authorities, and corporations.

Q: What should I consider before investing in a bond?

A: You buy and sell bonds in much the same way as you buy and sell stocks. *However, you may find that both information on bonds and the bonds themselves are not as readily available as stocks.* As with any investment decision, when you are considering a bond investment, you should review your general investment objectives and decide the role bonds should serve in your strategy to achieve these objectives. Once you have established how bond investments fit into your overall strategy, you can decide how to mix the different types of bonds and build a diversified portfolio of bonds. (See diversification discussion, page 154.) For assistance in establishing your strategy, you may turn to a professional at a brokerage house, bank, or other advisory firm. (See Chapter 14, Advisors).

Q: How do I select bonds to meet my objectives?

A: Some investors conduct their own firsthand bond research. The process of selection involves investment research to find *bond issuers* that are appropriate, as well as the *bond features* you are seeking.

Researching *bond issuers* resembles fundamental analysis of stocks. In both cases you are searching for issuers—whether corporations, government, or municipalities—that have the characteristics you are seeking. In researching bond issuers, you should pay particular attention to whether the issuer has adequate profits and cash flow to cover its debts, including bonds.

Researching *bond features* involves looking for bonds that have the appropriate maturity, interest rate, call features, etc. Unlike stocks, which are generally alike in their basic features, bonds issued by different entities differ greatly, as can even different bonds issued by the same entity.

Because of this complexity, you may find that information on bond features is not as readily available as general issuer information. Researching bond features can take more effort than researching the issuers, but it is equally as important.

Q: Are there published research sources I can consult?

A: Not all investors have the time, resources, or training to conduct firsthand bond research. Many use research prepared by professional analysts. Bond research is not as readily available as research on stocks. However, there are some sources. Many brokerage firms publish research reports on the bond market and particular issuers. Some brokerage firms also have access to highly specialized bond databases such as Bloomberg that keep track of the features of thousands of bonds.

Q: I often hear of a bond's rating being raised or lowered. Is this important for my research?

A: Yes. Bond ratings are a form of research. Rating agencies such as Standard & Poor's and Moody's perform very comprehensive research on bonds and publish reports, reference books, and databases that you may find at your public library. The ratings are widely used within the investment community as the standard credit quality rankings.

When one of the agencies announces a change in a bond's rating, there may be a significant effect on the bond's price as investors in the bond market react. If the rating is raised, generally the bond's price will increase. If the rating is lowered, generally the bond's price will decrease.

The rating agencies compile their data, then assign ratings to rank the quality of the issuers and the individual bond issues. Their ratings use letters to indicate the different levels of creditworthiness:

	Standard & Poor's	Moody's
Highest	AAA	Aaa
	AA	Aa
	A	A
	BBB	Baa
	BB	Ba
	B	B
	CCC	Caa
	CC	Ca
Lowest	C	C

Bonds that are rated BBB/Baa or higher are referred to as *investment-grade* bonds, appropriate for the general investing public. Bonds rated below that level are referred to by various terms, such as *below-investment-grade* bonds, *high-yield* bonds, or even *junk bonds*. Such bonds are not necessarily bad investments. However, they are considered to carry enough risk that you should carefully analyze them before you buy them.

Q: Where do I or my broker find bonds?

A: Bonds can be acquired from several different sources:

- Public offerings
- Treasury auctions
- Open-market purchases

Q: How do bonds originate in a public offering?

A: A public offering is the origination of new securities. A bond public offering is similar to a stock offering and will be accompanied by a *prospectus* describing the bond being offered. The prospectus, also called an *offering circular* or *offering statement*, is especially important in a bond offering. You should keep the prospectus, since it contains the bond indenture agreement, its features, and your rights as a bond-holder.

Q: Why do I need to keep my prospectus?

A: You may need the prospectus in the future for:

Identification: Since some issuers have more than one bond issue outstanding, the official description of your bond in the prospectus will assist you in distinguishing your bond when seeking price quotes or selling the bond.

Features: The prospectus contains the complete list of your bond's features, some of which may not come into play for years (such as sinking funds, call features, etc.). Keeping the prospectus allows you to keep track of all of your bond's features.

Contact information: The prospectus identifies the issuer, underwriter, legal counsel, trustee, payment agent, and transfer agent. Knowing who to contact will be important later if you have inquiries regarding your bond. (See page 204, "What do I do if I have a problem?")

BONDS

Q: How do Treasury auctions work?

A: The Treasury Department issues its bills, notes, and bonds through Treasury auctions, at which investors enter bids either directly or through their brokers. In the auction, the Treasury Department sells its bonds to the highest bidder—the bidder willing to accept the lowest interest rate for the new bond issue. You may see Treasury auction results cited in the news media as important indications of whether interest rates are rising or falling.

Q: How do I invest in Treasury issues directly through Treasury auctions?

A: You may participate in Treasury auctions either through a securities broker or directly through the *Treasury Direct* system. The Treasury Direct system allows you to set up an account directly with the Treasury Department. You may purchase and hold marketable Treasury securities in that account. You may also transfer securities from that account to a broker if you wish to sell them before maturity.

Q: How do I establish a Treasury Direct account?

A: To open a Treasury Direct account, you contact your nearest Federal Reserve office (see Illustration 8-25), which will send you a New Account Request form (see Illustration 8-13).

Once you submit the form, the Federal Reserve will establish a Treasury Direct account in your name.

Illustration 8-13
Treasury Direct—New Account Request

PD F 5182
(May 1990)

TREASURY DIRECT ®

OMB No. 1535-0069
Expires: 09-30-92

NEW ACCOUNT REQUEST

BONDS

INVESTOR INFORMATION

ACCOUNT NAME

FOR DEPARTMENT USE

DOCUMENT AUTHORITY

APPROVED BY

DATE APPROVED

ADDRESS

EXT REG ☐

FOREIGN ☐

BACKUP ☐

CITY   STATE   ZIP CODE

REVIEW ☐

TAXPAYER IDENTIFICATION NUMBER

1ST NAMED OWNER

SOCIAL SECURITY NUMBER   OR   EMPLOYER IDENTIFICATION NUMBER

CLASS ☐

TELEPHONE NUMBERS

WORK ( )   —   HOME ( )   —

DIRECT DEPOSIT INFORMATION

ROUTING NUMBER

FINANCIAL INSTITUTION NAME

ACCOUNT NUMBER

ACCOUNT TYPE ☐ CHECKING
(Check One)
☐ SAVINGS

AUTHORIZATION

I submit this request pursuant to the provisions of Department of the Treasury Circulars, Public Debt Series Nos. 1-86 and 2-86.

Under penalties of perjury, I certify that the number shown on this form is my correct taxpayer identification number and that I am not subject to backup withholding because (1) I have not been notified that I am subject to backup withholding as a result of a failure to report all interest or dividends, or (2) the Internal Revenue Service has notified me that I am no longer subject to backup withholding. I further certify that all other information provided on this form is true, correct and complete.

SIGNATURE   DATE

Q: How do I bid on Treasury issues?

A: You bid on Treasury issues by submitting a *tender* in the Treasury auction process. You enter your tender by completing a tender form (see Illustrations 8-19 and 8-20) and submitting it to the Federal Reserve, along with your payment. There are two methods of tenders that you may choose:

- A *noncompetitive tender*, in which you agree to accept the average yield from the auction of that issue
- A *competitive tender*, in which you specify the yield you are willing to accept

If your tender is accepted, the securities will be credited to your Treasury Direct account.

Note: Generally, it is not advisable for individual investors to use a competitive tender. If the yield you demand is too high, you will not receive the securities you seek. If the yield you specify is too low, you will receive a lower investment return than the average yield you would have received from a noncompetitive tender.

Q: After I invest, how do I follow my Treasury Direct holdings?

A: When you purchase a Treasury security, the Treasury Direct system sends you a Statement of Account. See Illustration 8-14. This statement lists all the holdings in your Treasury Direct account.

Illustration 8-14
Treasury Direct—Statement of Account

PD 5177 (DEC. 1991)

YOUR SERVICING OFFICE

STATEMENT OF ACCOUNT

TELEPHONE:

ACCOUNT NUMBER:

REASON(S) FOR THIS STATEMENT

PAYMENT INFORMATION

TELEPHONE:

TAXPAYER IDENTIFICATION NUMBER:

TAX WITHHOLDING STATUS/RATE:

DESCRIPTION OF HOLDINGS AS OF: ACCOUNT BALANCE:

LOAN	LOAN SUB-ACCOUNT	SCHEDULED REINVESTMENTS

CUSIP NUMBER DESCRIPTION MATURITY DATE INTEREST PAYABLE TOTAL PAR AMOUNT	NO.	PAR AMOUNT	ISSUE DATE	PURCHASE PRICE/$100 OF PAR	NUMBER REMAINING	LOAN TERM

Treasury Direct

IF YOU HAVE ANY QUESTIONS CONCERNING THIS STATEMENT, PLEASE CONTACT YOUR SERVICING OFFICE

Q: How do I receive my interest payments from Treasury Direct security holdings?

A: As a Treasury Direct investor, you will not receive checks for your interest payments. Your interest will be paid into your bank account by direct deposit. You supply your bank account information when you complete the tender form to bid for the securities.

Q: How can I transfer or sell the Treasury securities in the Treasury Direct account?

A: You may withdraw securities from your Treasury Direct account by submitting a Security Transfer Request form (see Illustration 8-21) to the Federal Reserve.

Your signature on the form authorizes the transfer of your securities to the financial institution you specify. Once the securities are deposited, they may be sold or pledged at your request.

Q: What happens when my Treasury securities mature?

A: When your securities mature, you may have the principal repayment sent to your bank account by direct deposit, or you may reinvest it in other Treasury issues. The method of choice differs depending on the type of security:

Treasury bills: You must make the choice at the time of your initial investment in Treasury bills, due to their short duration.

Treasury notes and bonds: You will receive a Notice of Maturing Treasury Security and a Reinvestment Request form (see Illustrations 8-22 and 8-23), which you may complete and return if you wish to reinvest.

Q: How do I buy bonds in the open market?

A: Most types of bonds, once they are issued through a public offering, trade freely in the open market, either on a *stock exchange* or in the *over-the-counter* market between dealers.

Trading procedures for bonds are much the same as those for stocks. Bonds are quoted differently: either as a percentage of par value (97 = $970 = 97 percent of par; 103 = $1,030 = 103 percent of par) or as a yield (6.75 percent = priced to yield 6.75 percent for the buyer).

Q: If I see a bond quoted in the newspaper, will I be able to buy it at that price?

A: You may not be able to buy it at that price, or even to buy that bond at all. Prices will vary from day to day and during the day as the market fluctuates. The published prices may also be applicable only to very large purchases, such as $100,000 or $1 million. A smaller investor may be able to buy only at somewhat less favorable prices.

You may also have difficulty in finding a bond from a particular issue available for purchase for several reasons:

Issue size: Except for large Treasury bond issues, most individual bond issues are smaller in total dollar terms than the typical stock issue. Since there are a smaller number of bonds in existence, there may not be as many of a particular bond readily available for purchase at a given time.

Trading activity: Bond investors tend to be long-term-oriented. They usually invest in bonds with the intention of holding them for an extended period, often until maturity. Therefore, if investors seek to buy a particular bond issue, that issue may not be readily available for purchase at a given time.

Q: How do I make a bond investment?

A: To purchase bonds, the first step is to open an account at a brokerage firm, bank, or discount broker, or directly at the Federal Reserve. Opening an account at an intermediary, such as a brokerage firm, is very straightforward and takes only a few minutes.

To open an account at the Federal Reserve, you must contact the nearest Federal Reserve office (see Illustration 8-25 for address and telephone numbers) and complete the proper documentation. (See page 192, "How do I establish a Treasury Direct account?").

BONDS

Q: When I open an account, may I specify how I want my bonds registered?

A: Not necessarily. If the bond you are buying can be issued in registered form, you may elect either to receive the certificate or to have it held by your broker in your name or in street name. In some cases, however, bonds will be issued in a form where you do not have a choice concerning the form of evidence of ownership. The two forms are:

- Bearer or coupon bonds
- Book entry bonds

Q: What are bearer or coupon bonds?

A: *Bearer bonds*, or *coupon bonds* are bonds owned by whoever holds the certificate. Interest is paid to whoever presents the "coupons" (see box) to a paying agent. Unlike registered bonds, whose ownership is officially registered and can be changed only by presentation of specific documentation, ownership of bearer bonds can easily be transferred simply by changing possession of the certificate. Ownership change is so easy, in fact, that concerns about theft and taxable income reporting led to a ban on any new bearer bonds after 1983.

> **Q: What does coupon clipping mean?**
> **A:** For a bearer bond, the owner receives interest by detaching (*clipping*) a coupon from the bond certificate and presenting it to the paying agent, either directly or through a bank. Each coupon usually represents one semiannual interest payment.

Q: What are book entry bonds?

A: *Book entry bonds*, which predominate today, are bonds that are never issued in certificate form. Ownership is registered in a ledger, by a *book entry*. Your ownership is established as securely as with any other type of registration, but your only physical evidence of ownership may be the confirmation and account statements you receive from your broker.

Q: What is the procedure for placing an order to buy or sell a bond?

A: Once you have established your brokerage account, you have several alternatives on how your order is entered and executed. If you are working with a broker, your choices of price and time are similar to those you would have with a stock order. Your broker will go to the source of bonds—the public offering, auction, or open market—and enter orders.

Q: How do I know whether and how my bond order was executed?

A: Once your order is executed through a broker, you will receive a written confirmation specifying the bond, its features, and the terms of your purchase. The confirmation contains many important items of information that you should keep for your records. Examples of confirmation statements are illustrated below.

BONDS

Illustration 8-15
Municipal Bond Purchase Confirmation

Scott & Stringfellow, Inc.
909 EAST MAIN STREET
RICHMOND, VIRGINIA 23219
804-643-1811

SIPC

CONFIRMATION / COMPARISON

PLEASE RETAIN THIS COPY FOR YOUR RECORDS

TO COMPLY WITH FEDERAL REGULATIONS PAYMENT FOR SECURITIES BOUGHT OR DELIVERY OF SECURITIES SOLD MUST BE MADE ON OR BEFORE

ACCOUNT NUMBER	TYPE	OFFICE	RR	SOC. SEC. / I.D. NO.	TRANS. NO.	MKT*	CAP*	TRADE DATE	SETTLEMENT DATE	ENTRY DATE	A* B* C*
18000001	1	MK	01	100-01-0001	00152	0	2	07/08/95	07/15/95		S B

ACCOUNT NAME OR CONTRA PARTY

Susan Q. Investor
1500 Investment Avenue
Richmond, VA 23132

SPECIAL INSTRUCTIONS

	QUANTITY	CUSIP / SYMBOL		SECURITY DESCRIPTION		COUPON	MATURITY
YOU BOUGHT	10,000	592650FA8 METFA8		METRO WASHINGTON AIRPORT SYS REV SER 1994A *AMT* MBIA INSD OID ORIG YLD 5.05		5.0000	10/01/00

YIELD DOLLAR PRICE 5.188911 TO MATURITY
INT FROM 06/01/95 TO 07/15/95
DTC

DATED: 06/01/95
FIRST: 10/01/95

RETURN ADDRESS

SCOTT & STRINGFELLOW, INC.
P.O. BOX 1575
RICHMOND,   VA   23213

PRICE	PRINCIPAL AMOUNT	COMMISSION	STATE TAX.	INTEREST	SEC FEE	MISC.	NET AMOUNT DUE
99	9,900.00			61.11			9,961.11

IN ACCORDANCE WITH YOUR INSTRUCTIONS WE ARE PLEASED TO CONFIRM THE ABOVE TRANSACTION FOR YOUR ACCOUNT AND RISK SUBJECT TO TERMS LISTED ON REVERSE SIDE.

CUSTOMER COPY

BONDS

Illustration 8-16

Treasury Note Purchase Confirmation

Scott & Stringfellow, Inc.
909 EAST MAIN STREET
RICHMOND, VIRGINIA 23219
804-643-1811

CONFIRMATION / COMPARISON

PLEASE RETAIN THIS COPY FOR YOUR RECORDS

TO COMPLY WITH FEDERAL REGULATIONS PAYMENT FOR SECURITIES BOUGHT OR DELIVERY OF SECURITIES SOLD MUST BE MADE ON OR BEFORE

SIPC

ACCOUNT NUMBER	TYPE	OFFICE	RR	SOC. SEC. / I.D. NO.	TRANS. NO.	MKT	CAP	TRADE DATE	SETTLEMENT DATE	ENTRY DATE	A • B • C •
18000001	1	MK	01	100-01-0001	00129	0	2	07/08/95	07/11/95		S

ACCOUNT NAME OR CONTRA PARTY

Susan Q. Investor
1500 Investment Avenue
Richmond, VA 23132

SPECIAL INSTRUCTIONS

	QUANTITY	CUSIP / SYMBOL	SECURITY DESCRIPTION	COUPON	MATURITY
YOU BOUGHT	2,130,000	912827J86 827J86	U S TREASURY NOTE 3.875% DUE 2/28/96	3.8750	02/28/96

DATED: 03/01/94

5.15 BEY

DTC   BOOK ENTRY

RETURN ADDRESS

SCOTT & STRINGFELLOW, INC.
P.O. BOX 1575
RICHMOND,   VA   23213

PRICE	PRINCIPAL AMOUNT	COMMISSION	STATE TAX	INTEREST	SEC FEE	MISC.	NET AMOUNT DUE
99.203124	2,133,026.56			29830.13			2,142,856.69

IN ACCORDANCE WITH YOUR INSTRUCTIONS WE ARE PLEASED TO CONFIRM THE ABOVE TRANSACTION FOR YOUR ACCOUNT AND RISK SUBJECT TO TERMS LISTED ON REVERSE SIDE.

CUSTOMER COPY

BONDS

Illustration 8-17
Treasury Bill Purchase Confirmation

BONDS

Scott & Stringfellow, Inc.
909 EAST MAIN STREET
RICHMOND, VIRGINIA 23219
804-643-1811

CONFIRMATION / COMPARISON

PLEASE RETAIN THIS COPY FOR YOUR RECORDS

TO COMPLY WITH FEDERAL REGULATIONS PAYMENT FOR SECURITIES BOUGHT OR DELIVERY OF SECURITIES SOLD MUST BE MADE ON OR BEFORE

SIPC

ACCOUNT NUMBER	TYPE	OFFICE	RR	SOC. SEC. / I.D. NO.	TRANS. NO.	MKT*	CAP*	TRADE DATE	SETTLEMENT DATE	ENTRY DATE	A * B * C *
18000001	1	MK	01	100-01-0001	00008	0	1	7/11/95	7/12/95		S

ACCOUNT NAME OR CONTRA PARTY

SPECIAL INSTRUCTIONS

Susan Q. Investor
1500 Investment Avenue
Richmond, VA 23132

	QUANTITY	CUSIP / SYMBOL	SECURITY DESCRIPTION	COUPON	MATURITY
YOU BOUGHT	20,000	912794P73 794P73	U S TREASURY BILL 0% DUE 1/5/96	0.0000%	01/05/96

4.76 DISC, 4.9418 BEY

DTC   BOOK ENTRY

DATED: 07/07/95
FIRST: 01/05/96

RETURN ADDRESS

SCOTT & STRINGFELLOW, INC.
P.O. BOX 1575
RICHMOND,   VA   23213

PRICE	PRINCIPAL AMOUNT	COMMISSION	STATE TAX	INTEREST	SEC FEE	MISC.	NET AMOUNT DUE
97.65965	19,531.93	48.00					19,579.93

IN ACCORDANCE WITH YOUR INSTRUCTIONS WE ARE PLEASED TO CONFIRM THE ABOVE TRANSACTION FOR YOUR ACCOUNT AND RISK SUBJECT TO TERMS LISTED ON REVERSE SIDE.

CUSTOMER COPY

Illustration 8-18
Corporate Bond Purchase Confirmation

BONDS

Scott & Stringfellow, Inc.
909 EAST MAIN STREET
RICHMOND, VIRGINIA 23219
804-643-1811

CONFIRMATION / COMPARISON

TO COMPLY WITH FEDERAL REGULATIONS PAYMENT FOR SECURITIES BOUGHT OR DELIVERY OF SECURITIES SOLD MUST BE MADE ON OR BEFORE

PLEASE RETAIN THIS COPY FOR YOUR RECORDS

SIPC

ACCOUNT NUMBER	TYPE	OFFICE	RR	SOC. SEC. / I.D. NO.	TRANS. NO.	MKT*	CAP*	TRADE DATE	SETTLEMENT DATE	ENTRY DATE	A* B* C*
18000001	1	MK	01	100-01-0001	00055	0	2	07/11/95	07/18/95		S

ACCOUNT NAME OR CONTRA PARTY

SPECIAL INSTRUCTIONS

Susan Q. Investor
1500 Investment Avenue
Richmond, VA 23132

	QUANTITY	CUSIP / SYMBOL	SECURITY DESCRIPTION		COUPON	MATURITY
YOU BOUGHT	10,000	74960LAQ9 60LAQ9	RJR NABISCO		8.3000%	04/15/00

DATED: 04/09/93

YIELD DOLLAR PRICE 9.735561 TO MATURITY
INT FROM 04/15/95 TO 07/18/95

RETURN ADDRESS

SCOTT & STRINGFELLOW, INC.
P.O. BOX 1575
RICHMOND,   VA   23213

PRICE	PRINCIPAL AMOUNT	COMMISSION	STATE TAX	INTEREST	SEC FEE	MISC.	NET AMOUNT DUE
94 5/8	9,462.50			214.42			9,676.92

IN ACCORDANCE WITH YOUR INSTRUCTIONS WE ARE PLEASED TO CONFIRM THE ABOVE TRANSACTION FOR YOUR ACCOUNT AND RISK SUBJECT TO TERMS LISTED ON REVERSE SIDE.

CUSTOMER COPY

BONDS

Q: After I buy a bond, how do I follow its progress?

A: The monitoring of your bond, like the research that led to your investment, will focus on your bond, the issuer, and the bond market in general. Following your bond's price and performance may not always be straightforward. Although some issues are listed on exchanges, the prices of many bonds are not reported on a regular basis in the financial media. If you hold your bond at a brokerage house in street name, your monthly statement may show its estimated value, and your broker should inform you of any change in your bond's performance, such as calls, interest payment interruption, etc. If *you* hold the bond certificate or it is held in *your* name, *you* are responsible for keeping current on its performance.

Just as you researched your bond's issuer before you invested, you should monitor the issuer's progress while you hold your investment. You are depending on the issuer's continuing ability to make interest and principal payments on your bond, so staying informed about the issuer's performance is very important. You may also want to watch developments in the bond market and the economy in general, since these broader developments may affect your bond's value, as previously discussed in this chapter.

Q: What do I do if I have a problem with my bond interest payment, calls, or maturity?

A: If you have a problem with your bond, you have several ways of seeking a solution. Before you inquire, it is important that you have at hand the critical details about your bond:

- Full description of the issuer
- Coupon rate (stated interest rate)
- Maturity date
- Series number, if applicable
- CUSIP number (see box)
- Your certificate number, if applicable
- Transfer agent information
- Interest/payment agent information

CUSIP: *Committee on Uniform Securities Identification Procedures.* A CUSIP number is assigned to every security issue. This number is used to identify the security you are buying or selling.

Once you have the identifying information, you will be able to get accurate answers about the status of your bond issue and your certificate specifically. If your bond is held at a brokerage firm in street name, you should be able to rely on your broker to research the problem and resolve it for you. If you bought a Treasury bond directly from the Federal Reserve, the Fed will be able to assist you.

Otherwise, if your bond's certificate is registered in your name, you should contact the *transfer agent* or *payment agent* (which is named on the bond certificate). The transfer agent, often a department of a bank or trust company, works for the issuer of your bond to administer the bond issue's record keeping. The payment agent is responsible for processing interest payments and for the final retirement of the issue when it matures or is called. Since the transfer agent and payment agent are responsible for an issue's records and activities, they will be able to tell you:

- If the mailing was delayed by a holiday or technical problem
- If their records show you at a wrong address
- If the payment was mailed properly and you did not receive it
- If the payment was interrupted and you missed the announcement
- If their records show that you received the payment and cashed the check

If you purchased the bond when it was issued, you will find the transfer agent's and payment agent's name, address, and/or phone number in the prospectus. If you purchased your bond after it was issued, you may ask your broker to assist you. Even if you hold your bonds yourself, a broker

BONDS

should be able to get the agent's name, address, and telephone number, or investigate the problem for you.

Q: If I own a corporate bond and its issuer is involved in a merger, what does this mean to me?

A: If your issuer is bought by or merged into another company, this is likely to affect your bond in one way or another. If the surviving company is bigger and stronger after the merger, your bond investment may be more secure. If the surviving company is bigger but weaker—heavily in debt, for instance—your bond investment may not be as secure. Also, depending upon the terms of your bond, the acquirer may have the right to call the bond when it acquires your issuer.

Q: If I own a corporate bond and its issuer announces a restructuring, how may this affect my investment?

A: In recent years many corporate issuers have made sweeping changes in the way their companies are organized or financed. If your bond's issuer announces a restructuring, this may or may not have a significant effect on your investment. For example, if your issuer were to spin off parts of the company into new companies, your bond's repayment could become the responsibility of the newly separate smaller company or remain with the original issuer, which is itself now smaller. On the other hand, your issuer may change its financial structure and borrow much more than before. This also would affect the security of your bond investment. In such a situation, you should investigate whether the bond continues to be a suitable investment.

Q: What does a bond default mean to me?

A: Your bond indenture lists obligations that the issuer must meet, including making timely payments of principal and interest. A corporate or municipal issuer may fail to perform such obligations, in which case the issuer is in default. The default may be very temporary, or only a *technical default* (see box), or it may be a serious threat to the issuer's existence. Your indenture agreement lists the course of action in the event of default, which may include immediate maturity of the issue and/or legal action. If a serious default persists, the trustee may be required to take action.

Q: What is technical default?

A: *Technical default* occurs when a bond issuer for some reason is not in compliance with all terms of the bond indenture, but is still able to maintain interest payments and anticipates payment of principal at maturity. The trustee is charged with dealing with this situation as required.

BONDS

Q: What would it mean to me if my bond issuer declared bankruptcy?

A: If your issuer has such grave problems that it can no longer meet its obligations and needs a court's protection, it may file for bankruptcy. Once such a filing takes place, the issuer usually suspends payment on obligations such as bonds. The issuer and its creditors, including representatives of bondholders such as yourself, will negotiate a reorganization that will enable the issuer to continue operations. In such a reorganization, the terms of your bond may be changed, or the bond may be changed into some other obligation entirely, such as a convertible bond or stock.

SUMMARY

When you invest in a bond, you are lending money to the bond issuer. The primary reason to invest in bonds is to earn an income from the time you invest in the bond until the bond matures. At maturity, you should be paid the face value of the bond.

Bond issuers have differing levels of quality, risk, and taxation. You need to be comfortable with the issuer and the structure of the bonds in which you invest as well as the maturities. This chapter should have answered many of your questions about investing in bonds, given you information on different issuers, and assisted you in working with investment professionals who are advising you on bond investing.

Illustration 8-19
Treasury Direct—Tender for 13-Week T-Bill

FORM PD F 5176-1
(February 1990)

OMB No. 1535-0069
Expires: 09-30-92

TREASURY DIRECT ®

TENDER FOR 13-WEEK TREASURY BILL

TENDER INFORMATION

AMOUNT OF TENDER: $_____

FOR DEPARTMENT USE

BID TYPE (Check One) ☐ NONCOMPETITIVE ☐ COMPETITIVE AT [ ] . [ ] %

TENDER NUMBER
912794

ACCOUNT NUMBER [   ] — [   ] — [   ]

CUSIP

ISSUE DATE

INVESTOR INFORMATION

RECEIVED BY

ACCOUNT NAME

DATE RECEIVED

EXT REG ☐

ADDRESS

FOREIGN ☐

BACKUP ☐

REVIEW ☐

CITY   STATE   ZIP CODE

TAXPAYER IDENTIFICATION NUMBER

1ST NAMED OWNER [   ] — [ ] — [   ] OR [ ] — [   ]
SOCIAL SECURITY NUMBER   EMPLOYER IDENTIFICATION NUMBER

CLASS ☐

TELEPHONE NUMBERS

WORK ([   ]) [   ] — [   ]   HOME ([   ]) [   ] — [   ]

PAYMENT ATTACHED

NUMBERS

TOTAL PAYMENT: $ _____

CASH (01): $ _____   CHECKS (02/03): $ _____

SECURITIES (05): $ _____ $ _____

OTHER (06): $ _____ $ _____

DIRECT DEPOSIT INFORMATION

ROUTING NUMBER

FINANCIAL INSTITUTION NAME

ACCOUNT NUMBER

ACCOUNT TYPE ☐ CHECKING
(Check One)

ACCOUNT NAME

☐ SAVINGS

AUTOMATIC REINVESTMENT

1 2 3 4 5 6 7 8 Circle the number of sequential 13-week reinvestments you want to schedule at this time

AUTHORIZATION

For the notice required under the Privacy and Paperwork Reduction Acts, see the accompanying instructions.
I submit this tender pursuant to the provisions of Department of the Treasury Circulars, Public Debt Series Nos. 1-86 and 2-86 and the public announcement issued by the Department of the Treasury.
Under penalties of perjury, I certify that the number shown on this form is my correct taxpayer identification number and that I am not subject to backup withholding because (1) I have not been notified that I am subject to backup withholding as a result of a failure to report all interest or dividends, or (2) the Internal Revenue Service has notified me that I am no longer subject to backup withholding. I further certify that all other information provided on this form is true, correct and complete.

_____   _____
SIGNATURE   DATE
SEE INSTRUCTIONS FOR PRIVACY ACT AND PAPERWORK REDUCTION ACT NOTICE

*U.S. GPO: 1990-268-403/20484

BONDS

Illustration 8-20
Treasury Direct—Tender for Treasury Bond

FORM PD F 5174-4
(January 1986)

TREASURY DIRECT ®

OMB No. 1535-0069
Expires: 01-31-89

TENDER FOR TREASURY BOND

BONDS

TENDER INFORMATION

AMOUNT OF TENDER: $_____

FOR DEPARTMENT USE

TERM _____

BID TYPE (Check One) ☐ NONCOMPETITIVE ☐ COMPETITIVE AT ☐☐ . ☐☐ %

TENDER NUMBER
912810

CUSIP

ACCOUNT NUMBER ☐☐☐☐ — ☐☐☐ — ☐☐☐☐

ISSUE DATE

INVESTOR INFORMATION

ACCOUNT NAME

RECEIVED BY

DATE RECEIVED

ADDRESS

EXT REG ☐

FOREIGN ☐

BACKUP ☐

REVIEW ☐

CITY   STATE   ZIP CODE

TAXPAYER IDENTIFICATION NUMBER

1ST NAMED OWNER ☐☐☐ — ☐☐ — ☐☐☐☐   OR   ☐☐ — ☐☐☐☐☐☐☐
SOCIAL SECURITY NUMBER   EMPLOYER IDENTIFICATION NUMBER

CLASS ☐

TELEPHONE NUMBERS

WORK (☐☐☐) ☐☐☐ — ☐☐☐☐   HOME (☐☐☐) ☐☐☐ — ☐☐☐☐

PAYMENT ATTACHED

TOTAL PAYMENT: $ _____

NUMBERS

CASH (01): $ _____   CHECKS (02/03): $ _____

SECURITIES (05): $ _____ $ _____

OTHER (06): $ _____ $ _____

DIRECT DEPOSIT INFORMATION

ROUTING NUMBER

FINANCIAL INSTITUTION NAME

ACCOUNT NUMBER

ACCOUNT TYPE ☐ CHECKING
(Check One)

ACCOUNT NAME

☐ SAVINGS

AUTHORIZATION

For the notice required under the Privacy and Paperwork Reduction Acts, see the accompanying instructions.

I submit this tender pursuant to the provisions of Department of the Treasury Circulars, Public Debt Series Nos. 1-86 and 2-86 and the public announcement issued by the Department of the Treasury.

Under penalties of perjury, I certify that the number shown on this form is my correct taxpayer identification number and that I am not subject to backup withholding because (1) I have not been notified that I am subject to backup withholding as a result of a failure to report all interest or dividends, or (2) the Internal Revenue Service has notified me that I am no longer subject to backup withholding. I further certify that all other information provided on this form is true, correct and complete.

_____   _____
SIGNATURE   DATE

*U.S. GOVERNMENT PRINTING OFFICE: 1987-188-550

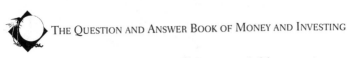
Illustration 8-21
Treasury Direct—Security Transfer Request

BONDS

FORM PD F 5179
(February 1990)

TREASURY DIRECT ®

OMB No. 1535-0069
Expires : 09-30-92

SECURITY TRANSFER REQUEST

ACCOUNT AND LOAN IDENTIFICATION

FOR DEPARTMENT USE

ACCOUNT NUMBER

ACCOUNT NAME

DOCUMENT AUTHORITY

APPROVED BY

DATE APPROVED

REFERENCE NUMBER

CUSIP   **DESCRIPTION**

AMOUNT TO BE TRANSFERRED: $ _____

NOTE: IF YOU ARE NOT TRANSFERRING ALL OF YOUR HOLDINGS FOR THE CUSIP SHOWN ABOVE, YOU MUST ALSO LIST THE SPECIFIC SUB-ACCOUNTS AND AMOUNTS TO BE TRANSFERRED (as shown on your Statement of Account).

SUB-ACCOUNT	AMOUNT	SUB-ACCOUNT	AMOUNT	SUB-ACCOUNT	AMOUNT
	$ _____		$ _____		$ _____
	$ _____		$ _____		$ _____

TRANSFER REQUESTED   CHECK ONE BOX AND PROVIDE THE INFORMATION REQUESTED FOR THAT TRANSFER.

☐ TO A FINANCIAL INSTITUTION

ROUTING NUMBER

FINANCIAL INSTITUTION NAME _____

SPECIAL HANDLING INSTRUCTIONS_____

☐ TO ANOTHER TREASURY DIRECT ACCOUNT

ACCOUNT NUMBER

ACCOUNT NAME

} Identify the TREASURY DIRECT account to which you want your securities transferred

TAXPAYER IDENTIFICATION NUMBER (IF AVAILABLE)

OR

SOCIAL SECURITY NUMBER   EMPLOYER IDENTIFICATION NUMBER

SEE INSTRUCTIONS FOR PRIVACY ACT AND PAPERWORK REDUCTION ACT NOTICE

Illustration 8-21
Treasury Direct—Security Transfer Request (cont.)

AUTHORIZATION

DO **NOT** SIGN THIS FORM UNTIL YOUR ARE
IN THE PRESENCE OF AN AUTHORIZED CERTIFYING INDIVIDUAL.

I SUBMIT THIS REQUEST PURSUANT TO THE PROVISIONS OF DEPARTMENT OF THE TREASURY CIRCULARS, PUBLIC DEBT SERIES NOS. 1-86 AND 2-86.

UNDER PENALTIES OF PERJURY, I CERTIFY THAT THE INFORMATION PROVIDED ON THIS FORM IS TRUE, CORRECT AND COMPLETE.

_____   _____
SIGNATURE(S)   DATE

_____
TITLE (IF APPROPRIATE)

CERTIFICATION

YOUR SIGNATURE MUST BE CERTIFIED BY AN AUTHORIZED CERTIFYING INDIVIDUAL.

I CERTIFY THAT THE ABOVE-NAMED PERSON AS DESCRIBED, WHOSE IDENTITY IS KNOWN OR PROVEN TO ME, PERSONALLY APPEARED BEFORE ME THIS _____ DAY OF _____ AT _____
AND SIGNED THIS REQUEST.   MONTH/YEAR   CITY/STATE

OFFICIAL SEAL
OR STAMP
(SUCH AS
CORPORATE SEAL,   _____
SIGNATURE   SIGNATURE AND TITLE OF CERTIFYING INDIVIDUAL
GUARANTEED
STAMP, OR
ISSUING AGENT'S   _____
DATING STAMP).   NAME OF FINANCIAL INSTITUTION

                          _____
                           ADDRESS

                          _____
                           CITY/STATE

CERTIFICATION BY A NOTARY PUBLIC IS NOT ACCEPTABLE

Illustration 8-22
Treasury Direct—Notice of Maturing T-Note

FORM PD 5261 (January 1988)
BUREAU OF THE PUBLIC DEBT
c/o FEDERAL RESERVE BANK OF PHILADELPHIA
TREASURY DIRECT, REINVESTMENT DIVISION
P.O. BOX 20
PHILADELPHIA, PA 19105-0020

OMB No. 1535-0085
Expires: 04-30-91

NOTICE OF MATURING TREASURY NOTE

STATEMENT DATE:

FOR OFFICIAL USE ONLY

THE TREASURY NOTE WITH CUSIP   IN YOUR ACCOUNT SHOWN BELOW IS DUE TO MATURE ON

THE AMOUNT OF THIS NOTE THAT IS AVAILABLE FOR REINVESTMENT IS $

IF YOU ARE INTERESTED IN REINVESTING THIS AMOUNT YOU SHOULD FOLLOW THESE STEPS:

1. SELECT A TERM AND FILL IN THE CORRESPONDING BOX WITH A BLACK PEN OR PENCIL. PLEASE NOTE THAT THIS FORM MAY ONLY BE USED TO REINVEST THE FULL AMOUNT LISTED ABOVE. IF YOU WISH TO REINVEST ONLY PART OF THESE PROCEEDS, YOU MAY REQUEST PARTIAL REINVESTMENT ON FORM PD 5262, WHICH CAN BE OBTAINED AT YOUR SERVICING OFFICE.

    BELOW IS AN **EXAMPLE** OF HOW A REQUEST FOR REINVESTMENT OF A TREASURY NOTE INTO A **2-YEAR TREASURY NOTE** WOULD LOOK:

    EXAMPLE ONLY

    2-YEAR ■
    4-YEAR □

2. SIGN AND DATE THE FORM. UNSIGNED FORMS CAN NOT BE PROCESSED AND WILL BE RETURNED.

3. ONCE COMPLETED, **RETURN THE ENTIRE FORM** IN THE ENVELOPE PROVIDED SO THAT IT IS RECEIVED BY_____
    YOU WILL RECEIVE A STATEMENT OF ACCOUNT WHEN THIS FORM IS PROCESSED.

IF THE MATURITY DATE FOR THIS SECURITY DOES NOT COINCIDE WITH THE ISSUE DATE FOR THE REINVESTMENT OPTION YOU HAVE SELECTED, THE ABOVE AMOUNT WILL BE PLACED IN A NON-INTEREST BEARING ACCOUNT UNTIL THE ISSUE DATE.

IF YOU DO NOT DESIRE REINVESTMENT PLEASE DISPOSE OF THIS FORM.

IF YOU HAVE ANY QUESTIONS ABOUT THE REINVESTMENT OF THIS NOTE PLEASE CONTACT YOUR LOCAL SERVICING OFFICE:

LISTED BELOW ARE THE ONLY REINVESTMENT OPTION(S) AVAILABLE FOR YOUR MATURING SECURITY.
INDICATE YOUR SELECTION HERE

ACCOUNT NUMBER: CUSIP: AMOUNT:

I submit this request pursuant to the provisions of Department of the Treasury Circulars, Public Debt Series Nos. 1-86 and 2-86. Under penalties of perjury, I certify that the information provided on this form is true, correct and complete.

SIGNATURE: _____   DATE: _____

Illustration 8-23
Treasury Direct—Reinvestment Request for Treasury Notes or Bonds

PD FORM 5262
Dept. of the Treasury
Bur. of the Public Debt

TREASURY DIRECT ®

OMB No. 1535-0068
Expires: 05-31-91)

REINVESTMENT REQUEST FOR TREASURY NOTES OR BONDS

BONDS

ACCOUNT AND LOAN IDENTIFICATION

ACCOUNT NUMBER ▢▢▢▢ – ▢▢▢ – ▢▢▢▢

ACCOUNT NAME

FOR DEPARTMENT USE

DOCUMENT AUTHORITY

APPROVED BY

DATE APPROVED

CUSIP

DESCRIPTION

TRANSACTIONS REQUESTED

CHECK THE BOX NEXT TO EACH TRANSACTION REQUESTED AND PRINT THE INFORMATION REQUESTED.

1. ☐ REINVEST $ —————— (PAR AMOUNT)   **TERM** FOR ▢▢ YEARS

2. ☐ REINVEST THE SUB-ACCOUNTS SHOWN BELOW FOR THE AMOUNTS AND LOAN TERMS INDICATED.
(Use this option **only** when you want to specify SUB-ACCOUNTS.)

SUB-ACCOUNT	AMOUNT	TERM
▢▢	$ ————————	▢▢ YEARS
▢▢	$ ————————	▢ YEARS
▢▢	$ ————————	▢▢ YEARS

SPECIAL NOTIFICATIONS:

● *If a four-year note is not available, the reinvestment will be made for two-years.*

● *If the maturity date of your security does not coincide but is within five calendar days of the issue date of the reinvestment option you have selected, the funds will be placed in a non-interest bearing account until the issue date. If the period is greater than five calendar days, the amount will be refunded.*

3. ☐ CANCEL **ALL** REINVESTMENTS.

4. ☐ CANCEL REINVESTMENTS **ONLY** FOR THE SUB-ACCOUNTS SHOWN BELOW.

SUB-ACCOUNT ▢▢   ▢▢   ▢▢

AUTHORIZATION

I submit this request pursuant to the provisions of Department of the Treasury Circulars, Public Debt Series Nos. 1-86 and 2-86. Under penalties of perjury, I certify that the information provided on this form is true, correct and complete.

_____   _____
SIGNATURE(S)   DATE

Illustration 8-24
Treasury Direct—Transaction Request

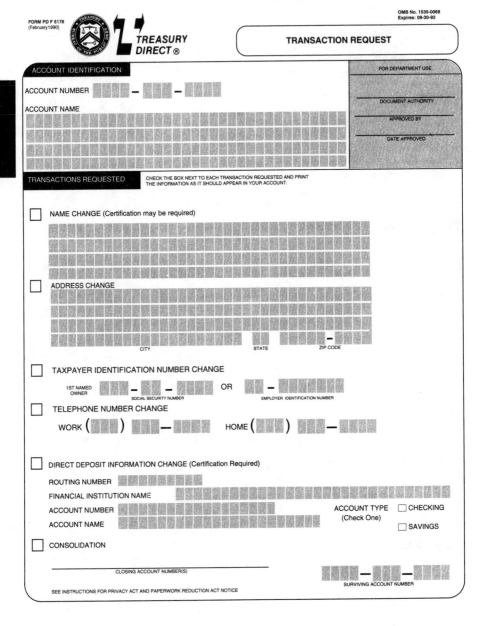

BONDS

Illustration 8-24
Treasury Direct—Transaction Request (cont.)

AUTHORIZATION

NOTE: IF YOUR SIGNATURE REQUIRES CERTIFICATION, DO **NOT** SIGN THIS FORM UNTIL YOU ARE IN THE PRESENCE OF A CERTIFYING OFFICER.

I SUBMIT THIS REQUEST PURSUANT TO THE PROVISIONS OF DEPARTMENT OF THE TREASURY CIRCULARS, PUBLIC DEBT SERIES NOS. 1-86 AND 2-86.

UNDER PENALTIES OF PERJURY, I CERTIFY THAT THE INFORMATION PROVIDED ON THIS FORM IS TRUE, CORRECT AND COMPLETE.

FOR TAXPAYER IDENTIFICATION NUMBER CHANGES ONLY: Under penalties of perjury I certify that the number shown on this form is my correct Taxpayer Identification Number and that I am not subject to backup withholding because (1) I have not been notified that I am subject to backup withholding as a result of a failure to report all interest or dividends, or (2) The Internal Revenue Service has notified me that I am no longer subject to backup withholding.

_____   _____
SIGNATURE(S)   DATE

_____
TITLE (IF APPROPRIATE)

CERTIFICATION

SIGNATURE CERTIFICATION IS REQUIRED FOR CERTAIN NAME CHANGES AND ALL DIRECT DEPOSIT INFORMA-TION CHANGES.

I CERTIFY THAT THE ABOVE-NAMED PERSON AS DESCRIBED, WHOSE IDENTITY IS KNOWN OR PROVEN TO ME, PERSONALLY APPEARED BEFORE ME THIS _____ DAY OF_____ AT_____
AND SIGNED THIS REQUEST.   MONTH/YEAR   CITY/STATE

OFFICIAL SEAL
OR STAMP
(SUCH AS
CORPORATE SEAL,
SIGNATURE
GUARANTEED
STAMP, OR
ISSUING AGENT'S
DATING STAMP).

_____
SIGNATURE AND TITLE OF CERTIFYING OFFICER

_____
NAME OF FINANCIAL INSTITUTION

_____
ADDRESS

_____
CITY/STATE

CERTIFICATION BY A NOTARY PUBLIC IS NOT ACCEPTABLE

Illustration 8-25
Federal Reserve Offices

For In-Person Visits	For Written Correspondence
Atlanta 104 Marietta Street, N.W. Atlanta, GA 404-521-8653 404-521-8657 (recording)	FRB of Atlanta 104 Marietta Street, N.W. Atlanta, GA 30303
Baltimore 502 South Sharp Street Baltimore, MD 410-576-3553 410-576-3500 (recording)	Baltimore Branch FRB of Richmond P.O. Box 1378 Baltimore, MD 21203
Birmingham 1801 Fifth Avenue, North Birmingham, AL 205-731-8708 205-731-8702 (recording)	Birmingham Branch FRB of Atlanta P.O. Box 10447 Birmingham, AL 35283-0447
Boston 600 Atlantic Avenue Boston, MA 617-973-3810 617-973-3805 (recording)	FRB Boston P.O. Box 2076 Boston, MA 02106
Buffalo 160 Delaware Avenue Buffalo, NY 716-849-5079 716-849-5158 (recording)	Buffalo Branch FRB of New York P.O. Box 961 Buffalo, NY 14240
Charlotte 530 East Trade Street Charlotte, NC 704-358-2410 or 2411 704-358-2424 (recording)	Charlotte Branch FRB of Richmond P.O. Box 30284 Charlotte, NC 28230
Chicago 230 South LaSalle Street Chicago, IL 312-322-5369 312-786-1110 (recording)	FRB of Chicago P.O. Box 834 Chicago, IL 60690
Cincinnati 150 East Fourth Street Cincinnati, OH 513-721-4787 Ext. 334	Cincinnati Branch FRB of Cleveland P.O. Box 999 Cincinnati, OH 45201
Cleveland 1455 East Sixth Street Cleveland, OH 216-579-2490 216-688-0068 (recording)	FRB of Cleveland P.O. Box 6387 Cleveland, OH 44101
Dallas 400 South Akard Street Dallas, TX 214-651-6362 214-651-6177 (recording)	FRB of Dallas Securities Dept. Station K Dallas, TX 75222

For In-Person Visits	For Written Correspondence
Denver 1020 16th Street Denver, CO 303-572-2470 303-572-2475 (recording)	Denver Branch FRB of Kansas City P.O. Box 5228 Terminal Annex Denver, CO 80217
Detroit 160 West Fort Street Detroit, MI 313-964-6157 313-963-4936 (recording)	Detroit Branch FRB of Chicago P.O. Box 1059 Detroit, MI 48231
El Paso 301 East Main Street El Paso, TX Call Dallas 915-544-4730	El Paso Branch FRB of Dallas P.O. Box 100 El Paso, TX 79901

Helena - The Helena Branch of the Federal Reserve Bank of Minneapolis does not deal in Treasury securities. Persons in the area served by the Helena Branch should instead contact the Minneapolis office listed in this Appendix.

For In-Person Visits	For Written Correspondence
Houston 1701 San Jacinto Street Houston, TX 713-659-4433 713-652-1688 (recording)	Houston Branch FRB of Dallas P.O. Box 2578 Houston, TX 77252
Jacksonville 800 West Water Street Jacksonville, FL 904-632-1179 904-632-1178 (recording)	Jacksonville Branch FRB of Atlanta P.O. Box 2499 Jacksonville, FL 32231-2499
Kansas City 925 Grand Avenue Kansas City, MO 816-881-2783 or 2409 816-881-2767 (recording)	FRB of Kansas City Attn. Securities Dept. P.O. Box 419440 Kansas City, MO 64141-6440
Little Rock 325 West Capitol Avenue Little Rock, AR 501-324-8272	Little Rock Branch FRB of St. Louis P.O. Box 1261 Little Rock, AR 72203
Los Angeles 950 South Grand Avenue Los Angeles, CA 213-624-7398 213-688-0068 (recording)	Los Angeles Branch FRB of San Fransico P.O. Box 2077 Terminal Annex Los Angeles, CA 90051
Louisville 410 South Fifth Street Louisville, KY 502-568-9236 or 9238 502-568-9240 (recording)	Louisville Branch FRB of St. Louis P.O. Box 32710 Louisville, KY 40232

For In-Person Visits	For Written Correspondence	For In-Person Visits	For Written Correspondence

Memphis'
200 North Main Street
Memphis, TN
901-523-7171
Ext. 622 or 629
Ext. 641 (recording)

Memphis Branch
FRB of St. Louis
P.O. Box 407
Memphis, TN
38101

Miami
9100 N.W. 36th Street
Miami, FL
305-471-6497
305-471-6257 (recording)

Miami Branch
FRB of Atlanta
P.O. Box 520847
Miami, FL
33152-0847

Minneapolis
250 Marquette Avenue
Minneapolis, MN
612-340-2075
612-340-2051 (recording)

FRB of Minneapolis
P.O. Box 491
Minneapolis, MN
55480

Nashville
301 Eight Avenue, North
Nashville, TN
615-251-7100
615-251-7236 (recording)

Nashville Branch
FRB of Atlanta
301 Eighth Avenue, North
Nashville, TN
37203

New Orleans
525 St. Charles Avenue
New Orleans, LA
504-593-3200
504-593-3290 (recording)

New Orleans Branch
FRB of Atlanta
P.O. Box 61630
New Orleans, LA
70161

New York
33 Liberty Street
New York, NY
212-720-6619
24-hour recording:
212-720-5823 (results)
212-720-7773 (new offerings)

FRB of New York
Federal Reserve P.O. Station
New York, NY
10045

Oklahoma City
226 Dean A. McGee Avenue
Oklahoma City, OK
405-270-8652
405-270-8660 (recording)

Oklahoma City Branch
FRB of Kansas City
P.O. Box 25129
Oklahoma City, OK
73125

Omaha
2201 Farnam Street
Omaha, NE
402-221-5636
402-221-5638 (recording)

Omaha Branch
FRB of Kansas City
P.O. Box 3958
Omaha, NE
68102

Philadelphia
Ten Independence Mall
Philadelphia, PA
215-574-6675 or 6680
215-574-6580 (recording)

FRB of Philadelphia
P.O. Box 90
Philadelphia, PA
19105-0090

Pittsburgh
717 Grant Street
Pittsburgh, PA
412-261-7863
412-261-7988 (recording)

Pittsburgh Branch
FRB of Cleveland
P.O. Box 867
Pittsburgh, PA
15230-0867

Portland
915 S.W. Stark Street
Portland, OR
503-221-5932
503-221-5931 (recording)

Portland Branch
FRB of San Francisco
P.O. Box 3436
Portland, OR
97208-3436

Richmond
701 E. Byrd Street
Richmond, VA
804-697-8372
804-697-8355 (recording)

FRB of Richmond
P.O. Box 27622
Richmond, VA
23261-7622

Salt Lake City
120 South State Street
Salt Lake City, UT
801-322-7944
801-322-7844 (recording)

Salt Lake City Branch
FRB of San Francisco
P.O. Box 30780
Salt Lake City, UT
84130

San Antonio
126 East Nueva Street
San Antonio, TX
512-978-1305 or 1303
512-978-1330 (recording)

San Antonio Branch
FRB of Dallas
P.O. Box 1471
San Antonio, TX
78295

San Francisco
101 Market Street
San Francisco, CA
415-974-2330
415-974-3491 (recording)

FRB of San Francisco
P.O. Box 7702
San Francisco, CA
94120-7702

Seattle
1015 Second Avenue
Seattle, WA
206-343-3605
206-343-3615 (recording)

Seattle Branch
FRB of San Francisco
P.O. Box 3567
Terminal Annex
Seattle, WA
98124

St. Louis
411 Locust Street
St. Louis, MO
314-444-8665 or 8666
314-444-8602 (recording)

FRB of St. Louis
P.O. Box 442
St. Louis, MO
63166

United States Treasury
Washington, DC

Bureau of the Public Debt
1300 C Street, S.W.
Washington, DC
202-874-4000
Device for hearing impaired:
202-874-4026

Mail Inquiries to:
Bureau of the Public Debt
Division of Customer Services
Washington, DC
20239-1000

Mail Tenders to:
Bureau of the Public Debt
Department N
Washington, DC
20239-1500

BONDS

CHAPTER 9

MUTUAL FUNDS: PROFESSIONAL MANAGEMENT

Mutual funds are investment pools that hold many of the investments discussed in earlier sections, including stocks, bonds, and other securities. Mutual funds exist in various different forms and allow investors with similar investment objectives to pool their investment capital. By investing in mutual funds, you are able to pool your capital with that of other investors to achieve goals collectively that you may not be able to achieve individually, such as diversification, full-time professional management, investment flexibility, and institutional power. This chapter seeks to answer questions about mutual fund features, as well as more pragmatic questions about how to select and invest in mutual funds.

To understand mutual funds, it is important that you understand certain basic features and terms.

Q: Where do mutual funds come from?

A: Investors have pooled investment capital and hired professional management for hundreds of years. From the era of Egyptian desert caravans through the days of the great Dutch and English merchant empires, investors spread the considerable risk of such ventures by pooling their investments so that no one would be ruined by the loss of any one caravan or the sinking of any one ship. The most famous English and Scottish pools, called *investment trusts*, made investments accessible to the growing middle class of modest investors.

Investors with moderate means entrusted their money to the management expertise of the professional merchants and trading companies. These were the models on which modern mutual funds are based.

American mutual funds developed during the late 1800s and the early 1900s. As the American middle class grew and developed demand for investments, individuals turned their money over to financial institutions to make their investment decisions. The first mutual fund in the form we have today was established in 1924. The American mutual fund industry has grown rapidly in recent years—the number of active mutual funds increased from 68 in 1944 to 3,952 in 1994.

MUTUAL FUNDS

Q: How are mutual funds formed?

A: Mutual funds are formed by a *fund sponsor*. The fund sponsor may be a company that specializes in marketing mutual funds, or it may be a bank or brokerage firm. Many sponsors establish several mutual funds with various investment objectives, or what is called a *fund family*. Each mutual fund established by the sponsor exists only to hold the types of investments specified in its charter.

An *investment company* is the legal term for a mutual fund. (The terms *investment company*, *mutual fund*, and *fund* are often used interchangeably.) The formal features of investment companies were established by the Investment Company Act of 1940 and the Investment Company Amendments Act of 1970. The laws were designed to protect investors by requiring registration of all shares being offered and full disclosure of the fund's investment goals; its advisors, sponsors, distributors, etc.; and all fees and charges. The investment company is required to issue a *prospectus* to fulfill full disclosure requirements (see box). The prospectus must be provided to any investor purchasing newly issued shares of the fund.

Prospectus: A document filed with the Securities and Exchange Commission that contains material information necessary for full disclosure for solicitation purposes by the issuer and the distributor of securities. For a mutual fund, material information may include the following: investment objectives, advisors, charges (fees), performance statistics, and purchase and liquidation instructions.

Q: Who carries out the business of a mutual fund?

A: The mutual fund shareholders elect *trustees* who are responsible for carrying out the activities of the fund. The trustees will appoint an *investment advisor*, or *management company*, which will be responsible for the fund's investment policies and management decisions concerning the fund's portfolio. The mutual fund usually pays the investment advisor a management fee based on a percentage of the fund's assets. The trustees may also appoint a *distribution company* to be responsible for the sales and marketing of the fund's shares. The distribution company may work with sales organizations such as brokerage firms, banks, etc.; arrange advertising for sales directly to investors; or do any combination of these in promoting the fund to investors. The trustees will also appoint a transfer agent to perform shareholder services such as accounting, communication, and administration of distributions.

MUTUAL FUNDS

Q: What are the different forms of investment companies?

A: There are three basic forms of investment companies:

1. Open-end
2. Closed-end
3. Unit investment trusts

Q: What is an open-end fund?

A: An *open-end* fund keeps itself "open" by offering new shares to each buyer and redeeming the shares of each seller. Shares may be bought only from the mutual fund and sold only to the mutual fund. The size of the fund will fluctuate not only with the value of its investment holdings, but also as money flows into the fund from buyers or flows out to sellers.

Q: What is a closed-end fund?

A. A *closed-end* fund originally issues a fixed number of shares and then "closes" itself to new money. The value of a closed-end mutual fund will fluctuate only with the increase or decrease in value of the investments in its portfolio, not as a result of buyer or seller activity. After the fund is established, its existing shares trade on a major exchange or in the over-the-counter market. They are usually bought and sold in the same way as any common stock.

Q: What is a unit investment trust?

A: A *unit investment trust (UIT)* issues a fixed number of shares, called *units,* and invests in a fixed portfolio of investments. Unlike open-end and closed-end investment companies, a unit investment trust does not actively buy or sell investments for its portfolio. Once it is established, a UIT simply holds the securities and distributes any interest or dividends as earned. The trust must distribute the proceeds to unit holders whenever it sells any of its holdings or as securities in its portfolio mature or are retired. As the holdings of the trust decrease and unit holders receive their proportionate share of all distributions, the size of the fund will decrease. The trust will generally have a final expiration date; most of the assets will have been liquidated before this, and a final distribution will be made to unit holders at this time.

Q: I have heard the term net asset value (NAV). What is it?

A: *Net asset value (NAV)* is the value of all the assets owned by a fund, net of liabilities. The *net asset value per share* is the fund's total NAV divided by the number of shares outstanding.

Q: Is the NAV the same as the market price of my mutual fund shares?

A: It depends on the type of mutual fund you own.

- *Open-end:* The market price (liquidating value) of your open-end shares is the NAV. In some open-end funds, the *offering* or *asked price* (purchasing price) may be higher than net asset value because it includes a sales charge (see page 224). Some open-end mutual funds have a contingent deferred sales charge (see page 225).

- *Closed-end:* The market price of your closed-end fund shares may be substantially above or below their net asset value. After their initial offering, closed-end fund shares are subject to market price fluctuations based on supply and demand (see page 226, "How are closed-end funds different?").

- *Unit investment trusts:* The market price of your UIT units will generally be the same as the NAV. Most UIT sponsors provide a secondary market for the units at NAV plus any accrued interest, if appropriate.

Q: What distributions can I expect from my mutual fund?

A: The mutual fund is required to distribute its income (via dividend distributions) and net realized capital gains (via capital gains distributions) to shareholders.

Dividend distributions from investment income consist of dividends and interest paid on by securities owned by the fund, net of expenses incurred by the fund. They may also include short-term gains from the sale of securities in the fund's portfolio.

Capital gains distributions consist of long-term profits realized by the sale of securities in the fund's portfolio. The distribution amount consists of net profits realized.

All distributions are calculated, paid, and reported on a per share basis. The amount you receive will be proportionate to the number of shares you own. The amount you receive will also reduce your net asset value per share when the distributions are made. If you reinvest your distributions, the number of shares you own will increase.

MUTUAL FUNDS

Q: I have heard of mutual fund expenses and fees. What are they?

A: All mutual funds incur expenses. Generally, the expenses are deducted from income before distributions to shareholders or deducted in the calculation of NAV. Some mutual funds also charge a sales fee (referred to as a "load"), which is added to the net asset value when purchasing new shares or deducted from the NAV when selling. All expenses and sales fees are disclosed in the prospectus.

Q: What expenses does a mutual fund incur?

A: The annual expenses a mutual fund incurs may include the following:

- *Administrative expenses*, such as accounting, legal, communication, shareholder services, and record-keeping costs.
- *Management fees*, which are paid to the appointed investment advisors for managing the assets of the fund. Management fees are usually based on the assets of a mutual fund.
- *12b-1 fees*, named for the regulation that created them, which may pay for distribution expenses such as advertisements, ongoing broker service, and other costs. This annual charge is based on a percentage of a fund's assets.

These expenses are deducted from investment income before distributions to shareholders, as stated above.

 Note: Such expenses, generally stated as a percentage of the fund's assets, can vary dramatically, ranging from under 1 percent to perhaps as much as 3 percent. To determine the expenses of any mutual fund, consult its prospectus.

Q: What sales fees may I incur when investing in mutual funds?

A: Many open-end mutual funds charge some form of sales fee, or load. Some funds offer a choice of several load structures. The types of load include:

- Front-end load
- Back-end load

- Level load
- No load

Q: What is a front-end-load mutual fund?

A: Funds that charge a *front-end load* usually depend on investment brokerage firms to attract and service investors. The fund charges a sales charge up front that is added to the NAV. On an ongoing basis, the fund may also deduct yearly expenses and 12b-1 fees from the portfolio's earnings. Shares sold with a front-end sales charge are often referred to as "A" shares.

Q: What is a back-end-load mutual fund?

A: Funds that charge a *back-end load* also usually depend on brokerage firms to sell their shares to investors. Investors pay little or no commission at the time the shares are purchased. Instead, they may be subject to redemption fees, called *contingent deferred sales charges (CDSC)*, on the "back end." If you sell shares before a certain date, your redemption proceeds will be reduced by the contingent deferred sales charge. CDSCs usually decline as the shares are held longer, disappearing altogether if the shares are held beyond a certain number of years (usually from three to seven years). Yearly expenses are also deducted from the portfolio's earnings. CDSCs are always disclosed in a fund's prospectus. The CDSC is waived upon the death of the shareholder if the prospectus contains such a provision. Shares sold with a back-end sales charge are often referred to as "B" shares.

Q: What is a level-load mutual fund?

A: Funds that charge a *level load* also usually depend on brokerage firms to sell their shares to investors. Such funds charge little or no fee upon purchase, but usually have a CDSC. The compensation to brokerage firms and sales organizations is included in the yearly 12b-1 fee, making the expenses higher. Shares sold with a level-load sales charge are often referred to as "C" shares.

MUTUAL FUNDS

Q: What is a no-load mutual fund?

A: *No-load funds* are those funds that do not charge a fee upon purchase or sale. They usually do not depend on brokerage firms to sell their shares to investors; instead, they depend on advertisements to attract investors and provide toll-free numbers for service. Since no-load funds rely on advertisements and direct marketing methods, their annual fees must cover all expenses, including sales and distribution costs.

Q: Do I have a choice between different load arrangements?

A: Many mutual funds (or families of mutual funds) will offer the same mutual fund to investors with a variety of load arrangements. A fund may be offered with an up-front load (A shares), a back-end load (B shares), or a level load (C shares). The fund may also offer no-load purchases for large investments. Each class of shares will have differing expense and fee charges.

The reason for the different acquisition costs for the same mutual fund shares is to allow the broker to accommodate whichever method you choose to pay for your mutual fund investment.

Q: How important are expenses and fees in mutual fund investing?

A: Expenses and sales charges obviously reduce a mutual fund's performance. Between two mutual funds with identical portfolio performance, the fund with lower expenses and fees will be a better investment. You must weigh the expense and fee factor against your other investment criteria, such as investment objectives and risk tolerance. How well a fund meets your investment objectives and the fund's long-term performance should be more important than expenses and fees alone.

Q: How are closed-end funds different?

A: Closed-end funds do charge management fees and expenses for the ongoing costs of running the fund, but they do not have the variety of sales charge arrangements that open-end funds have. Closed-end funds use brokerage firms in their initial public offering. Underwriting fees are generally deducted from the initial proceeds of the public offering. On any subsequent purchases by investors, the fund does not buy or sell shares. Instead, investors buy shares from and sell them to other investors on a stock exchange or in the over-the-counter market. They incur a brokerage commission as in any similar stock transaction. Since a closed-end fund does not incur ongoing sales or distribution costs, it usually does not impose sales loads or 12b-1 fees.

Closed-end funds are also unique in that their prices may be substantially above or below their NAV. After the initial offering, the market prices of closed-end fund shares fluctuate according to supply and demand. Unlike open-end fund shares, which are always redeemable at NAV, closed-end fund shares may trade at a *premium* above or a *discount* below their net asset value.

Bargain-hunting investors often seek closed-end funds priced at an unusually wide discount to their NAV. Investors may profit if the price rises along with the NAV, or if the NAV remains steady and the price rises closer to the NAV level (the discount narrows). Investors may also profit if the fund has a termination date. At such a date, the fund either liquidates its holdings or asks shareholders to vote on liquidation or conversion to open-end status. In either case, investors receive NAV from the proceeds.

 Note: Many closed-end funds will offer reinvestment of dividends and capital gains distributions at NAV or the current market price, whichever is less. For further information on dividend reinvestment plans, see Chapter 5, page 82.

Q: Why should I consider investing in mutual funds?

A: Mutual funds are an alternative form of owning the individual investments—such as stocks and bonds—that compose the fund's portfolio. Some investors prefer to hold the individual stocks or bonds, but others invest in mutual funds for several reasons, including:

- Professional management
- Diversification
- Investment convenience

Q: How does a mutual fund's professional management benefit me?

A: While you can perform your own research and invest directly in individual securities, you may lack the resources, time, and expertise to do so. By investing in a mutual fund, you are hiring professional investment advisors who do have the resources, time, and expertise to manage your assets pooled with the assets of others who have the same investment objective.

Q: How does a mutual fund's diversification benefit me?

A: The many investors who do not have large amounts of money to invest cannot buy enough individual stocks or bonds to build a diversified portfolio. Diversification, an important investment discipline, reduces an investor's dependence on any one issue's success or failure. A mutual fund offers investors instant diversification by providing a professionally managed portfolio suitable for your investment objectives.

An investor may achieve even wider diversification by holding a variety of mutual funds with different investment objectives or styles of management.

Q: How can mutual funds provide me investment convenience?

A: Mutual funds offer many features that are not always available to you in other investments. Such features may include:

- *Full and fractional shares.* With open-end funds, you can invest or withdraw the exact dollar amount you want, since the fund will issue full and fractional shares to accommodate the dollars invested. Fractional shares are usually carried to three decimal places (for example, 181.748 shares).
- *Rights of accumulation.* Most mutual funds with sales charges offer discounts when larger amounts of money are invested. For example, a sales charge may decrease from 5.75 percent to 4.5 percent for investments over $50,000. This means that the sales charge would be reduced when you make a $50,000 investment. *Rights of accumulation* allow you the discount on additional investments if your *total* balance, including the amount

you invest, is above the threshold, no matter how small the investment that sends the balance over the threshold. For example, if the value of your mutual fund account is $40,000 and you add $10,000 to your account, the additional investment would have a sales charge based on $50,000.

- *Periodic investment plans.* You may wish to invest a certain amount in several installments over a period of time. Under a periodic investment plan, you can mail checks to the fund on specific dates or the fund can arrange a withdrawal of specific amounts from your checking account for automatic investment on the dates specified.

    This feature may allow you to engage in the *dollar cost averaging* investment method rather than investing large amounts of money at one time. Periodic investing is a particularly good method for beginning investors, as it enables them to invest nominal amounts.

MUTUAL FUNDS

Illustration 9-1
Periodic Investing

Example of an initial investment of $250 and $50 monthly investing for ten years in a growth mutual fund. All dividends and capital gains distributions are reinvested.

Period End	Investment for Period	Dividends Reinvested	Capital Gains Reinvested	Year End Market Value
01/84	$250			$236
12/84	$550	14	5	$767
12/85	$600	20	80	$1,602
12/86	$600	38	107	$2,433
12/87	$600	51	203	$3,124
12/88	$600	71	136	$4,292
12/89	$600	164	536	$6,186
12/90	$600	160	274	$6,500
12/91	$600	135	412	$9,459
12/92	$600	83	39	$10,767
12/93	$600	56	449	$12,937

This illustration represents past performance of a sample mutual fund and should not be considered indicative of future results. The effects of taxes on this investment have not been reflected in the illustration. (The up-front maximum sales charge is 5.75 percent.)

- *Automatic reinvestments.* Most mutual funds offer you the ability to reinvest dividends and capital gains distributions into additional shares of the fund. Additionally, the fund may offer to invest the distributions in shares of another fund in the same sponsor's family of funds.

- *Systematic withdrawal* features allow you to designate a specific amount you wish to receive from your fund on a regular basis. Many funds will give you a choice of how you may receive your distribution. You may receive a check, or you may have the distribution deposited directly to your bank account. If you wish to receive $200 monthly, for example, a fund offering systematic withdrawal will send you that amount whether or not your investment produced $200 in the month. If your fund investment produced *more* than $200, the excess will remain in your mutual fund account, adding to your fund's investment value. If your investment earned *less*, the shortage would reduce the value of your account. Either way, you can count on receiving your planned distribution amount.

Note: You may want to establish a specified withdrawal rate lower than the anticipated total return of the fund so the value of the fund will continue to grow despite the withdrawals. If the value increases as anticipated, you should be able to increase future withdrawals. See Illustration 9-2.

Illustration 9-2
Systematic Withdrawal

Example of $2,400 per month (6%) withdrawal on $40,000 investment

Period End	Amount Invested	Amount Withdrawn	REINVESTED Income	Capital Gain	Total	Market Value
01/84	$40,000					$37,700
12/84	0	2,400	1,546	0	1,546	38,506
12/85	0	2,400	1,586	1,715	3,301	48,574
12/86	0	2,400	1,760	9,187	10,947	56,627
12/87	0	2,400	2,216	3,189	5,405	57,514
12/88	0	2,400	2,537	3,440	5,977	62,671
12/89	0	2,400	2,847	4,101	6,948	78,471
12/90	0	2,400	3,022	1,126	4,149	76,529
12/91	0	2,400	2,320	2,003	4,323	94,205
12/92	0	2,400	2,522	1,717	4,239	98,259
12/93	0	2,400	2,576	4,112	6,688	107,139

This illustration represents past performances and should not be considered indicative of future results. The effects of taxes on this investment have not been reflected in the illustration.

Q: How do I choose a mutual fund?

A: As with any type of investment, you should consider your needs and choose accordingly:

- Determine your investment objectives.
- Choose the *type* of mutual fund appropriate for your objectives.
- Gather information on the individual mutual funds within your chosen fund type.
- Choose the mutual fund that best suits your criteria for investment performance, risk, expense, etc.

Q: What types of mutual fund investment objectives are there?

A: In recent years the numbers of mutual funds with different investment objectives have grown. You may want to select one mutual fund or build a portfolio of funds. Mutual funds can be classified by investment objectives, including:

- Growth funds
- Aggressive growth funds
- Value funds

- Sector funds
- Growth-and-income funds
- Income funds
- Bond funds
- Balanced funds
- Dual-purpose funds
- Convertible funds
- International funds
- Global funds
- Index funds
- Money market funds

Q: What are growth funds?

A: *Growth mutual funds* define their goal as capital appreciation; their managers will invest in stocks that they believe hold the greatest potential for price appreciation. These may be stocks of large, established corporations, or they may be the first stocks issued to the public by smaller, emerging companies. Growth funds may also seek stocks with potential for regular dividend increases, but generally this is only a secondary investment objective. As pointed out in the common stock section, growth companies usually reinvest most or all of their earnings into the company for future expansion. Therefore, growth funds often do not generate much current income for shareholders. Also, the NAV of growth funds may experience more volatility than that of other types of mutual funds. Investors in mutual funds that have growth as a primary objective usually incur more risk than investors in other types of funds.

Q: What are aggressive growth funds?

A: *Aggressive growth mutual funds* specialize in stocks that the managers believe have the highest possible potential for growth, regardless of risk. Such stocks are often those of small, less-established companies or companies in riskier industries. These stocks thus tend to have greater price volatility. Aggressive growth funds accept the higher risks (hence the term *aggressive*) in order to seek higher returns than general growth funds.

Q: What are value funds?

A: *Value mutual funds* are similar to growth funds in that they seek capital appreciation, but different in that they invest in stocks whose prices are low relative to what the fund's managers believe is their actual value. In the search for unrealized value, managers of such funds may invest in out-of-favor stocks in low-growth industries. Because the managers tend to invest in stocks whose prices are already low, value funds tend to be less volatile than growth funds when the stock market is weak.

Q: What are sector funds?

A: True to their name, *sector funds* specialize in stocks of a certain sector, generally a specific industry group such as telecommunications or health care. Investing in a sector fund allows you to place emphasis on an area you believe will perform especially well. However, investing in sector mutual funds generally affords you less diversification.

Q: What are growth-and-income funds?

A: *Growth-and-income mutual funds* primarily seek capital appreciation. They may have a secondary objective of generating current income and growth of income for shareholders. Such funds invest primarily in stocks of well-established companies that pay dividends and have a record of steadily increasing these dividends, as well as potential to do so in the future. The funds may also invest in convertible preferred stocks or convertible bonds to earn additional income and participate in appreciation of the stocks underlying such securities. Since these funds invest in more established companies with less stock price volatility, investors in growth-and-income mutual funds incur somewhat less risk than those in pure growth funds.

Q: What are income funds?

A: *Income mutual funds* seek current income and sometimes growth of income. Capital appreciation may be a secondary goal. With such an emphasis, income mutual funds tend to invest in dividend-oriented stocks, such as electric utility stocks, and in preferred stocks and convertible securities.

MUTUAL FUNDS

They may also invest in bonds. As with growth-and-income funds, shares of an income fund will not be as susceptible to the price volatility of the overall stock market as shares of a growth fund would be. On the other hand, the value (price)of an income fund will react more to interest rates than would that of a growth fund.

Q: What are bond funds?

A: *Bond funds* invest in bonds, seeking income as their primary objective. Preservation of capital is often, but not always, a secondary objective. Some bond funds emphasize income, whereas others are willing to sacrifice some income to focus on preservation of capital. Bond funds are divided into a variety of categories according to type of bond (Treasury, municipal, or corporate), maturity range (short-term, intermediate-term, or long-term), and other distinctions. Usually, the income paid on the bonds in a fund's portfolio will retain the same character and tax treatment when it flows through to the fund's shareholders. For instance, the income paid by a fund that invests in tax-free bonds is received by shareholders as tax-free income. The prices of bond funds fluctuate with the prices of the bonds in their portfolios.

Q: What are balanced funds?

A: *Balanced mutual funds* are the middle ground between stock funds and bond funds. They invest in both stocks and bonds, with the percentage mix, or "balance," depending on the manager's view of current market conditions. The bonds in the portfolio provide the fund more income and generally less price volatility than a stock fund would have, and the stocks in the portfolio provide more growth potential than a bond fund would have.

Q: What are dual-purpose funds?

A: *Dual-purpose funds* are a type of closed-end fund that invests for both growth and income, and offers two classes of shares to allow investors to specialize. The two classes of shares are *income shares* and *capital shares*.

In most cases the *income shares* provide a specified income level, a claim on a certain dollar principal amount at maturity, and the right to any excess income produced by the fund. The fund's charter may also commit it to maintaining a certain percentage of the portfolio in dividend-paying common stocks and interest-bearing securities.

The remainder of the portfolio may be invested for growth on behalf of the *capital shares*. At the termination of the fund, all accumulated capital above the principal due to the income shareholders will be allocated to the capital shares.

Q: What are convertible funds?

A: *Convertible mutual funds* invest in securities that are convertible into common stocks. A convertible fund seeks higher income than is available from common stocks, but also seeks to participate in the potential capital appreciation of common stocks. Shares in a convertible fund generally pay less income and experience more price volatility than those of a bond fund, but pay more and fluctuate less than those of a stock fund.

Q: What are international funds?

A: *International mutual funds* invest in securities of companies and governments in foreign countries. There are international stock funds and international bond funds with investment objectives similar to those of domestic funds. These funds allow investors to diversify their holdings, balancing the opportunities and risks of international investing. Some international funds specialize in a region (such as Asia) or an individual country (such as Mexico or Brazil). Because of their specialization and management costs, international funds usually have higher fund expenses and management fees than most other funds.

Q: What are global funds?

A: *Global mutual funds* are similar to international funds, but they can also include U.S. securities in their portfolios. By including both domestic and foreign securities, global funds

MUTUAL FUNDS

can achieve greater geographic diversification than international funds. The managers can invest in the areas of the world that they believe are the most financially attractive.

MUTUAL FUNDS

Q: What are index funds?

A: *Index mutual funds* seek to mirror the performance of a particular securities index, such as the Standard & Poor's 500. These funds hold the same percentages of the same securities as are contained in the index, and adjust their portfolios only when the stocks in the index change. Index fund investors see the index as a reflection of the market and wish to achieve an investment return similar to that of the market.

Q: What are money market funds?

A: *Money market funds* seek to provide investors with immediate availability of their money, while offering a better return than is available on similar alternatives. The funds hold large quantities of short-term securities, some of which mature daily. This generally allows the funds to keep their share price stable, usually $1, and also results in slight changes in the fund's yield from day to day. Since money market funds are designed as an alternative to bank accounts, many of them have check-writing privileges to enhance investors' access to their money. They may also be linked to a companion brokerage account by a *sweep agreement*. A sweep agreement provides automatic transfer of funds into and out of the money market account when the investor sells or buys securities or receives dividends or interest.

Q: Where do I get information for choosing a mutual fund?

A: As with other types of investing, there are many types of investment information available on mutual funds. Major sources of information include the following:

- *The Investment Company Institute* is an information agency for the mutual fund industry. It publishes a variety of brochures, books, and videos on mutual funds, their performance, and methods of investing. You may contact the Institute at

Investment Company Institute
1600 M Street, NW, Suite 600
Washington, DC 20036
Tel.: (202) 326-5800

- *Mutual fund companies* themselves will provide you with a prospectus for their funds, along with a variety of sales materials describing their investment objectives, management style, and fund performance. Many mutual funds advertise in financial publications, and brokers can provide you with information and phone numbers.
- *Mutual fund rankings* published by several subscription services provide investors with objective comparisons between mutual funds. Some examples include

Morningstar, Inc.
225 West Wacker Drive
Chicago, IL 60606
Tel: (312) 696-6000

Value Line Publishing, Inc.
711 Third Avenue
New York, NY 10017
Tel: (800) 654-0508

CDA/Wiesenberger
1355 Piccard Drive
Rockville, MD 20850
Tel: (800) 232-2285

Lipper Analytical Services, Inc.
74 Trinity Place
New York, NY 10006
Tel: (212) 393-1300

In addition, several financial publications, such as *Business Week, Forbes, U.S. News & World Report, Barron's,* and *Money* issue periodic rankings of mutual funds throughout the year.

Note: You may be able to access these services at your local library, or your broker may be able to provide you with copies.

- Newsletters offer their subscribers advice on mutual fund investing; they are published by a large number of advisors. Some of the more popular mutual fund newsletters include

  Donoghue's Money Letter
  290 Elliot Street
  Box 91004
  Ashland, MA 01721-9104
  Tel: (508) 881-2800

  Mutual Fund Forecaster
  The Institute for Econometric Research
  3471 N. Federal Highway
  Fort Lauderdale, FL 33306
  Tel: (800) 327-6720

  Mutual Fund Investing
  7811 Montrose Road
  Potomac, MD 20854
  Tel: (800) 777-5005

  Mutual Fund Strategist
  P.O. Box 446
  Burlington, VT 05402
  Tel: (802) 425-2211

  Personal Finance
  1101 King Street, Suite 400
  Alexandria, VA 22314
  Tel: (703) 548-2400

Wall Street Digest Mutual Fund Advisor
One Sarasota Tower, #602
Two N. Tamiami Trail
Sarasota, FL 34236
Tel: (813) 954-5500

Your brokerage firm will generally have access to most of the information sources listed above and can review a wide range of funds to select a few choices that best suit your investment objectives and circumstances.

Q: Is my choice as simple as picking the fund with the best record and buying it?

A: As you read literature from different mutual funds, you will discover that investment performance can be measured in many ways. It often seems that *every* fund claims to be a performance leader among its peers, although this is statistically impossible. Your investment objective—whether aggressive growth, tax-free income, or something else—will narrow down the list of fund candidates appropriate for you.

Among the funds within your investment objective, the highest performer for the last three months or one year may not have the best long-term outlook. Often the past quarter's leader becomes a laggard in future periods. Most investors would be well advised to seek mutual funds with high performance rankings over longer periods, such as three, five, or ten years, to find funds that have performed well through different market environments.

Volatility may also be a factor. Several funds may have similar historical rates of return, but one may have less volatility in share price than its peers. Other investors look for a fund with lower expenses and managers that have been in place for a number of years to narrow down their choices.

Q: How do I go about buying a mutual fund?

A: Once you have set your investment objectives and chosen the appropriate fund or funds, how you buy the fund may depend on the type of fund. If you have been working with a broker, the way you purchase mutual funds is similar to the way you buy stocks and bonds. If you are purchasing a fund

MUTUAL FUNDS

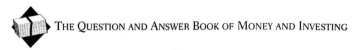

that markets itself directly to investors, you will contact the fund as directed in its prospectus and literature. In both cases, you will receive a confirmation of your transaction from the fund, your broker, or both (see Illustrations 9-4 and 9-5). Once a mutual fund account is open, you can usually make further investments by mailing a check to the fund or contacting the fund or your broker.

Illustration 9-3
Mutual Fund Quote Example

MUTUAL FUND QUOTATIONS

	Inv. Obj.	NAV	Offer Price	NAV Chg.	YTD	39 wks	5 yrs R
FLInsA p	MFL	8.88	9.30	...	-10.2	- 5.9	NS..
GrowthA p	GRO	11.67	12.38	-0.01	- 0.1	- 5.4	NS..
GrIncA p	G&I	11.49	12.03	+0.03	- 0.4	- 3.1	+7.5D
IntlGrA p	ITL	10.47	10.96	+0.03	- 1.8	- 4.4	NS..
NatMuA p	GLM	10.34	10.83	-0.01	- 7.7	- 4.5	NS..
STGIA p	WBD	2.25	2.33	-0.03	- 1.2	- 1.3	NS..
STHIQtA p	BST	2.30	2.38	-0.02	- 2.3	NA	NS..
USGovA p	MTG	9.11	9.54	-0.02	- 6.2	- 4.8	+5.9D
SIFE Trust	SEC	3.61	NA	-0.03	- 1.7	- 4.6	+11.3B
Skyline Fds:							
Europe	ITL	9.57	9.57	...	-13.9	-12.7	NS..
SpEquit r	SML	15.23e	15.23	-1.84	- 3.7	- 8.3	+18.2A
SpEquitII	MID	10.01v	10.01	-0.42	- 2.8	- 5.9	NS..
Smith Barney A:							
AdiGvA p	BST	9.73	9.73	-0.01	+ 2.2	+ 1.6	NS..
AgGrA p	CAP	26.14	27.52	+0.34	- 2.5	- 5.7	+10.6B
ApprA p	GRO	10.90	11.47	...	- 1.0	- 2.7	+8.1D
AzMuA p	SSM	9.34	9.73	-0.01	- 6.8	- 3.4	+6.4B
CapApA	CAP	13.24	13.94	-0.04	- 8.7	-14.1	NS..
ConvA	S&B	13.74	14.46	+0.01	- 6.1	NA	NS..
TelGA p	SEC	11.82	12.44	-0.07	- 8.1	- 5.4	+10.1B
TelIn	SEC	101.58	101.58	-0.11	- 1.2	+ 1.7	+6.1C
CaMuA p	MCA	14.37	14.97	-0.01	- 7.2	- 5.6	+6.1B
DvsInA	BND	7.50	7.85	...	- 3.2	- 3.0	NS..
EurpA	ITL	13.91	14.64	+0.02	- 3.9	NA	NS..
FdValA p	GRO	6.98	7.35	+0.01	+ 1.0	- 3.3	+11.5A
GlBdA	WBD	15.23	15.95	...	- 2.4	NA	NS..
GlGvtA	WBD	11.62	12.17	-0.01	- 4.0	- 3.0	NS..
GlOpA p	WOR	27.60	29.05	-0.07	- 5.1	- 9.0	+1.4E
GvScA	MTG	9.18	9.61	...	- 2.8	NA	NS..
GrInA p	G&I	9.54	10.04	+0.01	- 4.6	- 5.2	NS..
HiIncA t	BHI	10.53	11.03	+0.02	- 4.8	- 6.0	NS..
IncGrA p	G&I	12.29	12.94	+0.01	- 4.4	- 4.5	+6.8E
IncRetA	BST	9.36	9.55	...	+ 2.0	+ 1.9	+6.4B
IntCAA	IDM	7.80	7.96	...	- 5.2	- 2.5	NS..
IntNYA	IDM	7.88	8.04	-0.01	- 4.4	- 2.0	NS..
IntlA	ITL	16.93	17.82	-0.15	- 9.5	- 6.6	+11.8A
InvGdA	BND	10.98	11.50	-0.04	- 9.1	NA	NS..
LtdMuA p	STM	7.95	8.11	-0.01	- 0.3	+ 0.5	NS..
LtdTrA p	BST	7.08	7.22	-0.01	- 5.1	- 3.1	NS..
MgGvA p	MTG	12.08	12.65	...	- 1.9	- 0.5	+7.7A
MgMuA p	GLM	14.61	15.22	-0.01	- 5.1	- 3.8	+7.7A
MaMuA p	DMA	11.59	12.07	-0.02	- 8.8	- 5.2	+6.0E
MoGvtA	MTG	11.82	12.38	-0.02	- 1.7	- 1.1	+7.2A
MuCalA	MCA	11.55	12.03	...	- 6.1	- 3.4	+6.7A
MuFI A	MFL	12.15	12.66	...	- 5.8	- 3.4	NS..
MuLtd A	IDM	6.35	6.48	...	- 1.7	- 0.2	+6.4A
MunNtA	GLM	12.54	13.06	...	- 6.3	- 3.8	+7.3A
MuNJ A	MNJ	12.53	13.05	+0.01	- 6.7	- 3.7	NS..
MuNY A	DNY	12.08	12.58	-0.01	- 6.5	- 4.0	+7.1A
NiMuA p	MNJ	11.89	12.39	-0.01	- 7.6	- 4.4	+6.8A
NyMuA p	DNY	15.45	16.09	-0.01	- 7.3	- 4.5	+6.1C
PrMtA p	SEC	18.79	19.78	-0.06	-12.3	-11.5	+1.0D
PrTRA	G&I	15.17	15.97	-0.01	+ 3.0	+ 0.2	NS..
PrnRtA	S&B	9.43	9.43	...	- 0.4	- 0.8	+7.6D
PrinIIA p	S&B	7.78	7.78	-0.01	- 4.1	- 3.4	NS..
PrinIIIA p	S&B	8.35	8.35	+0.10	+ 0.8	+ 1.6	NS..
SHTSY	BST	3.91	3.91	-0.01	- 1.8	- 1.0	NS..
SpEqA p	SML	18.27	19.23	+0.08	- 9.7	-13.0	NS..
StrInA	S&B	15.99	16.83	-0.01	- 1.3	NA	NS..
TxExA	GLM	16.27	16.95	-0.01	- 6.5	NA	NS..
USGvtA	MTG	12.46	13.05	-0.03	- 1.8	- 1.1	+7.3A
UtltyA p	SEC	11.35	11.95	-0.02	- 8.7	- 6.5	NS..
UtilA	SEC	12.85	13.53	...	- 9.2	- 4.9	NS..
Smith Barney B:							
AgGrB t	CAP	25.75	25.75	+0.34	- 3.2	- 6.2	NS..
ApprB t	GRO	10.81	10.81	+0.01	- 1.3	- 2.8	NS..
CaMuB t	MCA	14.37	14.37	-0.01	- 7.7	- 6.0	NS..
ConvB t	S&B	13.74	13.74	+0.01	- 6.5	- 6.6	+6.6D
DvsInB t	BND	7.50	7.50	...	- 3.7	- 3.4	NS..
EurpB t	ITL	13.75	13.75	+0.03	- 4.6	- 5.1	+2.5D
FLMuB	MFL	9.11	9.11	...	- 9.1	- 5.8	NS..
FdValB t	GRO	6.98	6.98	+0.01	+ 0.4	- 4.0	NS..
GlBdB t	WBD	15.23	15.23	...	- 2.9	- 0.4	+7.8C
GlOpB t	WOR	27.13	27.13	-0.08	- 6.0	- 9.7	NS..
GrInB t	G&I	9.56	9.56	+0.01	- 5.0	- 5.4	NS..
GvScB t	MTG	9.18	9.18	...	- 3.3	- 1.5	+6.9B
HiIncB t	BHI	10.53	10.53	+0.02	- 5.3	- 6.4	+9.3D
InvGdB t	BND	10.98	10.98	-0.04	- 9.5	- 6.5	+7.9B
MgGvB t	MTG	12.08	12.08	...	- 2.4	- 1.0	NS..
MgMuB t	GLM	14.61	14.61	-0.01	- 5.6	- 4.2	NS..
MaMuB t	DMA	11.59	11.59	-0.02	- 9.2	NA	NS..
NiMuB t	MNJ	11.89	11.89	-0.01	- 8.1	- 4.8	NS..
NyMuB t	DNY	15.45	15.45	-0.01	- 7.8	- 4.9	NS..
CapAcc	S&B	14.50	14.50	-0.05	+ 2.1	- 2.4	NS..
DevMkt p	ITL	13.39	14.21	-0.16	- 8.8	- 7.9	NS..
Forgn p	ITL	8.79	9.33	-0.04	- 0.0	- 2.5	+9.9A
GlInfra	WOR	9.73	10.32	-0.02	NS	NS	NS..
GlbOp p	WOR	11.74	12.46	-0.04	- 4.9	- 5.8	NS..
Grwth p	WOR	16.17	17.16	-0.07	+ 0.4	- 2.6	+11.3A
Incom p	WBD	8.81	9.20	-0.01	- 3.7	- 2.9	+6.8D
RIEst p	SEC	12.50	13.26	-0.05	- 7.6	- 9.3	+8.5C
SmalCo p	WOR	7.30	7.75	-0.04	- 6.3	-10.5	+9.1B
World p	WOR	14.13	14.99	-0.05	+ 0.6	- 3.1	+9.3A
Templeton Instit:							
EmMS	ITL	11.17	11.17	-0.19	-11.7	- 9.9	NS..
ForEqS	ITL	12.77	12.77	-0.06	- 0.5	- 3.7	NS..
FEsafS	ITL	8.04	8.04	-0.03	- 3.0	- 3.0	NS..
GrwthS	WOR	10.86	10.86	-0.03	- 2.0	- 4.5	NS..
ThirdAve	SEC	17.20	18.01	-0.08	- 2.4	- 3.4	NS..
Thornburg Fds:							
IntMu	IDM	12.43	12.88	...	- 2.9	- 1.2	NS..
LtdCal	STM	12.13	12.44	...	- 2.3	- 1.4	+5.5B
LtdGv p	BST	11.80	12.10	-0.02	- 2.2	- 1.5	+6.4B
LtMu p	STM	12.90	13.23	...	- 1.8	- 0.8	+5.9A
LtdTIn	BST	11.39	11.68	-0.02	- 3.0	- 2.3	NS..
NM Int	IDM	12.47	12.92	-0.01	- 2.3	- 0.9	NS..
TocquevilleFd	GRO	11.56	11.56	-0.03	- 1.0	- 3.8	+10.3B
Tower Funds:							
CapAp	G&I	12.96	13.36	-0.01	- 2.7	- 3.9	+7.9D
LA Mun	SSM	10.26	10.58	...	- 5.2	- 2.9	+6.6B
TotalRet	BIN	9.43	9.72	-0.02	- 2.9	- 1.6	NS..
US Gv	MTG	9.60	9.90	-0.02	- 3.5	- 2.1	+6.5C
Trademark Funds:							
Equity	GRO	10.30	NL	+0.01	+ 0.5	+ 0.1	NS..
GovtInc	BIN	8.93	NL	-0.03	- 5.4	- 3.4	NS..
KYMun	ITL	9.00	NL	-0.01	- 6.2	- 3.8	NS..
SI Govt	BST	9.08	NL	-0.02	- 2.5	- 1.4	NS..
Transamerica:							
AdiGvA	BST	9.66	10.01	-0.01	+ 1.0	+ 0.8	NS..
CapGrA p	GRO	11.14	11.82	...	-12.0	-16.1	+5.8E
CATFA p	MCA	9.24	9.70	-0.01	- 9.9	- 6.7	+5.9C
CATFB	MCA	9.24	9.24	-0.01	-10.5	- 7.3	NS..
EmGA p	SML	25.15	26.68	+0.08	- 3.8	- 8.9	NS..
EmGB t	SML	24.39	24.39	+0.07	- 4.5	- 9.4	+14.5B
GlbRsB t	SEC	14.05	14.05	-0.15	-11.0	-10.9	+3.4D
GvInc t	MTG	8.68	8.68	-0.02	- 5.3	- 3.5	+5.4E
GvInvTr p	MTG	7.50	7.87	-0.02	- 4.1	- 2.4	+6.1D
GvSec p	MTG	7.39	7.76	-0.01	- 4.1	- 2.7	+6.7C
GrInA p	G&I	10.68	11.33	-0.01	- 8.8	- 8.1	+7.5D
GrInB t	G&I	10.69	10.69	-0.02	- 9.5	- 8.7	NS..
HiYldB t	BHI	6.97	6.97	...	- 6.6	- 8.6	+9.7D
HYTF t	HYM	8.68	8.68	...	- 6.0	- 4.7	+5.8D
InvQA p	BND	8.05	8.45	-0.03	- 6.0	- 3.9	+6.5E
TFBd A	GLM	9.33	9.80	-0.01	-10.0	- 6.7	NS..
TFBdB t	GLM	9.33	9.33	-0.01	-10.7	- 7.3	NS..
Tr for Credit Unions:							
GSP	BST	9.65	9.65	-0.01	+ 1.9	+ 1.4	NS..
MSP	BST	9.45	9.45	-0.02	+ 0.7	+ 0.8	NS..
TMP1996	BND	9.43	9.43	-0.02	+ 0.7	+ 0.7	NS..
TFEB97	BND	9.45	9.45	-0.02	NS	NA	NS..
TMay97		9.71	9.71	-0.01	NA	NA	NA..
TurnerGrEq	CAP	11.85	11.85	...	- 7.5	- 8.6	NS..
TweedyAmerVal	GRO	9.83	NL	-0.02	- 1.1	NA	NS..
TweedyGlVal	WOR	12.01	NL	+0.03	+ 4.1	- 4.3	NS..
20th Century:							
BalInv	S&B	15.18	NL	...	- 0.7	- 4.5	+8.7B
EqInc		4.95	NL	...	NA	NA	NA..
Gift	SML	18.30	NL	+0.12	+11.1	+ 4.2	+22.9A
Grwth	GRO	18.54	NL	-0.07	- 2.5	- 8.8	+10.0B
HerInv	GRO	9.22	NL	+0.04	- 7.6	-10.7	+9.4C
IntlEmGr	ITL	5.29	NL	...	NS	NS	NS..
IntlEq	ITL	6.69	NL	...	- 5.7	- 6.7	NS..
LTBnd	BND	8.86	NL	-0.02	- 4.6	- 2.8	+6.5E
Select	G&I	32.90	NL	-0.02	- 8.6	- 9.6	+6.3E
TxEIn	IDM	9.86	NL	-0.01	- 2.4	- 0.5	+6.0C
TxELT	GLM	9.61	NL	...	- 6.0	- 3.0	+6.2C
TxEST	STM	9.93	NL	...	+ 2.3	+ 2.2	NS..
Ultra	MID	19.64	NL	+0.12	- 5.1	-11.4	+19.9A
USGvShT	BST	9.17	NL	-0.01	- 0.5	+ 0.1	+5.3D
Value	G&I	4.91	NL	+0.01	+ 3.8	+ 2.6	NS..
Vista	MID	10.50	NL	+0.06	+ 2.5	- 1.2	+10.3D
USAA Group:							
AgvGt	SML	15.18	NL	+0.28	- 3.0	- 5.1	+8.3D
Balan	S&B	11.74	NL	-0.01	- 2.9	- 2.5	+6.3E
CA Bd	MCA	9.33	NL	...	- 9.8	- 6.5	+5.8D
Cornst	S&B	21.36	NL	+0.02	- 2.0	- 3.2	+6.6D
GNMA	MTG	9.56	NL	-0.03	- 0.3	+ 0.4	NS..
Gold	SEC	8.21	NL	-0.04	-13.4	- 9.1	-2.9E

Illustration 9-4

Redemption Confirmation

DAILY CONFIRMATION

MANAGED MONEY FUND-A

MANAGED MONEY FUND
P.O. BOX 0005, BOSTON, MA 02146
1-800-555-5555

Representative: Victor L. Harper
Rep No.: MK50

Confirmation Date: 08-02-94
Account No: 556-97706919

Scott & Stringfellow, Inc.
909 E. Main Street
Richmond, VA 23213

John P. Investor
1500 Investment Road
Richmond, VA 23213

Confirmation of Transactions

DATE	TRANSACTION	DOLLAR AMOUNT	FEE	TAX WITH-HELD	PRICE	NO. OF SHARES	TOTAL SHARES
	Beginning Balance						1368.426
7/7	Reinvested Income Dividend	46.49			6.40	7,264	1375.690
7/26	Redeemed through dealer	845.00			6.40	132.031	1243.659

Summary of Account

INCOME DIVIDENDS PAID THIS YEAR	GAINS/OTHER PAID THIS YEAR	SHARES ON DEPOSIT	CERTIFICATE SHARES	TOTAL SHARES YOU OWN
275.10	0.00	1,243.659	0.00	1,243.659

Dividend Option: Reinvest
Capital Gain Option: Reinvest

Agent: Managed Money Service Center, P.O. Box 0005, Boston, MA 02146

Additional Investment - Address Change

Please use this section to make additional investments or address changes to your account. Indicate the fund name and account number on your check.

John P. Investor	Managed Money Fd-A	Tax Year .....
1500 Investment Road	Acct: 556-97706919	Rep #: MK50
Richmond, VA 23213	Tax ID: 005-05-0005	Rep Name: Victor L. Harper
	Amount Enclosed: $.........	
	Minimum Investment $50.00	

Please verify all information to be correct. (1-800-555-5555)

MUTUAL FUNDS

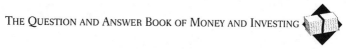

Illustration 9-5

Purchase Confirmation

DAILY CONFIRMATION

MANAGED MONEY FUND
P.O. BOX 0005, BOSTON, MA 02146
1-800-555-5555

MANAGED MONEY FUND-B

Representative: Victor L. Harper
Rep No.: MK50

Confirmation Date: 06-22-94
Account No: 555-97706808

Scott & Stringfellow, Inc.
909 E. Main Street
Richmond, VA 23213

Susan Q. Investor
1500 Investment Road
Richmond, VA 23213

Confirmation of Transactions

DATE	TRANSACTION	DOLLAR AMOUNT	FEE	TAX WITH-HELD	PRICE	NO. OF SHARES	TOTAL SHARES
	Beginning Balance						0.00
6-14	Purchase through dealer	50003.72			6.76	7397.00	7397.00

Summary of Account

INCOME DIVIDENDS PAID THIS YEAR	GAINS/OTHER PAID THIS YEAR	SHARES ON DEPOSIT	CERTIFICATE SHARES	TOTAL SHARES YOU OWN
0.00	0.00	7,397.000	0.00	7,397.000

Dividend Option: Cash
Capital Gain Option: Reinvest

Agent: Managed Money Service Center, P.O. Box 0005, Boston, MA 02146

Additional Investment - Address Change

Please use this section to make additional investments or address changes to your account. Indicate the fund name and account number on your check.

Susan Q. Investor
1500 Investment Road
Richmond, VA 23213

Managed Money Fd-B
Acct: 555-97706808
Tax ID: 001-01-0001
Amount Enclosed: $.........
Minimum Investment $50.00

Tax Year .....
Rep #: MK50
Rep Name: Victor L. Harper

Please verify all information to be correct. (1-800-555-5555)

MUTUAL FUNDS

Q: How can I keep track of my mutual fund's progress?

A: Mutual fund prices are quoted in the financial media on a daily basis. Prices of closed-end fund shares will be included in the stock quote section of newspapers. Open-end fund quotes have a separate section and a somewhat different format. The fund quotes are grouped together with the other funds in their family of funds. You may also call your broker or the fund directly for information such as current value, yield, and performance. Most mutual funds have toll-free telephone numbers for your convenience.

In addition, you will receive regular statements from your mutual fund and/or your broker. The statements will report any purchases, liquidations, or distributions that took place in your account during the period and will provide a cumulative total of the shares you own. It is important for you to keep these statements for your records, since they contain the cost basis information on any shares you bought during the period. You may need the information they contain at a future date for income tax purposes. This is particularly true if you are continually reinvesting your income and/or capital gains distributions into more shares.

Q: Will I receive a certificate for my mutual fund investment?

A: Generally, mutual fund shares are held at the fund on your behalf. However, most funds will send you a certificate if you specifically request it.

Q: How do I measure my mutual fund's performance?

A: Mutual funds use various methods to measure their performance, but as with direct stock and bond investments, the most common measurement is total return. The total return of your fund consists of the income distributions you receive and the capital gains you achieve from capital gains distributions plus or minus the change in the value of your mutual fund shares.

Q: How do I sell my mutual fund investment?

A: The way you sell your mutual fund shares is similar in principle to the way you bought your shares. With closed-end shares, the procedure is the same as that for selling any stock.

With open-end funds, you are selling shares back to the fund itself at NAV, either directly or through your broker. Although some mutual fund companies accept telephone instructions, you will generally need to send a letter of authorization requesting either a full or partial liquidation of your mutual fund account (see Illustration 9-6).

Illustration 9-6
Redemption Letter

1500 Investment Road
Richmond, VA 23213

August 24, 1994

High Income Bond Fund
P.O. Box 8888
Boston, MA 02468

RE: Account Number: 2516789
Fund Number: 307
Susan Q. Investor
Social Security Number: 100-01-0001

Gentlemen:

Please consider this letter a market order to liquidate all full and fractional shares in the above referenced account. Please mail a check for the proceeds to the address of record.

Enclosed is a stock power signed by me as registered owner and signature guaranteed by Scott & Stringfellow, Inc., members of the New York Stock Exchange.

If you need any further information, please call Victor Harper or Sarah Dale at Scott & Stringfellow, (800-446-7075).

Thank you for your help.

Sincerely,
Susan Q. Investor

Q: How are mutual fund investments taxed?

A: Generally, income and capital gains distributed from your mutual fund investment will be taxed in much the same way as those from other investments. Tax regulations require your mutual fund to distribute at least 90 percent of its taxable income. You will pay income taxes on income distributions (even if you are reinvesting them) unless your fund invests in tax-free securities such as municipal bonds. Your income distributions may include short-term gains from sales of securities in the mutual fund's portfolio.

You will pay capital gains taxes if:

- Your fund makes a capital gains distribution to you.
- You sell some or all of your mutual fund shares for a gain.

Your fund will distribute capital gains when it sells securities from its portfolio and makes a net profit. You should report all capital gains distributions as long-term capital gains, regardless of how long you have owned your mutual fund shares.

If you sell shares in your mutual fund for more than you paid for them, you will pay taxes on the gains. Calculating the gains may be complicated if you have purchased shares at different times and at different prices (for example, by reinvesting your dividend and capital gains distributions). If you incur losses instead of gains, you may be eligible for a deduction from taxable income. Consult your tax advisor for methods of reporting such gains and/or losses.

Note of Caution: Beware of purchasing mutual fund shares shortly before December. Since many mutual funds make their capital gains distributions in December, you could find yourself liable for taxes on the full year's gains even though you just purchased your shares.

Q: Do some older mutual funds have a large potential capital gain because of unrealized profits in the portfolio?

A: Yes. The amount of unrealized profits (potential capital gains) is usually disclosed in the prospectus.

SUMMARY

Mutual funds have become a popular and successful investment alternative. Investors may turn to mutual funds rather than selecting and monitoring individual securities. There are thousands of mutual funds and many types of funds from which to choose, and the choices can be quite intimidating.

This chapter should help you understand more about mutual funds and make you more comfortable in approaching mutual funds as an investment alternative. We have discussed the features of mutual funds, sources of information available, and the importance of matching your investment objectives when choosing a fund. Careful consideration of the issues discussed in this chapter may guide you to the appropriate mutual funds for your investment strategy.

MUTUAL FUNDS

Chapter 10

Insurance and Annuities

Insurance protects you and your family against possible financial losses due to property damage, illness, injury, or death. The risk of such losses has led people to seek protection for hundreds of years. Insurance allows the purchaser to transfer this risk to an insurer.

There are many different types of insurance protecting against many different types of risks, and entire books have been written about each type of insurance. Given our emphasis on investments, we will focus on the types of insurance—varieties of life insurance and annuities—that may assist you in building wealth. The investment characteristics of some forms of life insurance and annuities have made them popular investment alternatives.

Q: How does insurance work?

A: Insurance is a method of managing and shifting risk. You constantly assume risks in your daily life, most of which you accept because their consequences would be minor or avoidable. If you identify a risk that would have a measurable, significant economic impact, you may seek to avoid or shift the risk by obtaining insurance.

To obtain insurance, you fill out an application and, when your application is accepted, you sign an agreement, called a *policy*, with an insurance company. You agree to pay fees, called *premiums*, to the insurance company, which agrees to pay a specified amount, called the amount of *coverage*, if the loss you are insuring against occurs.

When it accepts your premiums and those of others, the insurance company is counting on being able to predict the likelihood, on average, of the various losses occurring. It does so by combining your risk with the similar risks of a large number of people. The insurer studies the past experience of similar groups, calculates the frequency with which it will have to pay off, and sets its premiums at a level that will enable it to do so. If losses occur more frequently than predicted, the insurance company loses money and will usually raise future premiums.

Q: What is life insurance?

A: Life insurance is a type of insurance that protects against the financial consequences of loss of life. Life insurance allows you to create an instant estate in case of your untimely death.

If you are the principal income earner in your household, for instance, your death would cause major financial hardship for your family. It would cause similar hardship for your business partners, your mortgage holder, or any number of other people with an economic interest in your survival. To protect against this financial hardship, you could purchase a life insurance policy that would pay a stipulated amount that you believe would be needed in the event of your death.

Many life insurance policies include investment features that provide for income tax deferral of cash flow.

Q: How does life insurance work?

A: Life insurance is intended to provide money to cover the financial loss caused by your death. You purchase a policy that will pay the amount that you determine would be needed to meet your financial obligations. The amount of coverage you purchase is called the *face amount* of the policy. If you die, the amount paid is called the *death benefit*.

Q: How does an insurance company determine its premiums?

A: When an insurance company issues you a life insurance policy, it predicts how much longer you will live. By studying population statistics, insurance companies have developed *actuarial tables* that predict the average life expectancy of people with certain characteristics, such as age, sex, and health. Using these actuarial tables, the insurance company can predict the likelihood of its having to pay the death benefit during the period covered by the premium. The premiums are set at a level that will compensate the company for this risk.

Q: Who are the parties to a life insurance policy?

A: There are several parties to a life insurance policy, each with different roles in the policy's benefits and obligations:

- Insurance company
- Insured
- Policy owner
- Premium payer
- Beneficiary

Q: What role does the issuing company play?

A: The *issuing company*, or *insurer*, is the insurance company. The policy creates a contract between you and the insurer. The insurer agrees to provide the death benefit. The insurer also agrees to a number of features concerning payment of premiums, ownership of the policy, value of the policy, and other factors. As with any complex contract, you should closely examine the insurer's rights and obligations as outlined in the policy.

Q: What are the different types of life insurer?

A: There are two major types of insurance companies:

- Mutual companies
- Stock companies

INSURANCE AND ANNUITIES

Q: What are mutual insurance companies?

A: *Mutual insurance companies* are insurance companies that are owned by the policyholders and rely on premiums for capital to support the company. Mutual companies generally charge higher premiums in order to create a pool of money that is sufficient for payment of claims. They return any excess money as dividends to the policyholders. The dividends are a return of overpaid premiums, so they are not considered taxable income to the policyholders.

Q: What are stock insurance companies?

A: *Stock insurance companies* are insurance companies that are owned by shareholders, like any other corporation. They rely on the shareholders for capital to support the company, so their premiums are generally lower than those of a mutual company. On the other hand, stock companies pay dividends to their shareholders, not to the policyholders. Without the dividends to partially offset premiums, stock company policyholders may actually pay more in premiums for their policies.

 Note: In comparing the net cost of insurance policies, you must project the level of future dividends that may be paid by mutual companies. The subject of net cost is very complex and will not be addressed in this book.

Q: What is the role of the insured?

A: The *insured* is the person whose life is covered by a life insurance policy. If you are the insured, it is your age, sex, and health characteristics that are used to determine the premium amounts charged. If the insured dies while the policy is in force, the policy matures and the death benefit is paid.

Q: Can a person automatically get insurance just by paying a stipulated premium?

A: No. The insurance company will review medical and other information on the individual or individuals to be insured to determine whether it wants to assume the risk. The insurance company will not automatically offer a policy to everybody, particularly those with health problems. An individual who obtains insurance protection is said to be *insurable*.

Q: If I have health problems, does that mean I cannot get life insurance protection?

A: Not necessarily. Some individuals with certain health problems may be able to acquire life insurance protection by paying extra premiums. If you are offered life insurance protection for extra premiums, you are said to be *rated*.

Q: Are health problems the only reason an insurance company may decline or rate individuals seeking life insurance protection?

A: No. People who engage in hazardous activities or who are in hazardous professions may have difficulty getting life insurance protection or will be rated.

Q: Can the insured be more than one person?

A: Yes, in some cases you may establish multiple insured parties. Two of the most popular types of such arrangements are joint life and survivor, or second to die.

Q: What are joint life policies?

A: *Joint life policies* name two or more people as the insured parties, with the death benefit payable upon the first death among the insured parties. Most often a joint life policy involves spouses or business partners providing for the security of the survivor.

Q: What are second-to-die policies?

A: *Last survivor policies*, or *second-to-die policies*, pay the death benefit only when the survivor dies. Such policies are popular for several purposes, the primary one being estate settlement for couples.

INSURANCE AND ANNUITIES

Q: What is the role of the policy owner?

A: The *policy owner* is the owner of a life insurance contract (policy). The owner usually pays the premiums and can exercise full control of the policy's rights as outlined in the policy provisions. The owner can usually change the beneficiary, authorize a change of ownership, or cancel (or modify) the policy.

Q: What is the role of the premium payer?

A: The *premium payer* is the party accepting the financial responsibility for making premium payments on an insurance policy. The policy owner is most often the premium payer, but this is not necessarily the case. In some situations, it may be advantageous to separate the two parties. For example, an employer could pay premiums and grant ownership of a policy as an employee benefit. Or, alternatively, grandparents may pay premiums on a policy to benefit a grandchild, but they may wish to place the ownership in their adult child's hands.

Q: What is the role of the beneficiary?

A: The *beneficiary* is the person, business, or organization to which the policy's death benefit will be paid upon the death of the insured. Beneficiaries have no control over the policy and may not even be informed that they have been named as beneficiaries.

The beneficiary may be one person, several people, a trust, a corporation, or some other entity. If the beneficiary dies before the insured, the policyholder may name another beneficiary. Many policies provide for *contingent beneficiaries* to provide an automatic succession in case of a beneficiary's death.

Q: What are the standard provisions of a life insurance policy?

A: Any contract, including an insurance policy, sets forth the rights and duties of the parties. Some complex policies may have numerous provisions, but certain *standard provisions* appear in all policies. Standard provisions include the following:

- Insuring clause
- Owner's rights

- Free look
- Incontestability
- Payment of premiums
- Grace period
- Reinstatement
- Policy loans

Q: What is the insuring clause provision?

A: The *insuring clause* in a life insurance policy establishes the basic contract between the insurer and the insured: that in return for payment of premiums, the insurer agrees to pay the benefits specified in the policy.

Q: What is the owner's rights provision?

A: The *owner's rights provision* establishes the policy owner's entitlement to certain specified powers over the policy and its operation. The specified owner's rights may include the right to:

- Assign or transfer ownership
- Change the policy payment schedule
- Change the beneficiary designation
- Receive dividends or cash value
- Terminate the policy

Q: What is the free look provision?

A: A life insurance policy is required to specify that the owner has a ten-day *free look*. This allows the owner to examine the policy after delivery and have the premium refunded if he or she decides to surrender the policy. Because of the complexity of insurance policies, the owner may need some time after receipt of the policy to understand any inappropriate features. Alternatively, the ten-day period may allow the owner to compare other competing policies and find a better bargain.

Q: What is the incontestability provision?

A: The *incontestability provision* gives the insurer two years from the date of the application to discover any incorrect information, error, or even fraud in the application and use such information to contest payment of a claim. After the two years, the policy becomes incontestable, and even suicide cannot negate a claim to the death benefit.

One exception to the incontestability provision is a misstatement of age. Even though age is central in establishing life expectancy and premiums, the insurer is not allowed to cancel the policy if the insured's age is misstated. Instead, the insurer may adjust the face amount to whatever amount the stated premiums would buy for a person of the insured's actual age.

Q: What is the payment of premiums provision?

A: The *payment of premiums provision* establishes the timing, method, and location requirements for premium payment. The conditions must be stated specifically and clearly for the protection of the owner. All payment of premiums provisions must also state that premiums are payable in advance.

Q: What is the grace period provision?

A: A life insurance policy is required to allow the premium payer a *grace period* of at least thirty-one days after the premium due date before terminating coverage. If the insured dies during the grace period, the death benefit must be paid. The insurer is allowed to charge interest for late premiums during the grace period, and may deduct the late premium and interest from the death benefit if the insured dies during the grace period.

Q: What is the reinstatement provision?

A: If a premium remains unpaid past the grace period and the policy is canceled, the owner has three years in which to apply to *reinstate* the policy. The insurer may require payment of unpaid premiums, charge interest on the past due amounts, and require renewed evidence of insurability (such as a physical exam).

Q: What is the policy loans provision?

A: A policy that provides for a buildup of cash value (see below) will usually allow *policy loans* to the insured. Such loans are based on the cash value balance, and interest is charged. In addition, the insurer may take an automatic loan from the cash value to cover a premium that remains unpaid after the grace period expires.

Q: What are some additional features that are common in life insurance policies?

A: Many insurance policies contain special arrangements that are not among the basic provisions. Such features are called *riders*, since they are attached as extra provisions. Some of the most common riders are:

- Accidental death rider
- Waiver of premium rider
- Guaranteed insurability rider

Q: What is an accidental death rider?

A: An *accidental death rider*, also called the *double indemnity rider*, increases the death benefit if the insured dies of accidental causes. Double indemnity refers to a doubling of the death benefit, but accidental death riders may use other multipliers, such as $1\frac{1}{2}$ times or 3 times coverage (*triple* indemnity).

Q: What is a waiver of premium rider?

A: A *waiver of premium rider* allows the suspension of premiums if the insured becomes disabled. During the disability, the coverage continues in force and the owner continues to enjoy all rights outlined in the policy. Most often, the policy will qualify a waiver if a disability persists for six months. Waiver of premium riders are generally inexpensive and can be quite valuable, so they are quite common.

Q: What is a guaranteed insurability rider?

A: A *guaranteed insurability rider* provides that on certain specified dates or occasions, the insured may purchase additional insurance without having to prove insurability. The occasions may be the insured's reaching a certain age or an event such as marriage or the birth of a child.

INSURANCE AND ANNUITIES

Q: How does life insurance benefit my financial and investment planning?

A: Life insurance can help you achieve your financial goals through death benefits and living benefits.

Q: How do the death benefits affect my financial planning?

A: Most directly, life insurance benefits your financial planning by protecting your heirs from financial hardship in the event of your death. For example, your financial plans most likely include a secure retirement for you and your spouse, a college education for your children, and payment of debts. Such plans would be threatened by your untimely death, but the death benefits provided by life insurance would provide the wealth (cash) needed to accomplish your plans.

Q: How could life insurance provide me living benefits?

A: In addition to protecting your heirs, some forms of life insurance can help you build wealth for future use. With such policies, tax laws allow for a tax-free or tax-deferred buildup of reserves—called *cash value*—within the policy.

Premiums on life insurance policies that accumulate cash value usually remain constant over the life of the policy. Therefore, you usually overpay for the pure life insurance protection in the early years. During the later years of the policy, you usually underpay for the pure protection. Your accumulated cash value assists in balancing out the premium payments. As a policyholder, you own the cash value within the policy. You may cancel the policy at any time and receive the cash value, or you may borrow against the cash value. Therefore, you may choose to use the cash value feature as a savings and investment vehicle to help you achieve your financial goals, such as retirement.

 Note: Appropriate life insurance policies can assist you in achieving your goals—whether for your heirs' protection or for your own future security. It is important that you understand your goals and carefully con-

INSURANCE AND ANNUITIES

sider how much life insurance and which type may be best for you.

A: The amount of insurance protection you need depends on the purpose you intend the policy to serve. The amount needed for some purposes, such as burial expenses, estate taxes, or debt payment, is easy to determine. In other situations, your insurance needs will require more analysis.

If you wish to provide income for your spouse, for instance, you have to calculate the amount of capital needed to produce the desired amount of income.

 Example: You have determined that in the event of your untimely death, your spouse would have the following income:

	Month	Annual
Social Security:	$900	$10,800
Retirement income:	$600	$7,200
Investments:	$400	$4,800
	$1,900	$22,800

You want your spouse to have a monthly income of $4,000, or an additional $2,100 a month or $25,200 a year. If you assume that invested capital could earn 7 percent, you would need $360,000 ($25,200 divided by 0.07) to generate $25,200 a year. So $360,000 is the amount of life insurance protection you would need.

Determining the amount needed for other purposes, such as a business buyout, can be even more complex. If you have such a need, you should get professional advice when deciding how much coverage you should have.

 Note: Estimating the amount of life insurance protection you may want or need can be very complex. You should consult an advisor to assist you in determining your needs.

Q: What are the types of life insurance?

A: Life insurance is a complex topic, with many different variables. Consequently, there are many types of life insurance policies. However, the two most basic types are *term* and *whole life* insurance, and many of the policies currently being offered are just variations or combinations of these. This chapter will focus on some of the major types of life insurance:

- Term life insurance
- Whole life insurance
- Endowment life insurance
- Universal life insurance
- Variable life insurance

Q: What is term life insurance?

A: *Term life insurance*, as its name implies, is a policy with a specific period of time, or *term*, of coverage. The term may be stated in years, such as ten years, or as covering to a certain age, such as age 65. A term policy pays only if the insured dies during the stated term of the policy. Generally, if the insured is still living when the term ends, the policy expires and the policyholder receives nothing in return for the premiums.

Many term policies provide for renewal of the policy for a new term or conversion into another type of insurance. The conversion feature may be especially valuable if the policy can be converted into a whole life policy, as this guarantees permanent *insurability* for the insured.

Generally, term insurance is inexpensive when the insured is young and healthy, since the risk of death is much smaller than when the insured becomes older. Because of its low cost, term insurance is often an excellent way for young families to acquire substantial amounts of protection at rates they can afford. As the insured ages, term insurance gets much more expensive. The cost may become prohibitive for people in their late fifties or older.

Q: What is whole life insurance?

A: *Whole life insurance*, in contrast to term life, is designed to provide coverage for the insured's "whole life" at a fixed premium. The coverage is permanent and cannot be canceled as long as the policyholder continues paying the premiums.

The premiums for a whole life policy are considerably higher than those for term life when the insured is younger, but they do not rise with age as term premiums do. Some whole life policies are designed so that premiums are paid only for a specified number of years until the insured reaches a certain age. Such features allow the policyholder to predict the total amount to be paid.

Q: Why are whole life policy premiums higher?

A: The risk to the insurer for whole life insurance rises as the insured gets older, just as for term life insurance. Since the premiums on a whole life policy remain at a fixed level, the policyholder is paying higher premiums in the early years to avoid having to pay increasing premiums in later years. The higher premiums also pay for the costs of setting up the policy, such as commissions, medical exams, and administration.

In addition, the premiums begin to build the cash value as the insurer invests the funds and credits earnings to the policy. As cash value builds, the policyholder may use it for policy loans or retirement income. If the issuing company is a mutual company, the cash value or dividends may also be used to purchase additional insurance coverage.

Q: How does whole life insurance sometimes serve investment purposes?

A: The cash value feature can give whole life insurance many investment characteristics. Though the cash value is designed as a reserve to support the higher costs of coverage in your later years, as a policyholder you own the cash value.

The cash value within a whole life policy will grow as you pay premiums and as the insurer adds earnings from investing the funds. As the cash value within your policy builds, it may become as important a source of wealth as any other investment.

Q: How could I use a whole life policy for investment purposes?

A: With whole life policies, as with other cash value policies, you may use the cash value in different ways, depending on the provisions of your policy. Among the possible alternatives open to you, you may:

INSURANCE AND ANNUITIES

- Cancel your policy and claim the cash value
- Buy paid-up life insurance
- Transfer your policy's cash value
- Borrow against your cash value

Q: What happens if I cancel a life insurance policy that has cash value?

A: If you cancel your policy, you are entitled to receive the cash value outright. The distributed cash value above and beyond the premiums you paid is considered taxable income. The amount net of taxes will then be freely available for any other purpose.

Q: What happens if I cancel or surrender my life insurance policy, but want to retain some protection?

A: Most life insurance policies that have cash value include a provision that permits you to convert the policy into a certain amount of fully paid life insurance; the amount is determined by the amount of cash value you have accumulated. You should review your policy or consult your advisor to determine the amount of paid-up life insurance you could have if you canceled your policy.

Q: What happens if I want to transfer my cash value?

A: Instead of canceling your policy, you may want to *transfer* your cash value by making a *1035 exchange.* A 1035 exchange, named for the regulation that created it, allows you to transfer the assets in your cash value policy into another insurance policy or into an annuity with another insurance company.

The ability to make a 1035 exchange gives your cash value more mobility. You may be able to move your accumulated cash value into a policy that is more suited to your investment goals or into an annuity, which is more investment-oriented. A 1035 exchange is not considered a withdrawal, so you would avoid any taxation by using this method. However, you should consult your tax advisor before engaging in a 1035 exchange.

Q: If I need cash, can I borrow some of the cash value?

A: Yes. Many policies allow you to take out *policy loans* of up to 90 percent of the cash value and still keep the policy in force. Loan balances are subtracted from your death benefit if you die while the loans are outstanding. Loans are also not considered withdrawals, so no tax would be due on the proceeds. Your life insurance policy will include the terms on which you can take out a policy loan and the rate of interest to be paid. You should consult your tax advisor concerning the deductibility of interest paid on policy loans.

Q: What is the advantage of building cash value in a life insurance policy rather than in other investments?

A: The principal benefit of a cash value life insurance policy is that the earnings and capital accumulation within the policy are tax-deferred. If you choose to build capital in an insurance policy rather than a mutual fund or certificate of deposit, its earnings are not subject to current income taxes. In contrast, earnings accrued in a certificate of deposit or a mutual fund (except one investing in tax-free bonds) are taxed as they are earned.

Since the cash value within an insurance policy is not reduced by income taxes, it will increase faster than the value of a taxable investment earning the same rate of return. After years of tax-deferred compounding, the value of your investment will be much larger. Illustration 10-1 exhibits the advantage of tax-deferred compounding in a cash value life insurance policy.

INSURANCE AND ANNUITIES

Illustration 10-1
Cash Value Life Insurance Policy:
Advantage of Tax-Deferred Compounding

Comparison of compounding results for a taxable investment versus a tax-deferred cash value life insurance policy. Investor contributes $1,500 annually, earns 8%, and pays taxes of 35%.

	Taxable Investment	Policy Cash Value	
Year	Balance	Balance	Difference
1	$1,500	$1,500	$0
2	$3,156	$3,240	$84
3	$4,898	$5,119	$221
4	$6,731	$7,149	$418
5	$8,659	$9,341	$682
6	$10,687	$11,708	$1,021
7	$12,821	$14,265	$1,444
8	$15,065	$17,026	$1,960
9	$17,427	$20,008	$2,581
10	$19,911	$23,228	$3,317
11	$22,524	$26,707	$4,182
12	$25,274	$30,463	$5,189
13	$28,166	$34,520	$6,354
14	$31,209	$38,902	$7,693
15	$34,409	$43,634	$9,225
16	$37,777	$48,745	$10,968
17	$41,319	$54,264	$12,945
18	$45,046	$60,225	$15,180
19	$48,966	$66,663	$17,697
20	$53,090	$73,616	$20,526
21	$57,429	$81,126	$23,697
22	$61,993	$89,236	$27,243
23	$66,795	$97,995	$31,200
24	$71,846	$107,454	$35,608
25	$77,160	$117,671	$40,510
26	$82,751	$128,704	$45,954
27	$88,632	$140,621	$51,989
28	$94,819	$153,490	$58,672
29	$101,327	$167,390	$66,062
30	$108,174	$182,401	$74,227
31	$115,377	$198,613	$83,236
32	$122,955	$216,122	$93,167
33	$130,926	$235,032	$104,105
34	$139,313	$255,454	$116,141
35	$148,135	$277,510	$129,375
36	$157,416	$301,331	$143,915
37	$167,180	$327,058	$159,878
38	$177,451	$354,842	$177,391
39	$188,256	$384,850	$196,593
40	$199,624	$417,258	$217,634

Q: What is a single-premium life insurance policy?

A: A single-premium life insurance policy is a whole life policy in which a certain amount of protection (face value) is purchased from an insurance company with the payment of a single premium. Most such policies have a cash value that will increase income tax-deferred.

Q: Who might be interested in single-premium life insurance policies?

A: People whose circumstances and the purposes for which they have life insurance have changed might be interested in single-premium life insurance policies. Many people purchase life insurance at an early age to provide an instant estate or to protect the financial security of their family in case of their untimely death. Later in life, the proceeds of life insurance are often intended to pay estate taxes rather than to protect one's family. In this case, some of the older life insurance policies may be outdated.

If you are in this situation, you may be able to consolidate the cash value of your policies with 1035 exchanges and acquire a new single-premium life policy. The combined cash value may be enough to acquire a policy that will satisfy your current or anticipated insurance needs.

 Note of Caution: When considering a consolidation of your life insurance policies to acquire a single-premium policy, consult your advisors to make sure you avoid any potential income tax liabilities.

Q: What is endowment life insurance?

A: *Endowment life insurance* pays the face value of the policy either at the insured's death or at a certain date. Unlike whole life, an endowment life insurance policy is designed primarily to provide a *living* benefit and only secondarily to provide life insurance protection. Therefore, it is more of an investment than a whole life policy.

Endowment life is a method of accumulating capital for a specific purpose and protecting this savings program against the saver's premature death. Many investors use endowment life insurance to fund anticipated financial needs, such as college education or retirement. Since endowment life premiums are substantially higher than the same amount of term coverage, one might achieve similar results by purchasing term life insurance and investing the difference. The endowment life premiums, however, force an investment discipline that many people appreciate.

Q: What is universal life insurance?

A: *Universal life insurance* segregates the insurance protection from the investment fund. The policy links a yearly renewable term life insurance contract to an investment fund. The rate of return earned on the investment fund is tied to an interest-rate index or the insurance company's own portfolio return. Thus, a universal life policy provides a wider range of benefits to suit different policyholders.

With a universal life insurance policy, a fixed expense fee (for commissions, administration, etc.) is deducted from premiums, then the balance is deposited into an investment fund. The segregated up-front fee is similar to the load charged by mutual funds. After net premiums are deposited in the fund, investment earnings are credited to the fund and the insurance coverage costs are deducted. As the fund accumulates value, any excess value may be used to increase coverage or reduce future premiums. In addition to its flexible insurance features, universal life can also serve investment purposes.

Q: How could I use universal life for investment purposes?

A: The universal life policy's investment fund was originally designed to provide flexibility of coverage and premiums within the insurance policy. However, the accumulation of value may also be used to achieve other financial goals.

The investment fund often guarantees a minimum interest rate, such as 4 percent. In addition, the fund will earn variable returns above that level, linked to a well-known index such as U.S. Treasury security interest rates. As long as enough balance remains to keep the policy in force, the policyholder may withdraw the cash value or borrow against it for other purposes.

The universal policyholder may thus build capital and have the option of using it for insurance purposes or for broader financial goals, such as retirement.

Note of Caution: If the performance of the investment part of a universal life policy is better than originally projected, more cash value may accumulate than anticipated, and so your future premiums may be reduced. However, if the performance is poorer than projected, you may have to reduce your insurance protection and you will have less cash value accumulation.

Q: What is variable life insurance?

A: *Variable life insurance* is similar to universal life in that it has both insurance features and investment characteristics. Like universal life, variable life segregates the insurance protection from the investment fund. The policyholder's ability to vary coverage and premiums or use the fund for investment purposes will depend on the performance of the investment fund. Beyond these similarities, however, there are some important differences.

Q: What is the difference between universal life and variable life policies?

A: As its name implies, variable life invests the policyholder's funds in investments, such as common stocks. This contrasts sharply with universal life's interest rate-based returns. A variable life policy may thus experience greater risks and returns than are typical of universal life policies.

Because of the higher risks involved, the policyholder's investment fund is further segregated into a *separate account*, apart from other policyholders' funds. The separate account protects the policyholder's funds from any financial problems in other separate accounts or in the company in general.

Q: How could I use a variable life insurance policy for investment purposes?

A: Although it is designed primarily to provide life insurance protection, variable life insurance is quite clearly investment-oriented in its features. The potentially rapid accumulation of value can create substantial funds beyond those needed for insurance purposes. The policyholder has access to these funds via withdrawal or borrowing. The excess value is thus available for general investment purposes.

The investment orientation is also evident in other features of variable life policies. Some policies resemble mutual fund "families" in that they offer a wide range of investment alternatives. The fee structure of many policies also mirrors that of the mutual fund industry, as the buyer has the choice of *front-end* or *back-end loads* (commissions).

Investors are attracted to variable life because of these features. A policy may become merely an extension of the investor's financial plan for retirement security.

 Note of Caution: As with a universal life insurance policy, your amount of protection, future premium payments, and cash value accumulation may be greatly affected by the performance of the investment part of the policy.

Q: What is an annuity?

A: An *annuity* is a contract with an insurance company under which the owner pays a premium and expects to receive a payment or a stream of payments that is directly tied to that premium plus accrued earnings. Most people now think of an annuity more as an investment than as an insurance policy. Unlike traditional life insurance, where the primary purpose is to provide a death benefit, annuities are specifically designed to provide wealth during your lifetime. They provide a death benefit, but the amount is generally limited to the investor's premiums plus any accumulated earnings.

Q: How could an annuity benefit me?

A: The principal benefit of an annuity is that it provides you with deferral of taxes on earnings and capital appreciation. The advantages of its tax-deferred compounding are similar to those of traditional cash value life insurance policies (see Illustration 10-1 on page 264).

An annuity may help you to achieve your long-term financial goals more quickly or completely by accelerating the growth of your capital. You must pay taxes on the earnings when money is paid out by your annuity, but the years of tax-deferred compounding still result in a larger after-tax value than would be available with taxable investments such as mutual funds.

Q: How is an annuity similar to an IRA or qualified retirement plan?

A: An annuity's ability to provide for long-term tax-deferred capital accumulation makes it similar to an IRA or qualified retirement plan. Since annuity contributions are not tax-deductible or made on a pretax basis, they are similar to non-deductible IRA contributions (except that there is no dollar maximum limit).

Also as with retirement plans, withdrawals from an annuity will be taxed as income. The exception to that rule (as with nondeductible IRAs) is that the original amount invested will not be taxed upon withdrawal.

Q: Is there a tax penalty if I withdraw money from an annuity before age 59¹/₂?

A: Tax laws discourage withdrawing money from an annuity before age 59¹/₂. Withdrawals before that age may be subject to a 10 percent penalty in addition to being taxed as ordinary income. However, there are provisions in the tax code that may allow you to withdraw from your annuity before age 59¹/₂ without a penalty. If you want to do so, you should consult your tax advisor.

Q: How does an annuity work?

A: The basic functioning of an annuity is fairly straightforward. You make premium deposits—either a single one or several over time—and choose a type of investment from the alternatives offered by the insurance company sponsoring the annuity. The earnings from your investment compound tax-deferred until withdrawal. This is often referred to as the *accumulation phase*. The *withdrawal phase* begins when you decide, usually at retirement, to begin distributions from an annuity account.

Q: Who are the parties to an annuity account?

A: As with a traditional insurance policy, there are several parties to an annuity contract. The parties to an annuity contract are:

- Insurance company
- Owner
- Annuitant
- Beneficiary

Q: What is the role of the insurance company in an annuity contract?

A: An annuity is a life insurance policy, and thus it is a contract between you and the *insurance company*. Just like a traditional insurance policy, the annuity contract contains a number of provisions specifying what the insurance company must do. These may include investing your funds as you indicate, allowing you to make withdrawals under certain conditions, and providing a death benefit, among others. You should understand the provisions in an annuity contract and their implications for you before you place your money in it. Also, as with any insurance policy, you must carefully consider the strength of the insurance company—its ability to provide the returns and fulfill its obligations under the contract.

Q: When I sign an annuity application and send money to the insurance company, am I obligated?

A: No. You generally have ten days from the date you receive the contract to review the policy. Within the ten days, you can rescind the policy and get your money back.

Q: What is the role of the contract owner?

A: The *contract owner* is the owner of an annuity policy. If you are the owner, you control the annuity contract. You control any deposits or withdrawals, any investment decisions, any changes in the annuitant or beneficiary, or cancellation of the contract. You can own the contract in your name alone or jointly with your spouse. You may also give or will the contract to another person, a trust, a corporation, or a partnership, as you choose. The contract is your property, and will pass to your heirs if you die while the contract is in force. Many annuity contract owners name a *contingent owner* who will contractually become the owner upon the death of the original owner. The value of your annuity contract will be included in your estate. For estate tax implications, see page 280.

Q: What is the role of the annuitant?

A: The *annuitant* is the person whose age, sex, and other characteristics are used to calculate the annuity payments when the owner decides to begin the withdrawal phase (annuitization). The annuitant is in a similar position to the insured person in a life insurance policy. His or her agreement is required to establish an annuity, but the annuitant has no authority to make deposits, withdrawals, or changes to the contract unless he or she is also the owner. An annuitant can be the owner, a family member, a friend, or a colleague. Generally, the person an annuity owner selects as an annuitant will be determined by their annuitization strategy or investment goals. The only requirement for an annuitant is that he or she must be under the insurance company's maximum allowable age (generally seventy to eighty years old).

Upon the death of the annuitant, the contract is terminated and the death benefit is distributed to the beneficiary, who may or may not be the owner. In practice, if you are establishing an annuity contract to provide for your retirement years, most likely you would designate yourself (and/or your spouse) as owner and annuitant.

INSURANCE AND ANNUITIES

Q: What is the role of the beneficiary?

A: The *beneficiary* of an annuity contract has the same role as the beneficiary of a life insurance policy. The beneficiary receives the death benefit when the annuitant dies. The beneficiary has no authority to control or change the annuity contract. The owner doesn't even have to ask the beneficiary's permission or inform the beneficiary that he or she has been named. If the beneficiary dies before the annuitant, the owner will need to name another beneficiary. Many contracts provide for naming a *contingent beneficiary* in case the annuitant survives the beneficiary.

Q: Why might I select an annuitant who is not the owner of an annuity contract?

A: Any investment should be structured to serve your financial strategy, and the annuity offers flexibility to help you in doing so. In some situations, you may choose to be the owner and not the annuitant. For example, if you are beyond the insurance company's maximum age for an annuitant, you will need to select another person as annuitant.

In other situations, you may choose to be the annuitant, but not the owner. For example, you may be trying to remove assets from your estate in order to reduce future estate taxes. As another example, if you are a grandparent providing funds for a newborn grandchild's future education, you may wish to be the annuitant, make your grandchild the beneficiary, and make the parent (your child) the owner. This would remove the contract value from your estate, benefit your grandchild, and place control in the parents' hands to ensure that the funds are managed properly.

 Note: Determining who should be the owner, annuitant, or beneficiary may involve both investment strategy and estate planning considerations. When establishing an annuity contract, carefully consider your choices of annuitant and beneficiary. If you already own an annuity contract, you may want to review your choices of annuitant and beneficiary periodically to make sure the contract continues to meet your changing needs. You should consult your investment and tax advisors when making these decisions.

Q: What are the different types of annuity contracts?

A: There are two major types of annuity contracts:

- Fixed annuities
- Variable annuities

The types may also be used in combinations, or *"split"* annuity form, to meet certain investment goals.

Q: What are fixed annuities?

A: *Fixed annuities* offer a specified rate of return for a specified period of time. For example, a fixed annuity might guarantee you a rate of 4.25 percent for a year or 5.5 percent for three years. When the contract term expires, the insurance company will offer a new rate for another specified term. At that time, you may withdraw the balance or leave it in the account and accept the new rate. If you withdraw the value of your annuity, the earnings are taxable income and some early withdrawal income tax penalties may be payable.

The financial strength of the company making the *guarantee* is very important to you in a fixed annuity. As the owner of a fixed annuity, you do not have a segregated account; you are a general creditor of the insurance company. Therefore, the guarantee is only as solid as the insurance company. You must rely on the company's financial stability to back up its guarantee of your principal and accumulated earnings. If the company were to fail, you could lose your money.

Q: What are variable annuities?

A: *Variable annuities* generally do not offer a fixed rate of return on your investment. Instead, they offer a number of investment accounts into which you can place your premium deposits. You may select accounts that invest in stocks, bonds, international securities, or other alternatives.

Like the investment alternatives available with variable insurance policies, variable annuity accounts can resemble mutual fund families in their variety and ease of switching between accounts. They are also like mutual funds in that the account value will rise or fall according to the market performance of the underlying investments. This feature is what

INSURANCE AND ANNUITIES

gives the variable annuity its name. Variable annuities remove the comfort of a guaranteed, fixed return and can expose you to greater investment risks, but they also allow you more investment control and potentially greater returns.

The insurance company places variable annuity deposits into a segregated account in your name. This protects your accumulated value regardless of what happens to the insurance company. Also, the insurance company will often guarantee that the death benefit will not decline below your initial investment and will increase this guarantee periodically as the value of your account increases. Some variable annuities have begun offering a specified rate of increase in the death benefit—say 5 percent per year.

Q: Are there other classifications of annuities?

A: Yes. Annuities may also be classified as:

- Immediate annuities
- Deferred annuities

Q: What are immediate annuities?

A: *Immediate annuities* do not have an accumulation period. Withdrawals begin as soon as the contract is established. Immediate annuities are appropriate if you wish to begin receiving income from your deposits immediately. You may select an immediate annuity instead of, say, a bond because the annuity guarantees you an income as long as you live. Alternatively, you could use an immediate annuity to fund a specific period of financial need, such as four years of college for a family member. Immediate annuities are also often used to guarantee payment of financial agreements such as court settlements and business purchases.

Q: What are deferred annuities?

A: *Deferred annuities* are designed to accept premium deposits, to compound the investment earnings over time, and to pay out the proceeds at a future date. They are appropriate if you are attempting to accumulate wealth for a future need, such as retirement, and do not need the money or income now.

Deferred annuities can be either fixed or variable during their accumulation period.

Q: What are "split" annuities?

A: *"Split" annuities* combine the features of different types of annuities. To reach specific financial goals, an investor may wish to have the guarantee of a fixed annuity and the growth potential of a variable annuity, or the income of an immediate annuity and the compounding power of a deferred annuity.

As an example of a fixed/variable split, you may want the growth provided by equity investing, but also want a long-term guarantee that will preserve your original principal. In such a situation, you might invest enough of your principal in a fixed annuity to compound to your original deposit (investment). You could invest the remainder for growth in a variable annuity, knowing that the fixed annuity guarantees that you will not lose money.

Illustration 10-2
Fixed/Variable Split Annuity

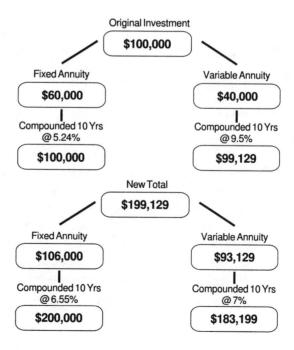

As an example of an immediate/deferred split, you may want to maximize your income and protect your principal amount as well. As in the previous example, you might invest enough in a fixed deferred annuity to replace the full principal amount over, say, nine years. You could then invest the remainder in an immediate annuity for current income. The immediate annuity's term could be set to match the nine-year replacement period.

Illustration 10-3

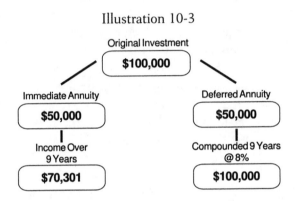

This split annuity allows you to maximize your income from one part of your investment and still maintain your principal intact. At the end of the period, you can repeat the strategy for another period.

Q: How can I structure distributions from an annuity?

A: Annuities got their name because traditionally their value was *annuitized* at the beginning of the withdrawal phase of the contract. In annuitization, the insurance company uses your accumulated value (the contract value) and the period of time over which you wish to receive income to calculate a stream of payments at regular intervals. The insurance company then begins sending the annuitant (or his or her designated beneficiary) regular checks as annuity income. Generally, you have alternative methods of structuring the annuity payments. Some of the types of annuitizations are:

- Life annuity

- Period certain annuity
- Life with period certain annuity
- Joint and survivor annuity

Each method is appropriate for different circumstances; their different features affect the amount that you will receive in each payment.

Q: What is a life annuity?

A: A *life annuity* is the classic annuity; it provides an income stream that is guaranteed to continue throughout the lifetime of the annuitant. It is particularly appropriate if you want an income that you cannot outlive, and you are not concerned about leaving any of the contract value to your heirs.

For a life annuity, the insurance company calculates your life expectancy from statistical averages, using actuarial tables similar to those used for traditional life insurance policies. Your life expectancy and the accumulated value in your account will determine the amount of income you will receive. The larger your accumulated balance and the shorter your life expectancy, the larger your annuity checks will be. Conversely, if you are expected to live a long time or have a smaller accumulated balance, your annuity payments will be smaller.

Q: What is the risk of a life annuity?

A: A life annuity favors you if you live much longer than the statistical averages. It carries substantial risk to your heirs if the reverse is true. If you die early, the annuity contract is terminated, and any remaining balance in your account reverts to the insurance company. This is the opposite of the basic nature of life insurance. If you select a life annuity, you are betting on being paid by the insurance company over a long remaining life. With traditional life insurance, it is the insurance company that is betting on being paid while you live a long life.

Q: What is a period certain annuity?

A: As its name implies, the *period certain annuity* guarantees that the annuitant and/or his or her beneficiary will receive the annuity income for a designated period of time regardless of the survival of the annuitant. Under the period certain structure, payments will be made to you or to a designated beneficiary if you die before the guaranteed number of payments are made. The period certain annuity method is often used to provide funds for education or some other goal requiring guaranteed payments for a specific period.

Q: What is a life with period certain annuity?

A: The *life with period certain annuity* combines the lifetime income of a life annuity with the shorter-term guarantee of a period certain annuity. For example, if you choose a life annuity with ten years certain, you will continue to receive your annuity income no matter how *long* you live. On the other hand, the insurance company will make payments to someone for ten years no matter how *short* your life after annuitization. If you die within the ten years period certain, your beneficiary will continue to receive the annuity income until the guaranteed period has expired.

Q: What is the price for a life with period certain annuity?

A: The life with period certain annuity may seem to be the best of both worlds, but the advantages come at a price. The insurance company takes a risk in guaranteeing the period certain, and must charge something for assuming this risk. The payments you receive will thus be lower than they would be with a straight life annuity.

Q: What is a joint and survivor annuity?

A: A *joint and survivor annuity* is a variation of a life annuity in which two annuitants' lives are included. The joint and survivor structure is appropriate if you wish to guarantee that your annuity income will continue for both your life and that of another person. It is most commonly used to provide for a spouse's financial security.

INSURANCE AND ANNUITIES

When the first annuitant dies, the contract continues without any interruption or delay. The second annuitant will continue to receive income for life, either the same payment amounts as before or some smaller amount (75 percent, 50 percent, etc.), as agreed in the contract. The annuity payments will stop only when the second annuitant dies; however, if both should die early in the contract, all remaining balances revert to the insurance company. As with the straight life annuity, the annuitants are counting on a long combined life, and the insurance company benefits if the reverse occurs. You may also have a period certain in joint and survivor annuity payment arrangements.

 Note: Compared to a straight life annuity, every guarantee you add to an annuitization will lower the amount of the annuity payments.

Q: Must I take my withdrawals in annuity form?

A: No. The annuity payment is just the traditional method. As annuities have come to be more widely used by people with different goals, some investors have elected not to annuitize their accounts. Instead of annuitizing, you might choose to accept distribution of the full account balance in a lump sum or to make a series of withdrawals appropriate for your financial plans and needs. Keep in mind, however, that nonannuitized distributions may have significant tax disadvantages (see question below).

Q: How are annuity withdrawals taxed?

A: The tax laws permit earnings on your annuity to compound on a tax-deferred basis during the accumulation phase. Income taxes on the earnings are deferred, not avoided. During the distribution phase, all earnings are taxed as ordinary income; however, distributions of your premium deposits are considered a return of your capital and are not taxed. The timing of your taxes due depends on whether or not you annuitize the distributions from your annuity contract. Before you decide whether or not to make annuitized withdrawals from your annuity contract, you should consult your tax advisor to determine how this would affect you.

Q: How are nonannuitized distributions taxed?

A: If you choose nonannuitized withdrawals, all payments are first assumed to be taxable distributions of your accumulated earnings. This tax treatment is called *LIFO* (last in, first out), since the most recent earnings accumulation is assumed to be the first money withdrawn. Therefore, with nonannuitized distributions, you may have to pay all the taxes in the early part of the withdrawal phase. Only when your annuity account is reduced to the amount of your original deposits are the subsequent payments considered a nontaxable return of your capital.

By requiring that all the taxes be paid in the early years, tax regulations ensure the schedule that is most advantageous to the government. By definition, this is less advantageous for you as a taxpayer.

Q: How are annuitized distributions taxed?

A: If you choose annuitized withdrawals from your annuity contract, you are establishing a uniform schedule of payments. Because of this uniformity, tax regulations consider a significant portion of each annuitized payment to be a return of your premium deposit. Tax regulations include formulas for calculating the nontaxable portion of annuitized distributions.

Because a portion of each annuitized payment is nontaxable, the taxes due on each of the early payments are less than would be due on a nonannuitized payment. This tax break begins with the first check, so annuitization carries important tax advantages early in your withdrawal phase.

Q: How are annuity values taxed at death?

A: The value of an annuity contract is the owner's property. If you are the owner and not the annuitant, that value is included in your estate and is subject to estate taxes along with your other property. The contract continues after your death until the annuitant dies or the new owner terminates the contract.

If you are a joint owner, the contract value passes automatically to the other joint owner at your death.

If you are both the owner and the annuitant, your death terminates the contract. If you die during the accumulation phase, the death benefit is included in your estate.

The taxation of the annuity contract value or death benefit will depend on your estate circumstances. You should consult your advisor to determine how this affects you.

Q: What is the cost of acquiring an annuity?

A: Generally, when you place money in an annuity, fixed or variable, you will not pay an up-front commission. The contract will usually provide for a deferred sales charge that is reduced each year you own the contract. If you withdraw your money, you will be assessed the deferred sales charge in effect at the time.

 Example: You may place your money in an annuity that has a deferred sales charge of 5 percent that decreases at a rate of 1 percentage point a year for five years. After you have owned the contract for five years, the assets in the annuity will no longer be subject to any sales charge if you withdraw them.

Q: Can I make small withdrawals from an annuity without being subject to the deferred sales charge?

A: Most annuities allow a policyholder to withdraw 10 percent of the deposits or current value without the withdrawals being subject to a deferred sales charge. Consult your annuity contract for details on any early withdrawal allowance.

Q: Are my annuity policies subject to other charges or expenses?

A: Most fixed annuities are not subject to charges other than a deferred sales charge.

Variable annuities are subject to annual expense and mortality (insurance) charges. These expenses, which are deducted from the policy's assets annually, may be $1\frac{1}{2}$ to 2 percent of the accumulated value.

Many fixed and variable annuities are charged an annual policy fee of $20 to $50.

 Note: Before placing money into any annuity, you should always ask about deferred sales charges, expenses, and policy fees.

Q: If I am unhappy with my annuity, how do I change contracts without the withdrawal being subject to taxation?

A: As with any insurance contract, if you are unhappy with your annuity, you can transfer the assets to another annuity with another insurance company through a 1035 exchange (see page 262).

 Note of Caution: When considering a 1035 exchange of an annuity contract, you should investigate whether or not the policy you want to exchange is subject to a deferred sales charge. The exchange may trigger the payment of a portion of the deferred sales charge, which would reduce the assets transferred.

SUMMARY

The protection and income tax deferral of cash value provided by life insurance and annuities are important factors for any family's plans, goals, and financial security. This chapter gives you a basic overview of the various types of life insurance and how they may fit your plans.

To accomplish your objectives, you will need to develop a specific plan that suits you. You should consult an insurance advisor or financial planner. Given the constant changes in life insurance policies, you should periodically review your life insurance program. The material in this chapter should be helpful to you in such a review.

Investing in annuities, which are increasingly popular because of the tax-deferral benefit they provide, offers both opportunity and risk. This chapter should help you in reviewing your annuities or in considering whether an annuity may be appropriate for you.

CHAPTER 11

RETIREMENT PLANS

Retirement plans are formalized arrangements to set aside money during working years in order to provide retirement income. During your working years, you or your employer make contributions, usually tax deductible, to a plan. Generally, you pay no current income tax on the earnings on retirement plan assets. When you withdraw pretax contributions and accumulated earnings, you will pay income tax on the distributions. Each type of retirement plan has its own rules and regulations, which will be briefly discussed in this chapter.

Any discussion of retirement plans in a book such as this must be brief and limited. The purpose of this section is to give an overview of retirement plans and their benefits to employees and employers.

Q: Is Social Security the most common retirement plan?

A: The best-known retirement plan is Social Security. Each of us and our employers make contributions to the Social Security system during our working years and receive retirement income, within limits. Social Security is more comprehensive than most retirement plans and is somewhat like an insurance policy. It has death benefits—income for surviving minor children and a spouse—and disability income provisions. To obtain an estimate of your Social Security benefits, call a local Social Security office and get a copy of Form SSA-7004-PC-OP1 (9-89), "Request for Earnings and Benefit Estimate Statement" (see Illustration 11-1). Shortly after sending the form to the Social Security Administration, you will receive an estimate and explanation of your estimated future benefits.

Illustration 11-1
Sample SSA-7004-PC-OP1 (9-89)
Request for Earnings and Benefit Estimate Statement

Form Approved
OMB No. 0960-0466

SP

SOCIAL SECURITY ADMINISTRATION
Request for Earnings and Benefit Estimate Statement

To receive a free statement of your earnings covered by Social Security and your estimated future benefits, all you need to do is fill out this form. Please print or type your answers. When you have completed the form, fold it and mail it to us.

1. Name shown on your Social Security card:

   First   Middle Initial   Last

2. Your Social Security number as shown on your card:

3. Your date of birth: Month   Day   Year

4. Other Social Security numbers you have used:

5. Your Sex: ☐ Male ☐ Female

6. Other names you have used (including a maiden name):

7. Show your actual earnings for last year and your estimated earnings for this year. Include only wages and/or net self-employment income covered by Social Security.

   A. Last year's actual earnings:
   $ __ , ___ . 0 0
   Dollars only

   B. This year's estimated earnings:
   $ __ , ___ . 0 0
   Dollars only

8. Show the age at which you plan to retire:
   (Show only one age)

9. Below, show the average yearly amount that you think you will earn between now and when you plan to retire. Your estimate of future earnings will be added to those earnings already on our records to give you the best possible estimate.

   Enter a yearly average, not your total future lifetime earnings. Only show earnings covered by Social Security. Do not add cost-of-living, performance or scheduled pay increases or bonuses. The reason for this is that we estimate retirement benefits in today's dollars, but adjust them to account for average wage growth in the national economy.

   However, if you expect to earn significantly more or less in the future due to promotions, job changes, part-time work, or an absence from the work force, enter the amount in today's dollars that most closely reflects your future average yearly earnings.

   Most people should enter the same amount that they are earning now (the amount shown in 7B).

   Your future average yearly earnings:
   $ __ , ___ . 0 0
   Dollars only

10. Address where you want us to send the statement:

    Name

    Street Address (Include Apt. No., P.O. Box, or Rural Route)

    City   State   Zip Code

I am asking for information about my own Social Security record or the record of a person I am authorized to represent. I understand that if I deliberately request information under false pretenses I may be guilty of a federal crime and could be fined and/or imprisoned. I authorize you to send the statement of earnings and benefit estimates to the person named in item 10 through a contractor.

Please sign your name (Do not print)

Date   (Area Code) Daytime Telephone No.

ABOUT THE PRIVACY ACT
Social Security is allowed to collect the facts on this form under Section 205 of the Social Security Act. We need them to quickly identify your record and prepare the earnings statement you asked us for. Giving us these facts is voluntary. However, without them we may not be able to give you an earnings and benefit estimate statement. Neither the Social Security Administration nor its contractor will use the information for any other purpose.

Form SSA-7004-PC-OP1 (9-89) Destroy Prior Edition

We estimate that it will take you about 5 minutes to complete this form. This includes the time it will take to read the instructions, gather the necessary facts and fill out the form. If you have comments or suggestions on this estimate, or on any other aspect of this form, write to the Social Security Administration, ATTN: Reports Clearance Officer, 1-A-21 Operations Bldg., Baltimore, MD 21235, and to the Office of Management and budget, Paperwork Reduction Project (0960-0466), Washington, D.C. 20503. Do not send completed forms or information concerning your claim to these offices. Send them to your nearest Social Security Office.

Moisten, fold, and seal before mailing.

RETIREMENT PLANS

Illustration 11-1
Sample SSA-7004-PC-OP1 (9-89) (cont.)
Request for Earnings and Benefit Estimate Statement

SOCIAL SECURITY
ADMINISTRATION

Request for Earnings and
Benefit Estimate Statement

The Social Security program belongs to you and you can count on it to be there for you. Social Security can protect you in many ways. It can help support your family in the event of your death and provide monthly payments and health insurance when you retire or if you become disabled.

To help you learn how Social Security is a part of your life, we are pleased to offer you a free Personal Earnings and Benefit Estimate Statement.

The Personal Earnings and Benefit Estimate Statement shows your Social Security earnings history and estimates how much you have paid in Social Security taxes. It also estimates your future benefits and tells you how you can qualify for benefits. When you receive your earnings statement, we hope you will use it to start planning for a strong financial future.

To receive your statement, please fill out the form on the reverse and mail it to us. You should receive your statement in 6 weeks or less. We look forward to sending it to you.

GWENDOLYN S. KING
Commissioner of Social Security

First
Class
Postage
Required

SOCIAL SECURITY ADMINISTRATION
WILKES-BARRE DATA OPERATIONS CENTER
P.O. BOX 20
WILKES-BARRE, PA 18711-2030

SOCIAL SECURITY . . . It never stops working!

RETIREMENT
PLANS

Q: Are there different types of retirement plans?

A: Yes. There are two general types of retirement plans. They are:

1. Nonqualified (unfunded) agreements
2. Qualified retirement plans

Q: What are nonqualified retirement plans?

A: In *nonqualified retirement plans*, an employer has a written, contractual obligation to pay an employee a certain amount of money in a lump sum or in monthly installments at some future date, usually retirement. The employee is not taxed on the benefits until the money is actually received, and the employer cannot deduct any of the benefits until the money is paid.

Some employers set aside money for nonqualified agreements and invest it, but the investments cannot be available to the employee or "mirror" the contract in any way. If the employee has any right to control such funds, he or she may be seen as having *constructive receipt* and be taxed on the contractual amount.

Anyone covered by a nonqualified agreement (contract) should seek tax and/or legal advice concerning his or her rights, risks, and potential tax liabilities. An employee covered by a nonqualified retirement plan is just like any other unsecured creditor of the employer. An unsecured creditor does not have money or assets guaranteeing a debt.

RETIREMENT PLANS

Q: What are qualified retirement plans?

A: *Qualified retirement plans* are those that are allowed by and conform to provisions of the Internal Revenue Code. Generally, money must be set aside in a *fiduciary account* (see box) by the employee and/or employer. The employer is allowed an immediate tax deduction for its contribution in the year the money is set aside. As an employee, you pay no current taxes on amounts contributed by your employer or yourself. All earnings and gains on the invested assets in the fiduciary account accumulate tax-deferred. Generally, money you withdraw from a retirement account is taxable income in the year in which it is distributed. Exceptions include distributions placed into an IRA rollover account, which will be discussed later in this section, and distributions of nondeductible contributions.

> A *fiduciary* is a person or institution to whom assets are entrusted for the benefit of someone else. The fiduciary is responsible for managing the assets. A *fiduciary account* is an account (like a retirement plan account) that holds assets on a beneficiary's behalf.

Q: Are there situations in which a part of the distribution from a retirement plan may not currently be taxable income?

A: Yes. Distributions of nondeductible (after-tax) contributions are not taxable income. Also, distributions placed directly into an IRA rollover account are not currently taxable income.

 Note of Caution: Other than such exceptions, any distributions from a qualified retirement plan before you reach age $59\frac{1}{2}$ may be subject to income tax at the ordinary income tax rates plus an early withdrawal penalty of 10 percent.

Q: Why should I take advantage of retirement plans?

A: You should take advantage of any retirement plan available to you primarily because it is the most beneficial means of saving money for your retirement years. As a fringe benefit, many employers will make contributions to such plans or provide you with the opportunity to make pretax contributions (salary reduction plans—see questions on 401(k), 403(b) on pages 290 and 291).

 Note: Perhaps the most important advantage of *qualified retirement plans* is tax deferral of the earnings. This means that earnings on the assets in such retirement plans are not taxable income until they are withdrawn. Since retirement plan assets are not decreased by taxes every year, they will compound faster than assets whose earnings are taxable. (Refer to Illustration 10-1 on page 264.)

RETIREMENT PLANS

Q: What types of qualified retirement plans may my employer have for me?

A: Generally, qualified retirement plans fall into two broad categories. They are:

1. Defined benefit
2. Defined contribution

Each of the categories and types of qualified retirement plans is discussed briefly below. Keep in mind that your particular plan will have specific rules; the documents spelling these out are always available to you at your employer's personnel or human resources office. Your employer has a duty to explain the features and rules of its retirement plans to you. If you do not understand the benefits and rights offered by your employer's retirement plan, you may also take the information to your tax advisor or another advisor, who will explain it to you.

Q: What are defined-benefit plans?

A: *Defined-benefit plans*, often referred to as pension plans, provide a definite retirement income (or defined benefit). This retirement income, which is usually paid as a monthly pension, is often a certain percentage of your salary before retirement. The employer makes annual tax-deductible contributions in an amount that, at an assumed rate of return, will provide the required benefit when you retire. Obviously, the older an employee, the larger the annual deposit required to provide the stipulated retirement benefit. Usually, an employee can receive the benefits of a defined-benefit, or pension, plan only in the form of a monthly income. It is mostly very large corporations and some unions that have pension plans for the benefit of their employees.

RETIREMENT PLANS

Q: What are the limits on contributions and benefits for defined-benefit retirement plans?

A: The limit on annual contributions that can be accrued for a participant in a qualified defined benefit plan is $118,800 for 1994. The maximum limit for annual benefits payable under defined-benefit plans is the lesser of 100 percent of the highest three years' preretirement compensation (income) or $90,000. These limits are to be adjusted annually for increases in the cost of living.

Q: What are defined-contribution plans?

A: *Defined-contribution plans* allow (but do not require) your employer to make a tax-deductible contribution each year to a qualified retirement plan. The contribution is defined, within regulations, and your benefit at retirement is the accumulated value of your account. The term *defined-contribution* means that your employer can determine the contribution it wishes to make each year. At retirement, termination of the plan, or separation from the company, the employee (participant) may receive the account balance as a lump sum or in the form of annuity payments (monthly income).

The maximum income (compensation) that can be considered for retirement contributions is $150,000 in 1994; this will be adjusted each year for increases in the cost of living.

Q: What is the limit on employer contributions to defined-contribution plans?

A: The limit for annual contributions to a participant's account in a defined-contribution plan is the lesser of 25 percent of earnings (compensation) or $30,000. Each year this limit will be adjusted for increases in the cost of living based on inflation.

RETIREMENT PLANS

Q: Are there different forms of defined-contribution plans?

A: Yes. While any defined-contribution plan allows employers to make contributions to a retirement plan that are defined within limits, as discussed above, there are different methods of computing the employer's allowed or required contributions. The method chosen usually determines the form of defined-contribution plan in which you are participating. The forms of defined-contribution plans are:

- Money-purchase pension
- Profit sharing
- Salary reduction

In a *money-purchase pension plan*, employers are required to make annual contributions even if they earn no profit. Even though annual contributions are required, this is not a defined-benefit plan; your retirement benefits are only the accumulated value of your account when you retire or withdraw from your plan.

A *profit-sharing plan* allows employers to make annual contributions to a retirement plan if they wish. Each year, your employer decides what percentage of its profits to contribute to its profit-sharing plan. Regulations for profit-sharing plans do not require that contributions be made every year.

A *salary reduction plan* allows employees to decide each year what percentage of their salary (income) they wish to contribute to a retirement plan (up to a maximum of $9,240 in 1994). Generally, employees do not pay current income tax on the amount that they contribute to a qualified retirement plan. Many salary reduction plans provide that the employer will match employee contributions up to some limit. The popular salary reduction plans are 401(k), 403(b), and SAR-SEP. These plans will be discussed later.

 Note: Generally, employers contribute to defined-benefit and most defined-contribution retirement plans. Employees usually make the contributions to salary reduction plans.

Q: What is a 401(k) plan?

A: A *401(k) retirement plan* is an employer-sponsored salary reduction plan and thus a type of defined-contribution retirement plan. Each year, employees who participate in a 401(k) plan may elect to take their full compensation in cash and pay current income taxes, or to have part of their salary placed into a qualified retirement plan. The full amount of employee contributions and the earnings on those contributions are fully *vested* (see box) immediately. Many employers will match a portion of an employee's salary reduction. If your employer has a 401(k) plan, most advisors strongly recommend that you participate at least up to the limit your employer will match. Limits on employee contributions to 401(k) plans were $9,240 in 1994 and will be adjusted each year for increases in the cost of living. Employer contributions are limited to the lesser of 15 percent of earnings or $30,000.

The amount an employee contributes to a 401(k) plan is subject to FICA (Social Security) tax. If your income is below the maximum to which Social Security applies, you will be paying Social Security tax on your full contribution.

> *Vesting* refers to the portion of your retirement plan account that belongs to you if your employment terminates before retirement. Generally, you will be fully vested (your entire retirement account will belong to you) if your employment terminates because of retirement, death, or disability. In most defined-contribution retirement plans, participants in the plans are vested over a number of years. After an employee terminates employment and withdraws his or her vested portion, the assets remaining in the employee's account are referred to as a *forfeiture*. Forfeitures are allocated to the remaining participants and can enhance the value of the accounts of the participants who remain.

Q: What is a 403(b) retirement plan?

A: *A 403(b) retirement plan* is technically not a qualified retirement plan, but a program for employees of certain charitable or nonprofit organizations such as schools, hospitals, or foundations. Employees can elect to forgo up to a certain percentage of their salary each year and place this amount in a annuity or mutual fund. Employers may also contribute to an employee's 403(b) account. The amount of the employee's or employer's contribution is not currently taxable income. As in qualified retirement plans, the earnings accumulate tax-deferred and withdrawals are taxable income. As with a 401(k) plan, employees participating in a 403(b) plan must

RETIREMENT PLANS

pay FICA (Social Security) tax on the amount they contribute. Employer contributions for employees are not subject to FICA withholding. The contribution limits are very complex, but are around 17 percent of compensation. There are *catchup provisions* in 403(b) regulations that allow employees who have not taken full advantage of contribution limits in previous years to make larger contributions that exceed the annual limits. If your employer has a 403(b) program, you should ask the human resources department to have your contribution limits calculated by one of the organizations providing investments for the program.

Q: What is a simplified employee pension plan (SEP)?

A: A *simplified employee pension plan*, known as a SEP, is basically an employee individual retirement account (IRA) (see page 296) to which an employer can make tax-deductible contributions. Employer annual contribution limits are the lesser of $30,000 or 15 percent of annual compensation. A law effective for 1994 places a limit of $150,000 of an employee's compensation that may be used to determine contributions to a SEP. Therefore, the maximum contribution in 1994 was $22,500 (15% times $150,000). In the future, the $150,000 will be adjusted for inflation until the above mentioned contribution limits again realistically apply. All employer contributions to an employee's SEP account are fully vested immediately. The employee's W-2 tax form must include SEP contributions as taxable income, but the amount of the contribution is a tax deduction for the employee and the employer.

 Note: The primary reasons why many employers establish SEPs rather than other retirement plans are the minimal rules, the minimal reporting requirements, and the low cost of establishing and maintaining the plan. Completing and filing IRS Form 305-SEP is all that is required. Employees must establish their own IRA accounts, to which their employers make the contributions.

RETIREMENT PLANS

Q: What is a SAR/SEP?

A: A *SAR/SEP* is a salary reduction SEP. It allows employees to contribute their own money to a separate SEP/IRA account. SAR/SEPs are limited to companies with twenty-five or fewer employees. An employee could contribute $9,240 to a SAR/SEP in 1994. This limit will be increased annually for increases in the cost of living. Nonprofit organizations and state and local governments may not establish SAR/SEPs.

 Note: The annual allowable limit for employee contributions (and salary reductions) applies to all of your plans. If you are a participant in a 401(k), a 403(b), and a SAR/SEP, your total annual contribution would be limited to $9,240 in 1994 (adjusted annually for cost of living).

Q: What is a Keogh plan?

A: A *Keogh plan* is usually a profit sharing plan for self-employed individuals. Most features and rules applying to Keogh plans are the same as for profit sharing plans (see p. 290). As in the case of profit sharing and pension plans, Keogh plans must be established by December 31. IRAs and SEPs can be established as late as April 15 following your tax year.

Q: If I have self-employed income outside my employer, can I establish a retirement plan on that income?

A: Yes. If you have income outside your employer such as consulting fees, part-time business, directors fees, etc., you can establish a retirement plan on that income.

Q: What is an ESOP retirement plan?

A: An *ESOP* retirement plan is an *employee stock ownership plan*. An ESOP is established to allow employers to make tax-deductible contributions to a qualified plan. The contributions are used to invest in the common stock of the employer.

RETIREMENT PLANS

Q: What is the advantage to an employer of establishing an ESOP?

A: The advantage to the employer is that the plan is a means of raising capital with tax-deductible contributions. An ESOP may also be a steady buyer of the employer's stock and thus support its price. Recent tax law changes have allowed extra tax benefits, in addition to deductibility, for employers who contribute to ESOPs.

Q: What is the advantage of an ESOP to an employee?

A: The advantage to an employee is the opportunity to own a part of his or her employer and to accumulate assets for retirement.

Q: How do retirement plans benefit me?

A: You benefit from your employer's having a retirement plan in one or several of the following ways:

- You do not pay any current income tax on your employer's contribution.
- Earnings on investments made by the plan build up tax-deferred.
- You will receive income at retirement.
- If your employment terminates, your employer terminates its retirement plan, or you become disabled or die, you will have the benefit of at least a portion and maybe all your employer's accumulated contributions. (See vesting, page 291.)

Q: How is any money withdrawn from a retirement plan taxed?

A: Generally, money withdrawn from a qualified retirement plan is taxed as ordinary income unless the distributions are placed in an IRA rollover account. (See page 304.)

The reason distributions from retirement plans are subject to income tax is simple: Neither you nor your employer paid income tax on the contributions to your plan, and no income taxes were paid on the earnings in the plan. Since the income was not taxed initially, the distributions from retirement plans are taxed.

Exception: After-tax employee contributions are not subject to ordinary income taxes.

 Note of Caution: If you withdraw assets from any retirement plan before you reach age $59^1/_2$, you will incur an early withdrawal penalty, and if your current income is higher than your income in later years, you may have created an unnecessary and substantial income tax liability. (See questions on IRA rollovers on page 304.)

Q: What happens to the assets in my retirement plans when I die?

A: At your death, the value of the assets in your retirement plans will be included in your estate and will be subject to estate taxes. In addition, when the assets in your retirement plans (including your IRAs) are withdrawn, the amounts of the distributions are taxable income to your estate or the beneficiary of your plans. Any balances left in retirement plans when you die will ultimately be subject to income and estate taxes. In addition, the assets in your retirement plans that are part of your estate may be subject to an *excess accumulation tax*.

Q: Is it more advantageous to leave assets in a retirement plan (or an IRA) as long as possible or to start withdrawals as soon as you can without income tax penalties?

A: Generally, it is more advantageous to leave assets in your retirement plan and delay paying income taxes as long as possible. However, if the amount of assets in your retirement plans and IRA accounts is large—over $1 million, for example—you should seek professional tax and estate planning assistance. By the time your heirs and/or your estate have paid possible excess accumulation tax, estate tax, and income tax, there may be less money available than you had anticipated.

RETIREMENT PLANS

Q: What is an excess accumulation tax?

A: An *excess accumulation tax* is a tax assessed against your estate if the total assets in *all* qualified retirement plans, including IRAs and tax-sheltered annuities, at the time of death exceed the cost of a single life annuity. The calculations are based on the individual's life expectancy in the year of death and annual distributions of $150,000. The estate will generally owe a penalty equal to 15 percent of the excess accumulation.

Q: What is the excess distribution tax?

A: The IRS imposes a 15 percent excise tax on annual distributions from all qualified retirement plans, tax-sheltered annuities, and IRAs that exceed $150,000.

 Note of Caution: If you are one of the lucky people with large balances in your retirement accounts, you may be in a Catch-22 after retirement. If you withdraw assets from your retirement plan too quickly, you may be subject to an excess distribution tax. If you withdraw them too slowly, you may be subject to an excess accumulation tax.

Q: Are all distributions in excess of $150,000 a year subject to the excess distribution tax?

A: No. Certain types of distributions may be excluded in determining an individual's total distributions for a year. Some examples of nontaxable distributions are as follows:

- Rollover amounts
- Nontaxable distributions, such as amounts representing after-tax employee contributions
- Some lump-sum distributions to which income averaging is applied (special rules may apply when individuals elect income averaging)
- Death distributions (beneficiaries are usually exempt from the excess distribution tax, but they may be subject to the excess accumulation penalty)

Q: What is an IRA?

A: *IRA* is the abbreviation for *individual retirement account*. It is an individual qualified savings plan that you set up and contribute to yourself. An IRA may offer you deductions for contributions and tax deferrals on earnings.

RETIREMENT PLANS

Q: Why should I consider establishing an IRA?

A: Two reasons you should consider establishing an IRA are:

1. You may be able to deduct some or all of your contributions to your IRA, depending on your income.
2. The earnings—interest, dividends, or capital gains—on your IRA are not taxed until they are distributed to you, which is usually after you retire.

In essence, by establishing an IRA, you will defer paying income taxes on the earnings on the money in the account and possibly on the money you invest. When you defer paying income tax on the money in the account, your capital will grow more quickly.

Q: Where can I establish an IRA?

A: To establish an IRA, you must have a custodian to hold the assets of your IRA. Most banks, brokerage firms, mutual funds, and insurance companies are qualified custodians. The investments you make in your IRA will vary depending on the investment opportunities offered by the custodian. You should consider your investment goals, risk tolerance, and other investments when choosing a custodian and the investments they offer. You can maintain multiple IRAs with several different custodians.

Q: Who is eligible to establish an IRA?

A: Any individual under the age of $70\frac{1}{2}$ who is receiving taxable compensation may establish an IRA.

Q: What is considered compensation?

A: *Compensation* is earned income. It is defined by the Internal Revenue Service as taxable earnings that are received in return for personal services. Generally, wages, salaries, commissions, and net earnings of self-employed persons are considered compensation. Taxable alimony and maintenance payments under a decree of divorce or separate maintenance agreement are also considered compensation.

RETIREMENT PLANS

Q: How much am I allowed to contribute to an IRA?

A: The maximum you can contribute to an IRA each year is the smaller of:

- $2,000
- Your total earnings (compensation)

 Note: If you had a part-time job and made only $1,500 in compensation during the year, for example, your maximum contribution to an IRA for that year would be $1,500.

Q: What is a spousal IRA?

A: A *spousal IRA* is an IRA established for a nonworking spouse. Two spouses cannot jointly own an IRA; each spouse must have his or her own account.

Q: What are the requirements for a spousal IRA?

A: To contribute to a spousal IRA:

- You must be married at the end of the tax year.
- Your spouse must be under the age of $70\frac{1}{2}$ at the end of the tax year.
- You must file a joint income tax return.
- Your spouse must have no compensation or elect to be treated as having no compensation.
- Married individuals filing separately who live apart during the year are treated as *not* married.

Q: What are the contribution limits for a spousal IRA?

A: The combined annual contribution to an individual IRA and a spousal IRA is $2,250. The contributions can be divided between the individual and spousal IRAs in any way so long as no more than $2,000 is contributed to either account.

Q: If my spouse and I both work, can we each establish an individual IRA?

A: Yes. You and your spouse can each contribute to an individual IRA if both of you work. If each of you has compensation of $2,000 or more, each of you may contribute $2,000 to your own IRA account, for a total of $4,000 rather than the $2,250 limit on an individual and a spousal IRA.

Q: When must I make contributions to my IRA?

A: You must make contributions to your IRA no later than the due date for filing your income tax return. For most people, this means that contributions for the previous year must be made by April 15.

Q: Do I need to inform anyone of the year to which my contribution applies?

A: You probably don't have to notify your custodian as to which year your contribution applies. However, if you make two contributions in one year and do not inform the custodian that one applies to the previous year, both contributions may be mistakenly reported as being for the same year and present an overcontribution problem.

Suggestion: When making an IRA contribution, always write on your check the year to which the contribution applies.

Q: What happens if I contribute too much to my IRA?

A: Any excess contribution to an IRA is subject to a 6 percent tax penalty in the year in which you make the excess contribution and each subsequent year until you correct the excess. You actually have two choices:

1. You can withdraw the excess contribution and any earnings on the excess. The earnings will be taxed at your regular rate, but the excess will be subject to a 10 percent early withdrawal tax penalty if you are under the age of $59\frac{1}{2}$.
2. You can leave the excess in the account and designate it as a contribution for the following year. You will still have to pay the 6 percent penalty until the excess is credited for the following year.

Q: How much of my IRA contribution is tax deductible?

A: The allowable deduction for your IRA contributions will depend on three factors:

1. Whether either you or your spouse is covered by an employer retirement plan for any part of the year

2. How much income you earn in the tax year to which your contribution is applied

3. Your filing status

Note: See Illustration 11-2 for a summary of the deductibility of IRA contributions.

Q: If neither my spouse nor I is covered by an employer retirement plan, can we deduct our IRA contribution?

A: If neither you nor your spouse is covered by an employer retirement plan for any part of the year, you can deduct your total allowable IRA contributions.

If you file as a single individual or head of household and you are not covered by an employer retirement plan for any part of the year, you can deduct the total allowable IRA contribution even if your spouse is covered by a retirement plan.

Q: How do we know if either of us is covered by an employer retirement plan for a tax year?

A: Generally, you and your spouse will know if you are covered by (often referred to as participating in) an employer retirement plan. The W-2 form you receive from your employer each year has a box indicating whether or not you were covered by the employer's retirement plan for the tax year. If you are covered, the box will be marked. If you are not covered, the box will be blank. If you are still not sure, ask your employer.

Q: Can we still deduct a part of our IRA contributions if either of us is covered by an employer retirement plan?

A: If either you or your spouse is covered by an employer retirement plan, the deductible amount of your IRA contributions will depend upon your level of income and filing status. See Illustration 11-2. Your allowable deduction declines as your income increases.

Illustration 11-2
Deductibility of IRA Contributions

Your contribution to an IRA can be deducted as follows:

Joint Returns:

1. *Neither spouse is an active participant in a qualified retirement plan:* Contributions are fully deductible regardless of income.

2. *Either spouse (or both) is an active participant in a qualified retirement plan and:*
   - *Adjusted gross income is less than $40,000:* Contributions are 100 percent deductible.
   - *Adjusted gross income is between $40,000 and $50,000:* Contributions are partially deductible based on by how much your income exceeds $40,000.
   - *Adjusted gross income is over $50,000:* Contributions are nondeductible.

Single Returns

1. *You are not an active participant in a qualified retirement plan:* Contributions are fully deductible regardless of income.

2. *You are an active participant in a qualified retirement plan and:*
   - *Adjusted gross income is less than $25,000:* Contributions are 100 percent deductible.
   - *Adjusted gross income is between $25,000 and $35,000:* Contributions are partially deductible based on by how much your income exceeds $25,000.
   - *Adjusted gross income is over $35,000:* Contributions are nondeductible.

Q: Do I have to report IRA contributions?

A: You do not have to report deductible IRA contributions other than to include the amount on your income tax return so as to receive the deduction. However, if you are making nondeductible contributions, you must file IRS Form 8606 with your income tax return. If you make a nondeductible IRA contribution, you must file this form with the IRS even if you do not file an income tax return.

RETIREMENT PLANS

Q: Why am I required to file a form for nondeductible IRA contributions?

A: The purpose of filing the form is to allow the IRS to track your nondeductible contributions. It is to your benefit to maintain a record of nondeductible contributions because when the nondeductible contributions are withdrawn, they are tax-free distributions. Only the earnings on the nondeductible contributions are taxable when withdrawn.

 Note: If you do not report nondeductible contributions, all of your IRA contributions will be treated as deductible contributions and taxed upon withdrawal.

Q: At what age may I begin withdrawals from my IRA?

A: You can begin making withdrawals, often referred to as distributions, from your IRA at age $59\frac{1}{2}$. Even if you are still working, you can make withdrawals from your IRA. Between age $59\frac{1}{2}$ and age $70\frac{1}{2}$, you can make withdrawals of whatever amount you wish. You may choose to make no withdrawals, in which case your IRA continues to compound income tax-deferred until you reach age $70\frac{1}{2}$, when you must begin withdrawals.

Q: Is there a way I can make withdrawals from my IRA before age $59\frac{1}{2}$ without paying the tax penalty?

A: Yes. You can make withdrawals from your IRA account before age $59\frac{1}{2}$ without paying the tax penalty if you establish a withdrawal schedule based on your life expectancy, the joint life expectancy of you and your spouse, or some other approved regular basis. The withdrawal schedule cannot be changed for five years or until you attain age $59\frac{1}{2}$. If you want to begin withdrawals from your IRA account before age $59\frac{1}{2}$, you should seek professional income tax advice to be sure you avoid the income tax penalty.

Q: How is the amount of the withdrawal taxed?

A: The amount of the withdrawal will be subject to income tax at ordinary income tax rates.

Q: Is there an age at which I must begin distributions from my IRAs?

A: Yes. You must begin to make withdrawals from your IRA in the year in which you become $70\frac{1}{2}$. If you fail to make the required withdrawals, a tax penalty of 50 percent is imposed on the difference between the amount you withdrew and the amount you are required to withdraw.

Q: How much of my IRA am I required to withdraw at age 70 1/2?

A: The amount you are required to withdraw depends on your life expectancy or the joint life expectancy of you and your spouse or other beneficiary. The IRS publishes tables showing life expectancy at certain ages. You may want to withdraw the required minimum amount, which is certainly acceptable. See Illustration 11-3 for some life expectancy assumptions.

Illustration 11-3
Life Expectancies

Single Individuals

Age	Life Expectancy
65	20 years
70	16 years
75	12.5 years
80	9.5 years

Joint Lives

Ages	Life Expectancy
65 and 60	27.6 years
70 and 65	23.1 years
75 and 70	18.8 years
80 and 75	14.9 years

Reprinted by permission of Quest For Value Distributors

RETIREMENT PLANS

Q: Is there a reason to make IRA contributions if we cannot deduct the contributions?

A: Yes. The main reason is that the earnings on the contributions are tax-deferred. This means that you will accumulate more money to produce more income when you retire. (See the tax-deferred advantage illustration on page 264.)

Q: What is an IRA rollover?

A: An IRA *rollover* is a special IRA into which distributions from qualified retirement plans can be deposited tax-free. All earnings on assets in an IRA rollover are tax-deferred.

Q: When might I use an IRA rollover?

A: If you are to receive a lump-sum distribution from a qualified retirement plan because you are changing jobs, your employment is terminated, or you retire, you have three choices:

1. You can take the distribution and pay income tax on it (and a 10 percent early withdrawal penalty if you are under the age of $59\frac{1}{2}$).
2. You can receive the distribution and subsequently deposit the funds into an IRA rollover (or another qualified retirement plan) within sixty days.
3. You can have your employer deposit the funds directly into an IRA rollover (or another qualified retirement plan). You will avoid current income tax on the distribution, and the earnings on the assets will continue to be tax-deferred.

Q: What will happen to my lump-sum distribution if it is not *directly* deposited into an IRA rollover?

A: Since January 1, 1993, your employer must withhold 20 percent of all distributions that are paid to you. This means that you will receive only 80 percent of the distribution. If you intend to roll the distribution over within the sixty-day limit for rollovers, you will have to come up with the remaining money from other sources or borrow it; otherwise, you will be subject to income tax *and* penalties on the amount withheld. The 20 percent tax withholding will be credited to your federal income tax liability like any other withholding.

Q: How can I avoid the 20 percent withholding?

A: You can avoid the 20 percent withholding by establishing an IRA rollover account with a bank, brokerage firm, or insurance company and instructing your employer to make the distribution directly to your IRA rollover account. Most employers will have the forms you must complete to enable them to make the distribution directly to your IRA rollover account.

Q: If I want to withdraw part of my distribution, what can I do?

A: If you want some of the distribution to spend, but you want most of it tax-deferred, you probably should have the distribution made to an IRA rollover, then make your partial withdrawal from the IRA. The amount you withdraw will be subject to current income taxes and a penalty if you are under age $59^1/_2$. Before making any taxable withdrawals, you should always consult a tax advisor.

Q: After I place my distribution in an IRA rollover, can it be put back into another qualified retirement plan?

A: Yes. Distributions from qualified retirement plans placed into IRA rollovers and the earnings on those distributions can later be rolled into another qualified retirement plan if the plan document provides for accepting such rollovers. This is true so long as you do not combine your distributions from qualified retirement plans with money you have contributed to an IRA.

Q: Can I roll after-tax contributions I have made to an employer plan into an IRA rollover?

A: No. Any distributions from after-tax contributions cannot be rolled into an IRA rollover. Your employer should tell you the part of any distribution that is your after-tax contribution.

RETIREMENT PLANS

Q: How many IRA accounts can I have?

A: You can have as many IRA accounts as you want. In fact, if you have a very large IRA, you may want to consider splitting it into several smaller IRAs. Also, if you have rollovers from several employers, you may want to place each in a separate

IRA account. However, many people who have several IRAs consolidate them so as not to have so many small accounts.

Q: After I have established an IRA account, can I change it to another institution?

A: Yes. You can change the institution that has your IRA in two ways: *rollover* or *transfer*. In a *rollover*, you can take a distribution from one IRA and place it into another IRA; you avoid tax on the distribution if it is placed into another IRA within sixty days. This is not advisable. In a *transfer*, you authorize your new custodian to have the distribution made directly from your existing IRA to your new one; the new custodian should provide the necessary forms. You are limited to one *rollover* a year, whereas you may *transfer* IRAs as often as you wish.

Q: What are the income and estate tax rules concerning distributions from an IRA rollover?

A: The same tax rules that apply to distributions from IRAs also apply to IRA rollovers. Again, when planning distributions, you should consult a tax advisor.

Q: Can I make nontaxable withdrawals by borrowing from my retirement plans?

A: You cannot borrow from your IRA accounts or use them as security for loans. If you do so, the amount of the loan will be considered a distribution subject to income tax and the tax penalty if you are under the age of $59^{1}/_{2}$. However, if the plan documents provide, you may be able to borrow from employer-sponsored retirement plans. If you wish to do so, you should check with the human resources department of your employer. Loans may be approved only in case of "hardship," which will be determined by the trustees of your employer retirement plan.

RETIREMENT PLANS

SUMMARY

Retirement plans are the most advantageous means of investing and saving for your retirement. Through the years, regulations of retirement plans have constantly been improved to protect employees. You should take advantage of all opportunities to participate in retirement plans. Most often, contributions to your retirement plans are tax-deductible and all earnings accumulate tax-deferred. You will pay income taxes when you make withdrawals from the plans.

Since retirement plans have become so important, it is imperative for you to understand the opportunities and rules of the retirement plans in which you may participate. This chapter has briefly covered some of the important aspects of the various types of retirement plans that may be available to you. You should always seek additional information about the retirement plans available to you and how they fit into your overall financial situation. As you get closer to retirement age, you will need to begin in-depth planning concerning how much income your retirement plans will produce and the income tax and estate tax situations for your retirement plans.

Your retirement plans will perhaps be the most important asset for your comfortable retirement years.

RETIREMENT
PLANS

CHAPTER 12

RETIREMENT PLANNING

A secure retirement is perhaps our most compelling goal. Other goals, such as keeping the bills paid and educating children, often temporarily take priority because of their immediacy. But always present on the horizon, looming larger with every passing year, is the importance of retirement security.

The preceding chapters of this book have answered questions about many vehicles—investments, savings, retirement plans—that you may use in planning for a secure retirement. However, your use of those vehicles will be most effective if you have a road map that shows where you are and how to get where you want to go. Retirement planning is the act of building such a road map.

Retirement planning requires gathering a great amount of information about yourself—your spending habits, your resources, and your retirement goals—and trying to predict the future. Such tasks can seem intimidating or even insurmountable in our busy day-to-day lives. A complete discussion of all aspects of retirement planning could fill several books—and has. The longest journey, however, begins with single steps. Our goal in this chapter is to answer a number of common questions to help you start your retirement planning process.

Q: Are Social Security and my employer responsible for my retirement security?

A: No. Ultimately, *you* are responsible for planning for your own retirement security. Many people believe that funds from outside sources, such as Social Security income or their employer's retirement plans, will enable them to have a financially secure retirement. Such a false sense of security may lead you to neglect retirement planning. It may, in fact, be true that Social Security and your employer's pension will provide you with retirement security, but you cannot blindly assume that they will without engaging in some retirement planning to determine the extent of such income and your income needs.

Q: What do I do to take control of my retirement security?

A: It is increasingly evident that Social Security and employer retirement plans, the traditional sources of retirement income, are becoming less dependable. They may provide only part of the income that you will need during your retirement. Many advisors compare your retirement income to a three-legged stool, with the first two legs being Social Security and income from your employer's pension. The third leg is income from your own retirement savings. Just as a stool cannot be stable on just two legs, your retirement income needs the third leg of your planning and saving. Retirement planning allows you to estimate how much retirement income must come from your own retirement savings, and to start building toward that goal.

Q: How do I start retirement planning?

A: Like any large task, retirement planning can best be accomplished one step at a time. Using the road-map analogy, your retirement planning should answer these questions:

● Where am I?
● Where am I going?
● How do I get there?

On the surface, retirement planning appears to be a fairly simple financial journey. However, the process of finding comfortable landmarks raises more questions, which we will address below.

Q: How do I determine where I am in retirement planning?

A: One of the most helpful features on maps in museums, shopping malls, etc., is the indicator "You are here." It is always easier to head toward a goal when you know where you are starting from. In retirement planning, where you are will influence how challenging your job will be. To find out where you are, you will need to:

- Determine your current retirement capital
- Analyze your current income needs

Q: How do I determine my current retirement capital?

A: Your *retirement capital* consists of all financial resources that you are likely to own long-term and that you plan to use in the future to generate retirement income. The retirement capital you have currently is your starting point in retirement planning.

Determining your current retirement capital is not always easy or straightforward. A good starting point is to consider your net worth. You may already have prepared a net worth statement for other financial purposes, such as loan applications (see Illustration 12-1). Your net worth consists of *all* of your assets minus your liabilities; therefore, it is generally more inclusive than your retirement capital.

Illustration 12-1
Sample Net Worth Statement

Assets
- Cash
- Checking accounts
- Savings accounts
- Money market balances
- Securities holdings and mutual funds
- Employer retirement plan balances (profit sharing, 401(k), etc.)
- IRA balances
- Life insurance cash value
- Homes
- Investment real estate
- Personal property (furniture, autos, etc.)

　　Total Assets

Liabilities
- Mortgages
- Credit card balances
- Other debts

　　Total Liabilities

　　Net Worth

RETIREMENT PLANNING

Q: How is my retirement capital different from my net worth?

A: Your retirement capital excludes some items that are part of your net worth because they are not related to retirement. Short-term liquidity items like your cash and money market balances should not be included, for example, because they are intended to cover more immediate needs. Also, any cash you maintain for "rainy day" emergencies should not be included. However, if you perpetually have highly liquid assets over and above such dedicated funds, and you believe you will keep these assets until retirement, you may include them in retirement capital.

Your home is probably the most significant exclusion from your retirement capital. Although it may be your largest asset, if you plan to keep your home after retirement, it will not produce income. The same may be true of any vacation home you intend to keep for your general enjoyment after you retire. Excluding these items will reduce your retirement capital substantially. On the other hand, you should also exclude your mortgages and other debt that is likely to be paid off before retirement.

Once you have excluded nonretirement items, the revised total will consist of the resources you have that you expect to generate income to support you during retirement years. This is your current retirement capital, an important starting point in your retirement planning.

Q: How important is my retirement capital in my retirement planning?

A: Your current level of retirement capital is an important factor in determining where you are in retirement planning, but it is not the only factor. No matter how much you have or do not have, it can be overridden by later developments. It is not an all-powerful fact of life that should deter you from engaging in retirement planning.

Having substantial current capital will not necessarily ensure your retirement security and allow you to avoid the effort of retirement planning. An impressive-looking capital level could become inadequate if you do not add enough to it over time. Conversely, a low level of capital is not a fatal flaw. Over time, you can overcome your current disadvantage by saving more, investing well, and controlling your income needs, or spending.

Q: How do my current income needs affect my retirement planning?

A: Your current income needs are another important factor in determining where you are in retirement planning. Analyzing your spending habits will also help you predict how far you have to go and how difficult it may be to get there.

Since your ultimate goal in retirement planning is to have ample retirement income, it is important for you to examine your income needs. You may already manage your household budget on an active basis and categorize your current expenses (see Illustration 12-2). Thus, you may know what your expenses are in each category and the total amount of your typical monthly bills. (For the example we will develop in this chapter, we will use $2,000.)

Knowing the level of your expenses is important in several ways. First, it will help you anticipate how much retirement income you will need. Also, managing your expenses (reducing some expenses) will help you save for retirement.

Illustration 12-2
Sample Monthly Budget

Housing costs (mortgage, insurance, taxes, utilities, repairs)	$750
Food costs (groceries, restaurant)	$300
Auto costs (loan, insurance, gas, repairs, tolls)	$250
Education costs (tuition, fees, supplies)	$100
Medical costs (insurance, fees)	$100
Clothing costs (clothes, cleaning)	$100
Entertainment costs (baby-sitters, clubs, subscriptions, etc.)	$250
Miscellaneous	$150
Total	$2,000

RETIREMENT PLANNING

Q: How do I determine where I am going in retirement planning?

A: In any process, once you have an idea of where you are, you need to set your sights on where you are going. In retirement planning, you need to set reasonable and measurable goals. Many experts believe that having specific *written* goals greatly boosts a person's motivation and likelihood of achieving the goals. Indeed, you cannot measure your success unless you have goals.

When you think of your retirement goals, you should consider such issues as being able to retire when you want to and having enough income to meet your needs. Setting your goals involves the following steps:

- Setting your planned retirement age
- Considering your life expectancy
- Estimating your retirement income needs
- Estimating your sources of retirement income
- Determining the adequacy of your sources of income relative to your income needs

These factors are straightforward and can be stated in measurable terms. In fact, stating them may appear so easy that you may overlook the importance of beginning your goal setting with some careful examination.

Q: What is involved in setting my planned retirement age?

A: Setting your planned retirement age may seem easy, but a surprising number of considerations can affect it. Your retirement age is both a *date* in time and a *distance* away from where you are right now. Both the date and the distance deserve careful consideration.

Q: How is retirement age a complex issue?

A: Your planned retirement age may not be as easy to determine as you might think at first. On the one hand, it may be partially dictated by an official retirement age established by your employer, commonly age 65. On the other hand, some employer's pension plans offer the option of early retirement at a younger age such as 62 or $59\frac{1}{2}$. Other employers, recognizing that many employees now remain vital past age 65, are setting their mandatory retirement age higher or eliminating it entirely.

Whatever your employer's policy may be, you may wish to set a different retirement date—one that better conforms with your personal goals. You may plan to retire early, perhaps when the children finish school or when your mortgage is paid off. Alternatively, you may plan a second career (perhaps part-time), or you may enjoy your occupation so much that you *never* plan to stop working entirely. Another factor to consider is whether health problems might affect the length of your career. Whatever your circumstances, you should carefully consider when you ideally would like to stop depending on your earned income and begin living on your retirement income.

Q: How is the amount of time before my retirement an important factor?

A: Once you have set a retirement date, you must consider the distance. Your planning will center around the fact that you have a limited, measurable amount of time between today and your proposed retirement date to achieve financial independence. That amount of time is perhaps the most important factor in your retirement planning.

The growth of your retirement capital is a function of the additions you make to it and the compounded returns on your capital. In any compounding process, the longer you allow compounding to continue, the more powerful it is.

Q: How can I control the time factor?

A: In retirement planning, starting early is very important. As shown in Illustration 12-3, people who start investing earlier allow the power of compounding to greatly multiply their

RETIREMENT PLANNING

capital, whereas the late starters have to save much more to catch up.

Q: Is getting an early start the only way to manage time in my retirement planning?

A: No. Because of the power of compounding over time, it is also important that you do not stop saving and investing too early. If you plan an early retirement, you must realize that this will come at a high price. You will be shortening the period of time during which you allow your retirement capital to build. The last five or ten years of your career are likely to be your highest earning years, allowing greater additions to your retirement capital. The compounded earnings on your retirement capital would also be greatest in those last years, since the earnings would be based on larger amount of capital than before.

You should also consider that early retirement may mean that you do not have any Social Security or retirement plan income in the first years of your retirement. This could force you to use more of your retirement capital than you anticipated.

Your planned retirement age, then, deserves careful consideration. But once you have weighed the alternatives and set a desired date, you have established your schedule for achieving financial independence.

Illustration 12-3

The "Early Bird" Factor

You would assume that someone who saved for thirty-two years would accumulate more capital than someone who saved the same yearly amount for only eight years. But when those eight years are earlier, they can be more powerful. At 10 percent compounding, the "early bird" and the "late bloomer" would accumulate the following amount of capital:

Year	"Early Bird" Contribution	Capital	"Late Bloomer" Contribution	Capital
1	$2,000	$2,200	$0	$0
2	$2,000	$4,620	$0	$0
3	$2,000	$7,282	$0	$0
4	$2,000	$10,210	$0	$0
5	$2,000	$13,431	$0	$0
6	$2,000	$16,974	$0	$0
7	$2,000	$20,872	$0	$0
8	$2,000	$25,159	$0	$0
9	$0	$27,675	$2,000	$2,200
10	$0	$30,442	$2,000	$4,620
11	$0	$33,487	$2,000	$7,282
12	$0	$36,835	$2,000	$10,210
13	$0	$40,519	$2,000	$13,431
14	$0	$44,571	$2,000	$16,974
15	$0	$49,028	$2,000	$20,872
16	$0	$53,930	$2,000	$25,159
17	$0	$59,323	$2,000	$29,875
18	$0	$65,256	$2,000	$35,062
19	$0	$71,781	$2,000	$40,769
20	$0	$78,960	$2,000	$47,045
21	$0	$86,856	$2,000	$53,950
22	$0	$95,541	$2,000	$61,545
23	$0	$105,095	$2,000	$69,899
24	$0	$115,605	$2,000	$79,089
25	$0	$127,165	$2,000	$89,198
26	$0	$139,882	$2,000	$100,318
27	$0	$153,870	$2,000	$112,550
28	$0	$169,257	$2,000	$126,005
29	$0	$186,183	$2,000	$140,805
30	$0	$204,801	$2,000	$174,995
31	$0	$225,281	$2,000	$174,995
32	$0	$247,809	$2,000	$194,694
33	$0	$272,590	$2,000	$216,364
34	$0	$299,849	$2,000	$240,200
35	$0	$329,834	$2,000	$266,420
36	$0	$362,817	$2,000	$295,262
37	$0	$399,099	$2,000	$326,988
38	$0	$439,009	$2,000	$361,887
39	$0	$482,910	$2,000	$400,276
40	$0	$531,201	$2,000	$442,503
Investment		$16,000		$64,000
Earnings		$515,201		$378,503

Q: How will my life expectancy affect my retirement goals?

A: Your life expectancy will affect how long your retirement will be. When Social Security was first established in the 1930s, the average retiree lived only a few years beyond age sixty-five and thus had a very short retirement. Now, the average person of age sixty-five can expect to survive past eighty, and so retirees must plan to support themselves for twenty years or more. Some people, in fact, live longer in retirement than they worked during their careers.

Q: What factors should I use in estimating my life expectancy?

A: In estimating your life expectancy after retirement, you should consider your planned retirement age, your general health expectations, and your heredity. You cannot predict your life span accurately, but it is important for your retirement planning that you make an estimate.

Your goal will be to accumulate an amount of capital that will generate enough income to meet your needs throughout the entire period of your retirement.

Q: How do I estimate my income needs during retirement?

A: The amount of retirement income needed is one of the primary concerns of most people considering retirement. Your basic goal in planning, saving, and investing is to have ample income to maintain your standard of living during retirement. You can determine your retirement income needs by considering such items as:

- Your current spending habits
- The compounding effects of inflation

Q: How do my current income needs affect my retirement income goal?

A: Your current income needs (see Illustration 12-2 on page 314) reflect your standard of living. Assuming that you wish to maintain your standard of living during retirement, your goal should be sufficient retirement income to buy the goods and services to which you are accustomed. However, you must consider the fact that your lifestyle will change.

RETIREMENT PLANNING

Q: How will my retirement income needs differ from my current income needs?

A: In setting your retirement income goal, you should consider which of your current expenses you will still have after you retire and how the level of expenses may be managed.

Some of your expenses may not continue. One of your largest monthly expenses, your mortgage payment, will disappear when you pay off your mortgage. Similarly, you probably will not have education and commuting costs. Because of these factors, many advisors suggest that your retirement expenses will be only 70 to 80 percent of your preretirement expenses.

Q: Is it possible that my income needs will not be reduced after I retire?

A: Yes. The traditional 70 to 80 percent rule for retirement income needs may not apply to current trends or to your plans. Although your mortgage may not be an expense anymore, your house will be getting older and will probably require a larger repair budget. Since you too will be aging, medical costs are likely to be a larger factor in your retirement budget.

Your plans for retirement may also include new expenses, such as travel or gifts to grandchildren. Because of these and other possible unforeseen expenses, many advisors now recommend that you anticipate needing 100 percent or more of your current expenses in retirement.

Taking these factors into account, you can estimate what your retirement income needs would be if you retired today. You can then adjust this estimate for inflation and use the result in your retirement planning.

Q: How can inflation affect my retirement income needs?

A: Just as the power of compounding assists you in building retirement capital (see page 317), it works against you in the form of inflation of your expenses. No matter what happens to the economy and your financial situation, the cost of the goods and services you need will almost certainly continue to increase each year after you retire. Illustration 12-4 shows how even moderate inflation over time will greatly affect the cost of the things you need.

RETIREMENT PLANNING

Illustration 12-4
Inflation: The Only Constant Risk

INFLATION:
The Only CONSTANT Risk

First Class Stamp

1973: 8¢

1993: 29¢

Gallon of Milk

1973: $1.30

1993: $2.79

Olds Cutlass

1973: $2,995

1993: $14,875

Q: How can I estimate my inflation-adjusted retirement income needs?

A: In your retirement planning, you should estimate the effect that inflation will have on your expenses, both between now and retirement and during retirement. Since inflation multiplies your expenses over time, you can use a multiplier to estimate your costs at retirement. Thus, using the table in Illustration 12-5, you could assume that twenty years of 5 percent inflation, on average, would multiply your expenses 2.65 times.

As an example, if your estimated required monthly retirement income is currently $2,000, it will increase to $5,300 ($2,000 times 2.65) in twenty years. You will thus need $5,300 a month in after-tax retirement income to maintain your current standard of living in twenty years.

Illustration 12-5

Compounding Multiplier Table Years of Compounding

Period	1%	2%	3%	4%	5%	6%	7%
1	1.010	1.020	1.030	1.040	1.050	1.060	1.070
2	1.020	1.040	1.061	1.082	1.102	1.124	1.145
3	1.030	1.061	1.093	1.125	1.158	1.191	1.225
4	1.041	1.082	1.126	1.170	1.216	1.262	1.311
5	1.051	1.104	1.159	1.217	1.276	1.338	1.403
6	1.062	1.126	1.194	1.265	1.340	1.419	1.501
7	1.072	1.149	1.230	1.316	1.407	1.504	1.606
8	1.083	1.172	1.267	1.369	1.477	1.594	1.718
9	1.094	1.195	1.305	1.423	1.551	1.689	1.838
10	1.105	1.219	1.344	1.480	1.629	1.791	1.967
11	1.116	1.243	1.384	1.539	1.710	1.898	2.105
12	1.127	1.268	1.426	1.601	1.796	2.012	2.252
13	1.138	1.294	1.469	1.665	1.886	2.133	2.410
14	1.149	1.319	1.513	1.732	1.980	2.261	2.579
15	1.161	1.346	1.558	1.801	2.079	2.397	2.759
16	1.173	1.373	1.605	1.873	2.183	2.540	2.952
17	1.184	1.400	1.653	1.948	2.292	2.693	3.159
18	1.196	1.428	1.702	2.026	2.407	2.854	3.380
19	1.208	1.457	1.754	2.107	2.527	3.026	3.617
20	1.220	1.486	1.806	2.191	2.653	3.207	3.870
25	1.282	1.641	2.094	2.666	3.386	4.292	5.427
30	1.348	1.811	2.427	3.243	4.322	5.743	7.612

Period	8%	9%	10%	12%	14%	15%	16%
1	1.080	1.090	1.100	1.120	1.140	1.150	1.160
2	1.166	1.186	1.210	1.254	1.300	1.322	1.346
3	1.260	1.295	1.331	1.405	1.482	1.521	1.561
4	1.360	1.412	1.464	1.574	1.689	1.749	1.811
5	1.469	1.539	1.611	1.762	1.925	2.011	2.100
6	1.587	1.677	1.772	1.974	2.195	2.313	2.436
7	1.714	1.828	1.949	2.211	2.502	2.660	2.826
8	1.851	1.993	2.144	2.476	2.853	3.059	3.278
9	1.999	2.172	2.358	2.773	3.252	3.518	3.803
10	2.159	2.367	2.594	3.106	3.707	4.046	4.411
11	2.332	2.580	2.853	3.479	4.226	4.652	5.117
12	2.518	2.813	3.138	3.896	4.818	5.350	5.926
13	2.720	3.066	3.452	4.363	5.492	6.153	6.886
14	2.937	3.342	3.797	4.887	6.261	7.076	7.988
15	3.172	3.642	4.117	5.474	7.138	8.137	9.266
16	3.426	3.970	4.595	6.130	8.137	9.358	10.748
17	3.700	4.328	5.054	6.866	9.276	10.761	12.468
18	3.996	4.717	5.560	7.690	10.575	12.375	14.463
19	4.316	5.142	6.116	8.613	12.056	14.232	16.777
20	4.661	5.604	6.782	9.646	13.743	16.367	19.461
25	6.848	8.623	10.835	17.000	26.462	32.919	40.874
30	10.063	13.268	17.449	29.960	50.950	66.212	85.850

Q: How can I estimate my income needs throughout retirement?

A: During your retirement, your income needs will continue to increase as a result of inflation. To estimate how inflation may affect your income needs year by year, you should begin with your estimated retirement-year budget and increase it by an anticipated percentage rate of inflation each year. Using this method, you can create a schedule of retirement income needs. Illustration 12-6 shows a retirement income need schedule using the $5,300 initial income level from the example above and a 5 percent rate of inflation.

Illustration 12-6
Retirement Income Need Schedule

Retirement Year	Retirement Income Need
1	$5,300
2	$5,565
3	$5,843
4	$6,135
5	$6,442
6	$6,764
7	$7,103
8	$7,458
9	$7,831
10	$8,222
11	$8,633
12	$9,065
13	$9,518
14	$9,994
15	$10,494
16	$11,018
17	$11,569
18	$12,148
19	$12,755
20	$13,393
21	$14,062
22	$14,766
23	$15,504
24	$16,279
25	$17,093
26	$17,948
27	$18,845
28	$19,787
29	$20,777
30	$21,816

RETIREMENT PLANNING

Q: How do I estimate my sources of income during retirement?

A: Generating retirement income is the central goal of retirement planning. Your sources of retirement income will determine whether your retirement will be secure or a financial struggle. Some of your sources of retirement income are provided by others, but it is important for you to determine how much retirement income you must provide on your own.

In your retirement planning, it is important that you estimate what your sources of income will be and how much income they will provide. Only after you have an idea of the extent of your retirement income will you know how much additional capital you will have to accumulate to achieve retirement security. The main sources of retirement income are:

- Social Security income
- Employer pension income
- Retirement savings income

To meet your estimated retirement income needs, you should estimate your income sources net of taxes, since only your after-tax income will be available to pay your expenses.

Q: What role does Social Security play in my retirement income?

A: You have probably noticed that your paycheck is reduced by an item called *FICA* each pay period. That item represents a mandatory payment into the Social Security system. Your employer also contributes on your behalf each pay period. The Social Security system is discussed further in Chapter 11, page 283.

After you and your employers have made payments throughout your career, the Social Security Administration will provide a specified level of income during your retirement years.

Q: How do I estimate my Social Security income during retirement?

A: The amount of Social Security income you will receive depends to some extent on how many years you will have worked and the extent of the contributions in your name. You can get an estimate of the amount of Social Security income you can expect at your retirement from the Social Security

Administration. If you send in the appropriate form, you will receive an estimate of the amount of Social Security income you will receive in the first year you are fully eligible (currently age sixty-five).

Since Social Security income is adjusted for inflation, you can create a schedule of the estimated year-to-year increases during your retirement at an anticipated rate of inflation. By doing this, you can create a Social Security income column to match your retirement income need schedule (see Illustration 12-7, column B, page 331).

Q: Can I count on receiving the Social Security income specified in the estimate I get from the Social Security Administration?

A: Not necessarily. A number of factors have decreased the certainty that you will benefit as much from Social Security income as you might think. When Social Security was first established, the over-sixty-five population was relatively small, and people generally did not live long past that age. The number of workers per retiree (37 in 1935) was great enough to comfortably support the Social Security benefits. Since that time, a combination of lengthening life expectancies and a growing population has placed severe strains on the Social Security system. The number of workers supporting each retiree has dropped to 3.5, and it is estimated that it will fall to 1.78 by the year 2020.

These factors will force some reform of the Social Security system. This may well affect your retirement planning. The level of Social Security income that will be available to you in retirement is unlikely to increase; any change will probably reduce the level you can count on. Such a reduction would increase the importance of maximizing your other sources of income in your retirement planning.

Q: Is it possible that I will receive no Social Security income?

A: It is unlikely, but possible. If enough strain is placed on the Social Security system, one possible reform might be to provide benefits for only the most needy of retirees. In such a case, anyone with other income or resources above a certain level might be disqualified from receiving any benefits.

RETIREMENT PLANNING

Recent tax increases on Social Security payments to higher-income retirees are a step in this direction.

In your retirement planning, it may be wise to take a look at how sufficient your retirement income would be if Social Security were severely limited or unavailable. Though such a situation is not likely, it is possible enough that you should consider it in your plans.

Q: How is Social Security income taxed?

A: At present, Social Security income is partially taxable. The current tax laws provide that up to 85 percent of Social Security income is fully taxable if your total income is above certain levels.

For further detail on Social Security income taxation, see your tax advisor. You should also consult your tax advisor on how income taxes may affect your anticipated Social Security payments.

Q: How do I estimate my income from my employer's pension plan during retirement?

A: If your employer's retirement plan provides a defined level of retirement income, it is important that you estimate the level of payments you will receive at retirement. Often your pension income will be a certain percentage—say 80 percent—of your preretirement income. If you are many years away from retirement, it may be difficult for you to predict what this amount will be.

The human resources department of your employer should be able to give you an estimate of your pension income. This estimate will assume that you continue working until retirement and that your pay increases by a reasonable percentage each year for the remainder of your career. The estimate that the human resources department provides for you should indicate both the level of pension income at retirement and whether the payments are fixed or will be indexed to increase with inflation. You can use your employer's estimate to write a schedule of estimated pension income to supplement your schedule of Social Security income.

Q: How is pension income taxed?

A: Generally, pension income is taxed as ordinary income when you receive it during retirement. Some exceptions may apply, depending on the source of the pension and your tax situation. Consult your tax advisor as to the tax status of your pension income.

Q: Are there other pension income sources I should consider?

A: Yes. You may be eligible for pension income from other sources. Previous employment or military service may entitle you to pension income that you have forgotten about or overlooked. It is worthwhile for you to investigate such possible sources and include any that you find in your schedule of retirement income.

Q: How do I estimate my income from my retirement savings during retirement?

A: With the increasing uncertainty of other sources of retirement income, the income from your own savings becomes a more crucial part of your retirement planning. This is also the income source most under your control. It is the source that you can manage in order to achieve retirement security.

In your retirement planning, you should estimate the income that you will have if you continue your current retirement savings habits. To do so, you will need to estimate:

- What your current capital will be worth
- What your contributions at your current rate will add
- What income your accumulated savings will produce

Q: How do I estimate the approximate value of my current retirement capital at retirement?

A: As discussed above, your current retirement capital is an important starting point in your retirement planning. You must consider the assets that make up your retirement capital (such as retirement plan balances, IRA balances, and other investments) and estimate how they will grow. To estimate how your capital will compound between now and retirement, you can apply a multiplier just as you did for your income needs (see Illustrations 12-5 and 12-6, pages 322 and 323). However, to determine the multiplier, you should use the rate of return you expect to earn on your capital.

RETIREMENT PLANNING

Example: Assume you currently have $100,000 in retirement capital and are twenty years from retirement. You expect to earn 7 percent (after taxes) on your capital. Since the corresponding compounding multiplier is 3.87, you can estimate that your current capital will be worth $387,000 at retirement. This may seem a generous amount of capital, but hopefully it will be only a part of your available resources.

Note: Your retirement capital may include several different types of assets that will grow at different rates. You can either compound each one separately, or use a reasonable average rate of return to compound the total.

Q: What role will my additional savings contributions play in my retirement planning?

A: Your ability to add to your retirement capital may determine whether you achieve your goal of retirement security. In many cases, your analysis will show that an increase in your savings is the answer to achieving a secure retirement. To determine that answer, however, you must first estimate how adequate your savings will be to provide the desired income if you continue to accumulate them at your current rate.

Q: How do I estimate how much my additional savings contributions will be worth at retirement?

A: Essentially, you can estimate how much each year's contribution to your retirement savings will add to your retirement-year capital the same way you estimated the future value of your current capital. Using the compounding multipliers from Illustration 12-5, page 322, you can calculate how much your savings will be worth at retirement at an assumed earnings rate.

If you are saving $250 per month, for instance, your yearly contribution to your retirement capital would be $3,000. If you earn 7 percent after taxes on your capital and you have twenty years to retirement, this year's contribution will add $11,610 to your capital by retirement. The next year's contribution will compound for only nineteen years, so it will add slightly less, and so on for subsequent years. You can make this calculation for each year—twenty years' contributions—to give you the total retirement capital that you would accumulate by your retirement year if you continued to save at your current rate.

 Note: If you are having difficulty computing the estimated future values of your various sources of capital or income needs, ask your advisors for help. They will generally have computers or calculators that can quickly determine the estimated future value of a sum of money or a savings program at an assumed earnings rate.

Now that you have estimated the retirement-year value of your current capital and all future contributions at your current savings level, the next step is to estimate the retirement income your capital may produce.

Q: How do I estimate the income my retirement savings will produce during my retirement?

A: Estimating the initial income from your retirement savings is simply a matter of applying a reasonable percentage to your estimated total retirement capital. If you have accumulated $500,000 and you earn 7 percent on this amount during your first year of retirement, your retirement income for that year will be $35,000. Subsequent years' income may be more difficult to estimate. You may be adding to or withdrawing from your capital, depending on how adequately your retirement income sources are meeting your retirement income needs, and this will change the amount of income you receive.

Q: How do I determine whether my income sources will be adequate to meet my income needs during retirement?

A: The preceding steps in retirement planning have provided the information you need in order to estimate whether your current retirement accumulations will provide adequate retirement security. To summarize, you have calculated:

- A schedule of estimated income needed in retirement (Column A)
- A schedule of estimated Social Security income (Column B)
- A schedule of estimated pension income, if any (Column C)

- Surplus (deficit) of income need versus Social Security and pension income (A deficit is the amount that must come from earnings on your own retirement capital.) (Column D)
- Your estimated retirement capital (Column E)
- Your estimated initial income from your retirement capital (Column F)

Putting together these estimates, you can make a consolidated schedule estimating the adequacy of your retirement income. For the example in this chapter, the schedule shown in Illustration 12-7 compares estimated income needs (Column A) with the combined income from Social Security and pension sources. You may find that those two sources will provide all the income you estimate you will need. It is more likely, though, that, as in this example, there will be a shortfall between income needed and estimated income produced.

Illustration 12-7
Retirement Income Adequacy Schedule

Inflation: 5%
Capital Earnings Rate: 7%

Year	A Monthly Income Need	B Social Security Income	C Pension Income	D Surplus (Shortfall)	E Retirement Capital	F Income on Retirement Capital
1	$5,300	$1,200	$1,800	($2,300)	$500,000	$2,917
2	$5,565	$1,260	$1,890	($2,415)	$507,400	$2,960
3	$5,843	$1,323	$1,985	($2,536)	$513,938	$2,998
4	$6,135	$1,389	$2,084	($2,663)	$519,485	$3,030
5	$6,442	$1,459	$2,188	($2,796)	$523,898	$3,056
6	$6,764	$1,532	$2,297	($2,935)	$527,023	$3,074
7	$7,103	$1,608	$2,412	($3,082)	$528,689	$3,084
8	$7,458	$1,689	$2,533	($3,236)	$528,711	$3,084
9	$7,831	$1,773	$2,659	($3,398)	$526,885	$3,073
10	$8,222	$1,862	$2,792	($3,568)	$522,989	$3,051
11	$8,633	$1,955	$2,932	($3,746)	$516,781	$3,015
12	$9,065	$2,052	$3,079	($3,934)	$507,999	$2,963
13	$9,518	$2,155	$3,233	($4,130)	$496,353	$2,895
14	$9,994	$2,263	$3,394	($4,337)	$481,532	$2,809
15	$10,494	$2,376	$3,564	($4,554)	$463,196	$2,702
16	$11,018	$2,495	$3,742	($4,782)	$440,973	$2,572
17	$11,569	$2,619	$3,929	($5,021)	$414,463	$2,418
18	$12,148	$2,750	$4,126	($5,272)	$383,228	$2,235
19	$12,755	$2,888	$4,332	($5,535)	$346,794	$2,023
20	$13,393	$3,032	$4,549	($5,812)	$304,647	$1,777
21	$14,062	$3,184	$4,776	($6,103)	$256,229	$1,495
22	$14,766	$3,343	$5,015	($6,408)	$200,933	$1,172
23	$15,504	$3,510	$5,265	($6,728)	$138,106	$806
24	$16,279	$3,686	$5,529	($7,065)	$67,037	$391
25	$17,093	$3,870	$5,805	($7,418)	$0	$0
26	$17,948	$4,064	$6,095	($7,789)	$0	$0
27	$18,845	$4,267	$6,400	($8,178)	$0	$0
28	$19,787	$4,480	$6,720	($8,587)	$0	$0
29	$20,777	$4,704	$7,056	($9,016)	$0	$0
30	$21,816	$4,939	$7,409	($9,467)	$0	$0

Q: What does it mean if my estimated retirement income appears to be sufficient?

A: If your estimated retirement income appears sufficient to meet your estimated expenses, congratulations! You are on track for retirement security. Your sources of income, including earnings on your own retirement savings, should meet the challenge of providing you a secure retirement.

If your capital continues to earn more than the rate of inflation, you will never need to deplete your capital to meet expenses. It will continue to grow, providing a reserve for any emergencies and a substantial estate for your heirs.

You should not become complacent just yet, however. If some of your assumptions prove to be too optimistic, your retirement security could still be threatened. You should run your calculations again with more pessimistic assumptions on inflation, earnings on retirement capital, or other factors to see how sensitive your retirement security may be to changing conditions. You can have true peace of mind if your estimates of retirement security can stand some harsher conditions.

Q: What does it mean if my estimated retirement income appears to be insufficient?

A: If your estimated retirement does not appear to be adequate, you run the risk of having to deplete your capital each year to meet expenses. As the example in Illustration 12-7 shows, this would decrease your subsequent income. The problem would get worse every year, as you would have less capital available to produce income. Your capital would be depleted by an accelerating amount until it was exhausted.

Q: Does insufficient income create a crisis?

A: Not necessarily, but it is troubling. Your retirement security will not necessarily be threatened if your capital decreases a bit each year. If the rate of depletion is slow enough, you may live years past your life expectancy (without sacrificing your lifestyle) before your capital is exhausted.

Some people actively plan to use their entire capital over a reasonable life expectancy. Such people are not concerned about leaving an estate for their heirs. They may place their retirement capital in an annuity that maximizes their income and has no residual value at death.

Q: Should I plan to deplete my capital during retirement?

A: If your goal is a secure retirement, you should aim to produce enough income to make capital depletion unnecessary. For most people, continually depleting retirement capital is never ideal. A perpetual decline leaves you without a margin for error in case of unexpected costs or emergencies.

An insufficient level of estimated retirement income generally indicates that you need to make some changes in your retirement planning. Improving your savings habits for retirement a bit today will greatly improve your chances of reaching your retirement goals years from now. The challenge, once you have determined where you are and where you are going, is determining how to get there from here.

Q: How do I determine how to get there in retirement planning?

A: If your preliminary retirement planning scenario shows you falling short of your estimated retirement income needs, you have plenty of company. Experts estimate that most people are not on track to enjoy the kind of retirement security they seek. Now that you have done the work required to estimate the income you will need at retirement, you can plan to eliminate your estimated shortfall.

The real work of retirement planning comes after you have answered the questions "where am I?" (your current status) and "where am I going?" (your retirement needs and goals). You now need to determine how to get there. Your retirement planning efforts will now focus on improving your chances to achieve your goal. In continuing your retirement planning, you can estimate the effects of changes such as:

- Starting a savings program earlier
- Increasing your savings contributions
- Adjusting your spending habits
- Maximizing investment performance
- Planning to work to a later age

Each of these changes would affect your estimates and improve the likelihood that you will have a sufficient retirement income. You may want to change just one factor at a time to see how powerful each might be in your case.

RETIREMENT PLANNING

Summary

Our purpose in this chapter was to answer some questions you might have when you begin to engage in retirement planning. As with any large undertaking, the first few steps will at least start you on the journey. The questions and answers in this chapter were designed to provide a road map on the basics of retirement planning. More involved planning should take you much farther.

Just as retirement planning is too important to do tentatively, the subject is too broad to cover fully in these pages. As you continue in your planning efforts, you may wish to seek the aid of an advisor. Together you may determine the provisions you must make in order to ensure a secure and comfortable retirement in your later years.

CHAPTER 13

ESTATE PLANNING

You will have spent a lifetime accumulating assets to achieve financial security. As discussed throughout this book, the way to achieve financial security is to develop a plan to accumulate wealth that will provide for you after you no longer have earnings or earning power.

The same planning effort will help you provide for your loved ones after you die. This is called *estate planning*. While you are alive, you should develop a plan for transferring your wealth to your beneficiaries in accordance with your wishes. If you do not develop an estate plan and draft the proper documents, your assets will be distributed in accordance with state laws, which may not be what you would want. Without proper planning and the proper documents, the settlement of your estate will also be more expensive, leaving fewer assets for your heirs.

Like the material in other chapters in this book, estate planning could be a book in itself. This chapter will cover the highlights and provide introductory information. The questions and answers should give you some ideas about ways in which you may reduce your estate taxes and establish trusts for your benefit and for the benefit of your heirs.

Many people do not create an estate plan because they do not know how to design and execute a specific plan and how to use estate planning techniques to preserve assets and transfer these assets to their heirs. This chapter seeks to make you aware that you can do this and give you enough information to let you work with your advisors to create an estate plan that meets your objectives.

Q: What is estate planning?

A: *Estate planning* is the process of arranging your assets in a way that will minimize estate taxes and ensure that your assets will be distributed to your heirs as you wish rather than as dictated by state law.

Q: Why would I need estate planning?

A: You will still have goals to achieve when your life ends. Estate planning can assist you in achieving such goals as:

- Providing for the support of your spouse and children
- Minimizing estate taxes
- Avoiding delays and expenses in estate settlement
- Distributing your assets as you wish
- Granting you peace of mind

Q: What is my gross estate?

A: Your *gross estate* consists of all assets that you own at the time of your death, including some items that are not necessarily listed on a personal financial statement.

Q: What are some of the assets that will be included in my gross estate?

A: The most obvious assets in your gross estate are cash, securities, and your home. Less obvious assets may include:

- The fair market value of any real estate you own or in which you have an interest
- The proceeds from any life insurance policies for which you are both the owner and the insured, and the cash value of any others that you own
- The value of any vested retirement benefits, which may include an employer's retirement plan, a 401(k) plan, and your IRAs
- The value of your interest in assets registered as joint tenants with the right of survivorship (one half of the total value)
- The value of your personal items, such as collections, household furniture, jewelry, and automobiles in your name

Q: What is my net taxable estate?

A: Your *net taxable estate* is your gross estate minus certain allowable deductions. A partial list of possible deductions from your gross estate may include:

- General expenses to settle your estate
- Expenses of a last illness
- Funeral expenses
- Expenses for administration of your estate
- Bona fide claims against your estate (debts)
- Mortgages against real estate or other debts
- Charitable transfers
- Marital transfers to your surviving spouse upon your death

Note: These lists of assets included in your gross estate and deductions from your gross estate are partial lists. In order to develop a complete list of the specific items included in your estate and deductions from it, you will have to consult with your advisors.

Q: What is a will?

A: A *will* is a legal document that details what you wish to do with your assets and instructs your executor or executrix to carry out your wishes upon your death. A will contains a number of legal clauses designed to ensure that your wishes are carried out. Some of these legal clauses do the following:

- Name an executor or executrix to carry out the instructions in the will
- Name legal guardians for minor children
- Arrange for the provision of income to your family while the estate settlement is being processed
- Detail special bequests you may want to make
- Designate a source for the payment of taxes
- Incorporate the marital deduction (page 341)
- Distribute the property that remains after all expenses and specific bequests

ESTATE
PLANNING

A will can be simple or complex, depending on the size of your estate and how you want your assets distributed.

Q: How can I ensure that my assets will be distributed as I wish?

A: If you have executed a proper will, the probate process will ensure that your instructions are carried out. Your will should include complete instructions on how you want your assets distributed after your death.

Q: What is probate?

A: *Probate* is a court process that provides a systematic method of paying a decedent's debts and fulfilling the instructions in the decedent's estate documents. Generally, a public official of accounts or an officer of the court in the locality in which a person resides at the time of his or her death will oversee the executor to ensure that all of the decedent's wishes as expressed in the will are carried out.

Generally, a small percentage of a decedent's assets will be paid as a probate fee in the settlement of the estate.

Q: What does it mean if a person dies intestate?

A: If a person dies *intestate,* he or she dies without a properly executed will. In such a case, a court will appoint an administrator to oversee the distribution of a decedent's assets. The court-appointed administrator will distribute the decedent's estate in accordance with state law, which may not be how the deceased would have distributed his or her property.

Q: If I have a will, will an administrator be appointed?

A: No. If your will names one or more executors or executrices, the person, persons, or organization named will be legally responsible for distributing your assets according to the instructions in your will.

Q: What is an executor?

A: An *executor* is a person or organization, such as the trust department of a financial institution, named in a will that is responsible for carrying out the decedent's instructions as stated in the will.

Q: What is an executrix?

A: An *executrix* is a female who is named in a will as the person responsible for carrying out the decedent's instructions as stated in the will.

Q: Who should I name as executor or executrix in my will?

A: There is no easy answer as to who you should name as executor or executrix in your will. For years, many individuals have named the trust department of a bank as their executor. Recently, many individuals have named one of their advisors or a close family member who has the expertise to settle their estate as executor or executrix. Some people name several executors. Often, a will names a backup executor in case the named individual or individuals cannot serve.

Q: Why would I not want to name the trust department of a financial institution as executor of my will?

A: You may not want to name the trust department of a financial institution as executor of your will because of the fees that it will charge and the amount of time many financial institutions take to settle an estate.

Also, as financial institutions have become larger and larger, many of them have transferred their trust operations to distant locations. If this has happened or if it happens before your death, a trust officer may not be readily available to your heirs or beneficiaries on a timely basis. In such a case, your heirs or beneficiaries may have to deal with executors through long-distance phone calls; this may or may not affect the settlement of your estate, but may not be the best of situations. This is a possibility that you must consider when drafting your will and naming an executor or executrix.

Q: Will an individual charge my estate the same fees as a trust department?

A: Not necessarily. You should talk to the individual or individuals you may want to name as executors or executrices and establish fee arrangements before you sign your will. Your legal advisor can write into your will that your executor is to be paid *hourly fees* rather than a *flat fixed percentage fee*.

Whether you have an individual or the trust department of a financial institution serve as your executor, your estate will still have to pay legal expenses, accounting expenses, court filing fees, and tax return preparation costs. These charges would be in addition to executors' fees.

Q: What is a living will?

A: A *living will* is a written expression of your instructions should you be physically incapacitated beyond recovery and unable to make your wishes known. You may use a living will to instruct that you *not* be kept on artificial life support in such a case.

Just as a will makes your financial wishes known, a living will puts your physical wishes clearly on record.

Q: What are estate taxes?

A: If the value of your estate is above a certain level, the amount above this level may be subject to *estate taxes*. Estate taxes are assessed by the federal government and often by state governments as well. They are a means of raising revenue for the government and, in consequence, reduce the amount of decedent's assets that are available to his or her heirs.

Q: At what level would my estate be subject to estate taxes?

A: Under current law, any estate valued in excess of $600,000 would be subject to estate taxes. You should check with your advisors periodically to see if this amount has changed and if your estate plan has to be changed as a result.

Q: What are the estate tax rates?

A: Illustration 13-1 shows the current Unified Federal Gift and Estate Tax schedule. Most states also impose inheritance taxes on the assets of a deceased individual. Estate inheritance taxes are often based on the federal estate tax, but are usually smaller.

Illustration 13-1
Gift and Estate Tax Rates

Taxable Transfer (thousands of dollars)	Tax on Col 1 (dollars)	% Tax on Next Dollar
0	0	18
10	1,800	20
20	3,800	22
40	8,200	24
60	13,000	26
80	18,200	28
100	23,800	30
150	38,800	32
250	70,800	34
500	155,800	37
750	248,300	39
1,000	345,800	41
1,250	448,300	43
1,500	555,800	45
2,000	780,800	49
2,500	1,025,800	53
3,000	1,290,800	55
10,000	5,140,800	60
21,040	11,764,800	55

Q: What is the unified credit?

A: Each person is entitled to a unified transfer tax credit (the *unified credit*) that can be used to offset tax liability for either gifts made during an individual's lifetime or estate taxes payable at death. The allowable credit is $192,800, which is the equivalent of exempting gifts or estates valued at up to $600,000. A person who has not used the unified credit during his or her lifetime can expect the first $600,000 of his or her estate to pass to heirs without estate taxes.

Q: What is the marital deduction?

A: The *marital deduction* is a deduction that offsets the transfer taxes when transfers, either during one's lifetime or at death, are made to a spouse. Currently, the deduction is unlimited, which means a couple may transfer any amount of assets to one another without incurring any gift taxes. After one spouse dies, there is no estate tax liability on transfers made to the surviving spouse under the will.

In essence, assets distributed to a spouse will not be subject to gift or estate taxes.

Q: If I leave all my assets to my spouse, will my estate avoid estate taxes?

A: Yes and no. If your estate is worth less than $600,000 and your estate combined with your spouse's is less than $600,000, there will be no estate tax on either estate no matter who you leave your assets to.

However, if your estate combined with that of your spouse is valued at more than $600,000 and you leave all of your assets to your spouse, you will create an estate tax liability for your spouse. The value of your spouse's estate will be the combined value and will be taxed accordingly.

The result of combining the assets of a decedent and his or her spouse may result in an unnecessary estate tax liability.

Q: How can my spouse and I avoid taxation on our combined estate?

A: You and your spouse can avoid taxes on a combined estate of up to $1,200,000 if you arrange your assets so that each of your estates can utilize the full $600,000 unified credit.

Since placing exactly $600,000 in each of your names may be impractical, you may automatically allocate the proper amounts by using a *bypass trust* (see page 349).

Q: How can we avoid paying estate tax if most of the assets are in the name of one spouse?

A: If one spouse has substantial assets, in order to save on estate taxes, the spouse with the assets should transfer at least $600,000 worth of the assets to the other spouse so that the family trust can be funded regardless of which spouse dies first.

Q: Could there be a problem with jointly owned assets or assets that pass to a designated beneficiary?

A: Jointly owned assets and assets with a designated beneficiary (such as insurance death proceeds or retirement plans) pass automatically to the surviving owner or to the beneficiary. Such assets may complicate the full utilization of the unified credit and *cannot* pass into a bypass trust.

 Note: You should review assets owned jointly and assets that pass to a designated beneficiary to ensure you are minimizing estate taxes.

Q: What are the advantages of making gifts during my life?

A: By making gifts during your lifetime, you are removing the value of the gifts and any appreciation on the gifted assets from your estate.

Q: How much am I allowed to give without having to pay a gift tax?

A: Any individual may make gifts of up to $10,000 per year to an individual who is not a spouse without invading the unified credit. You may make $10,000 worth of gifts to each of an unlimited number of individuals each year.

Q: Can a husband and wife increase the gift limit by making joint gifts?

A: Yes. A husband and wife may jointly make annual gifts of up to $20,000 to as many individuals as they like without invading the unified credit. The gifts can be made even if all the assets come from one spouse's account.

Q: If I give an individual other than a spouse more than $10,000 in a calendar year, what do I have to do?

A: If you make gifts of more than $10,000 in a calendar year to any individual other than a spouse, you will be required to file a gift tax form with your income tax return. The amount by which the value of a gift to an individual exceeds $10,000 may be subject to a gift tax. Alternatively, you may choose to pay no gift tax and draw on your unified credit. If you draw on the unified credit, you will decrease the amount of the credit available to offset estate taxes at your death.

ESTATE PLANNING

Q: What is the cost basis of any assets I give?

A: When you give someone an asset whose value has increased, the recipient retains your original cost basis and must use your (the donor's) date of acquisition. If the asset is worth less than you paid for it, the recipient's cost basis is the market value on the date of the gift. You cannot gift a loss.

Q: What is the cost basis of assets distributed as a result of the death of the original owner?

A: The cost basis of assets transferred from an estate is "stepped up" to the market value on either the date of the decedent's death or the alternative evaluation date, six months after the decedent's death. The market value of marketable securities (stocks and bonds) is the mean value on the date of death. The mean is the average of the high and low prices of the day. If the date of death is a weekend or holiday, the average from the mean on the day before and the day after is the market value.

Q: Would I want to give assets with a very low cost basis to children or grandchildren?

A: Probably not. In general, an older individual would not give children or grandchildren assets with a low cost basis relative to their current value, but would retain the assets as part of his or her estate so that their cost basis will be stepped up at the individual's death.

Q: What is a trust?

A: A *trust*, whether created during an individual's lifetime or by his or her will, is a written document specifying the creator's wishes (instructions) and directing that they be carried out. The trust document spells out how the assets in the trust are to be managed as well as when and to whom distributions are to be made. The document names the trustees as well as the beneficiaries.

 Note: The instructions in a trust can be as restrictive or as broad as the creator wishes. If a beneficiary is extravagant, the creator may want to restrict distributions. Alternatively, the creator may want to give the trustee very broad distribution authority.

Q: Why are trusts valuable in estate planning?

A: Trusts have many advantages in estate planning. A trust can be extremely valuable as a means of conserving and managing assets, and some types of trusts can be used to reduce income and estate taxes. Because a trust can exist long after your estate is settled, it can be more powerful than a will. A trust may be a more durable vehicle for achieving such estate planning goals as:

- Saving income taxes
- Saving estate taxes
- Avoiding court delays in the settlement of estates
- Protecting the interests of beneficiaries
- Specifying the time and manner of distribution of principal and income
- Providing for the special needs of individuals who are not able to manage for themselves

The advantages of establishing various types of trusts will be briefly discussed in the following pages. Each type of trust has its own advantages and limitations. The discussion of trusts in this book is not intended to be all-inclusive. How a particular type of trust may benefit you and your personal situation is something you should discuss thoroughly with your advisors.

Q: What terms should I know in order to better understand trusts?

A: The terms you should know in order to better understand trusts and how a trust operates are:

- Trustee
- Beneficiaries
- Creator (grantor)
- Funding

Q: What is a trustee?

A: A *trustee* is a person or organization, such as the trust department of a financial institution, that is named in the trust document as being responsible for the management of the assets in the trust. Trustees are responsible for carrying out the instructions of the creator (grantor), as written in the trust document, for the benefit of the beneficiary or beneficiaries.

Q: Who are the beneficiaries of the trust?

A: Usually, the *beneficiaries* of a trust are the individuals or organizations who are to receive assets from the trust. The two most common types of beneficiaries are income beneficiaries and remaindermen. A trust may distribute its income or part or all of its principal to income beneficiaries, depending on the instructions in the trust document. When the trust terminates, all remaining assets will be distributed to the remaindermen as stated in the trust document. The beneficiary or beneficiaries of a trust can be the creator, family members, or charitable organizations.

Q: Who is the creator of a trust?

A: The *creator*, often called the *grantor*, of a trust is the person or persons who have the trust document prepared and deposit assets (stocks, bonds, cash, real estate, and so forth) into the trust. The assets will be managed by the trustee or trustees for the benefit of the beneficiary or beneficiaries.

Q: What does funding a trust mean?

A: Generally, cash or other assets will be deposited into a trust so that they can be managed by the trustee or trustees for the benefit of the beneficiary or beneficiaries. Depositing assets into a trust is generally referred to as *funding* the trust.

Q: Are there different types of trusts?

A: Generally, trusts are classified as follows:

- Living trusts
- Testamentary trusts
- Irrevocable trusts
- Revocable trusts

Q: What is a living trust?

A: A *living trust* is a trust established during the lifetime of an individual or individuals.

Q: What is a testamentary trust?

A: A *testamentary trust* is a trust created after the death of an individual by the provisions of his or her will.

Q: What is a revocable trust?

A: A *revocable trust* is a trust that may be terminated at the discretion of the creator. The creator can usually also change trustees, investment managers, or beneficiaries.

Generally, all income produced by the assets in a revocable trust is taxable to the creator, since the creator still controls the assets and may benefit from them. The assets in the trust are also usually included in the creator's estate for estate tax purposes.

Q: What is an irrevocable trust?

A: An *irrevocable trust* is a trust that cannot be terminated by its creator. Such a trust is created to avoid income or estate taxes. In order to avoid these estate taxes and remove assets from his or her estate, the creator must surrender irrevocably his or her rights to the assets deposited into the trust. The creator usually cannot receive any income earned by the assets of an irrevocable trust, nor can he or she invade the property or change the beneficiaries.

 Note of Caution: Anyone who is considering establishing an irrevocable trust should give a great deal of thought to the reason for establishing the trust and to its provisions. Establishing an irrevocable trust is usually a way to make gifts to the beneficiaries, and the assets deposited into the trust may be subject to gift taxation. The amount of any potential gift tax liability will depend on the value of the gift. If you are considering establishing an irrevocable trust, you should consult your tax advisor concerning the potential gift tax liability and restrictions.

Q: What is a revocable living trust?

A: A *revocable living trust* is a trust that you create during your life in which you place some or all of your assets. You can change the conditions of the trust or revoke the trust at any

ESTATE
PLANNING

time. You can withdraw or add assets for any reason. Because you have complete control over the trust and its assets, you are viewed as the owner for federal income and estate tax purposes.

Q: Why would I consider establishing a revocable living trust?

A: One reason to establish a revocable living trust is to manage and pass along control of your assets. If you want uninterrupted professional management of your trust, you can name a money manager as the trustee who will take over upon your death. A revocable living trust can also provide for your guardianship if you should become incapacitated. This will avoid the expense and delay of guardianship court proceedings. A revocable living trust is sometimes used instead of a power of attorney.

A revocable living trust can also be designed to meet your specific family needs, such as supporting minor children or handicapped relatives or limiting distribution to future beneficiaries who have a tendency to overspend. Most individuals who create revocable living trusts provide for the trusts to continue after their death until the beneficiaries are able to manage their own assets.

In addition, the assets in a revocable living trust are not subject to the expense of the probate process, nor do they become matters of public record.

Q: Who should be trustee of my revocable living trust?

A: Usually, you will name yourself as trustee of your revocable living trust and continue managing the assets in the trust just as you did before you had a living trust.

You may want to name a standby trustee who would assume the role of trustee if you were to become disabled. Also, a standby trustee would have the responsibility for carrying out the instructions in the trust document after your death.

Q: What is a power of attorney?

A: A *power of attorney* is a written document that empowers another party—individual, individuals, or organization—to manage your affairs or perform some action on your behalf.

ESTATE PLANNING

A person holding your *general* power of attorney can usually pay your bills, withdraw money from your bank or investment accounts, buy or sell securities, and often buy or sell real estate. You may revoke a power of attorney any time you wish.

You can also give someone a *limited* power of attorney authorizing the person to take certain actions on your behalf. In such a case, the person holding the power of attorney can take only the actions specified.

 Note of Caution: You should be very careful about giving a general power of attorney. If the party holding your power of attorney is less than scrupulous, he or she may be able to clean you out!

Q: How can I protect myself when I give a power of attorney?

A: You can instruct your lawyer to *hold* the executed document giving another party your power of attorney and not to turn over the document to the party named until it is verified that you are disabled or unable to act on your own behalf.

 Note: Any questions you may have about a powers of attorney and authority over your affairs should be directed to your lawyer.

Q: What is a bypass trust?

A: A *bypass trust,* or *family trust,* is a type of trust that ensures that the full $600,000 unified credit is utilized in each spouse's estate. It provides that at the time of the death of the first spouse, up to $600,000 of the first spouse's assets are transferred to the trust. These assets are included in the decedent's estate for estate tax purposes.

The surviving spouse will be able to receive income and/or distributions from principal, under some circumstances, from the trust. However, at the death of the survivor, the assets in the family trust are not included in the survivor's estate for tax purposes. They will be distributed tax-free to the beneficiaries of the trust as designated in the trust document.

The first spouse to die will be the creator of the trust. The trust document will direct the distribution of the trust's

ESTATE
PLANNING

income and assets during the surviving spouse's life and at his or her death. The assets in the survivor's estate are subject to tax only if they exceed $600,000.

The result of using a family or bypass trust in each of your wills is that as a couple, you can pass a total of $1,200,000 to your heirs before paying estate tax. The trust allows you to pass an additional $192,800 to your heirs instead of paying it to the estate tax collector.

Q: What is a QTIP trust?

A: A *QTIP trust* (qualified terminal interest property) is traditionally used in conjunction with a family trust. Like a family trust, assets deposited into the QTIP trust are free of estate taxes to a surviving spouse. Unlike a family trust, the QTIP trust makes use of the unlimited marital deduction. The trust is usually intended to provide income support during the spouse's life, but preserve the capital for other beneficiaries.

Upon the death of the spouse, the assets in the trust are not included in the spouse's taxable estate. They are usually distributed to the creator's children as irrevocably designated by the creator in the trust document.

You might establish a QTIP trust if you have children by a previous marriage. The reason is that if your spouse has control over the assets after your death, he or she may dispose of them or leave them to someone other than *your* children. By using a QTIP trust, you are assured the assets in the trust will ultimately be passed to your children.

Q: What is a life insurance trust?

A: A *life insurance trust,* sometimes referred to as a pour-over trust, is an irrevocable trust. At the death of the creator, insurance and corporate fringe benefit proceeds, which have usually been made payable to the trust, are deposited into the trust.

For a life insurance trust to save estate taxes, it must be irrevocable. The creator must give up all rights to change the trust after it is created and all control over any assets that may be placed in the trust before or after his or her death. The trust will become the owner as well as the beneficiary of all insurance policies placed into it. If you decide to create an irrevocable insurance trust, you may incur some gift tax liability. You should always check with your tax advisor for potential gift or estate tax liabilities when you create such a trust.

The advantage of a life insurance trust is that it can provide immediate liquidity to your estate or beneficiaries and avoid the distress sale of real estate or closely held family businesses. Upon the creator's death, the trust receives liquid assets from insurance policies or corporate fringe benefits. These funds can then be used to buy illiquid assets from the creator's estate and create more estate liquidity.

Q: What is a Crummey trust?

A: A *Crummey trust* is a type of life insurance trust. In fact, what many people call a Crummey trust is a life insurance trust that includes Crummey provisions.

Crummey provisions allow the creator of an irrevocable life insurance trust to make annual gifts to the trust so that the trustee can pay the premiums on the life insurance policies owned by the trust. As long as the beneficiary or beneficiaries of the trust have a right to withdraw their proportionate part of these annual gifts, the death benefits paid by the insurance policies are *not* included in the creator's estate. However, the deposit is considered to be a gift of a present interest and is subject to the annual gift exclusion. The right of withdrawal allows the death benefits paid to the trust *not* to be included in the creator's estate.

Q: What are the risks in establishing an irrevocable life insurance trust with Crummey powers?

A: The use of Crummey powers in a life insurance trust can be extremely complex. If the trust document does not include the correct language and required procedures are not followed, the death benefits of the life insurance policy may be included in the creator's estate.

 Note of Caution: Because of their complexity, if you are considering making use of the Crummey powers, you should carefully consult with your advisors as to how the trust may benefit your personal situation. You must also understand and follow all required procedures.

Q: What is an educational trust?

A: An *educational trust* is an irrevocable living trust established primarily to pay for the education of a beneficiary. It is usually created to allow you or other family members to make gifts to children or grandchildren while retaining more control over the assets than you would have if they were registered under the Uniform Gifts to Minors Act. As previously discussed, you can give a minor up to $10,000, or you and your spouse can give $20,000, without paying any gift tax. Instead of making gifts to a minor, you or other family members may make them to a trust. Since the trust, or the minor, is usually in a lower income tax bracket, the income tax savings may be substantial. Also, assets you give to an education trust usually avoid taxation in your estate.

Q: What is a charitable remainder trust?

A: A *charitable remainder trust* is a trust whose income is paid to one or more beneficiaries, usually including the creator, for their lifetimes, with the remainder distributed to a named charity upon the death of the last beneficiary. You can deposit appreciated assets into such a trust, avoid taxation on the gain, and increase your current income.

Generally, you will receive a significant income tax deduction for the assets you place in the trust. This income tax deduction is based on what is called the *remainder interest*, which is the percentage of the initial value that IRS calculations assume will remain upon the creator's death. Any income you receive before you die will reduce the remainder interest, so your income tax deduction will be lower if you are young and receive a high income from the trust.

Since the trust does not pay income taxes, it can sell highly appreciated assets with no capital gains tax liability. For this reason, it will be able to reinvest a larger amount and earn more than you would have been able to earn if you had sold these assets and paid taxes on the gain. Traditionally, the income paid to the income beneficiary will be higher than the income paid on the assets deposited into the trust.

Upon the death of all income beneficiaries, the remaining value of the charitable remainder trust is usually distributed to a designated charity. Therefore, the assets in the trust will not be included in the creator's estate.

Q: What are the forms of charitable remainder trusts?

A: A charitable remainder trust generally takes one of two forms. They are:

- Unitrust
- Annuity trust

Q: What is a charitable remainder unitrust?

A: With a *charitable remainder unitrust*, the income beneficiary or beneficiaries must receive annual payments of a fixed percentage of the net market value of the trust assets. The net market value must be determined each year on a stated valuation date. As the value of the assets in the trust increases or decreases, the beneficiary's income will increase or decrease.

Q: What is a charitable remainder annuity trust?

A: With an *annuity trust*, a specific fixed dollar amount rather than a percentage of the value must be paid out annually. Generally, the payout from a charitable remainder annuity trust must remain constant for the term of the trust, or for the life of the income beneficiaries.

 Note: Computing the current tax deduction that may be available to you if you establish a charitable remainder trust can be quite complex. You should have your tax advisor determine all the income and estate tax considerations involved before you establish a charitable remainder trust and deposit assets into it.

Q: If I create a charitable remainder trust, who can be the income beneficiaries?

A: If you create a charitable remainder trust, you can name anyone, including yourself, as an income beneficiary. You can also name yourself and your spouse as joint beneficiaries. If you did this, the income would continue until both of you died. You can also include other people as joint beneficiaries.

ESTATE
PLANNING

 Note: Generally, the more income beneficiaries you include, the lower your income tax deduction will be when you establish the trust.

Q: Why should I consider establishing a charitable remainder trust?

A: You should consider establishing a charitable remainder trust if you would like to increase your income from low-yielding, highly appreciated assets. You should remember, however, that at your death, or at the death of the last income beneficiary, the assets in the trust will be distributed to the named charity or charities. They will *not* be available to your family or other heirs.

Q: Is there a way to replace in my estate the value of the assets deposited into a charitable remainder trust?

A: Yes. If you want to replace the value of the assets deposited into a charitable remainder trust, you can use part of the income tax savings or other assets to purchase a life insurance policy if you are insurable. You should purchase enough insurance to replace the assets deposited into the trust. The death benefits would be available to your heirs. If properly arranged, the death benefits from the life insurance policy may not be included in your taxable estate. In that case, you have saved both capital gains taxes and estate taxes.

Q: What is a charitable lead trust?

A: A *charitable lead trust* is a trust that provides for the distribution of income to a charity or charities for a term of years. At a specified date in the future, the assets in the trust will be returned to the creator or the creator's designated beneficiaries as designated in the trust document. A charitable lead trust may provide income tax benefits, but its primary use is to substantially reduce federal estate taxes and possible generation-skipping taxes.

 Note: The use and advantages of a charitable lead trust to reduce federal estate taxes and generation-skipping taxes are very complex and will not be addressed in this book. If you have an interest in a charitable lead trust, you should investigate the subject with your advisors.

ESTATE
PLANNING

SUMMARY

Two things in our society are inevitable: death and taxes. By having a basic knowledge of estate planning and planning for the distribution of your wealth at the time of your inevitable death, you may increase your heirs' potential inheritance. Effective estate planning will also ensure that your assets will be distributed as you wish.

This chapter is not intended to be a complete guide to planning your estate or utilizing trusts. Rather, its purpose is to provide you with enough information so that you can work with your advisor to develop an appropriate estate plan.

As with accumulating wealth, you need an effective plan to distribute your wealth after your death.

CHAPTER 14

ADVISORS

One of the most important decisions you have to make in your quest to accumulate wealth is the selection of an advisor or advisors. Competent guidance in selecting investments that have the potential to accomplish your objectives can be crucial to your financial security.

Over the last few years, the numbers of investment opportunities and financial organizations offering investments have greatly expanded. Banks no longer offer you just the usual personal finance services, such as checking accounts, savings accounts, and loans. They now offer trust services, brokerage services, and investment vehicles and products. Insurance agents no longer offer just insurance; they now offer investments. There are many investments available today that are only suitable for certain types of investors. Therefore, finding the right advisor and financial institution is crucial in locating investments that will meet your objectives with a risk level that you find comfortable.

The wrong advisor could be a serious roadblock in your path toward achieving financial security. Selecting a good advisor could be your best decision in seeking financial security.

This chapter will answer questions on the different types of advisors, what to expect from each, how to find them, and their fees and commissions.

To assist you in working with advisors, this chapter will also discuss the types of ownership of securities and the types of accounts in which you can transact business.

Q: What are the types of advisors you may want to consult?

A: Some of the professionals who can offer you investment advice and recommendations are:

- Accountants
- Bankers
- Insurance agents
- Stockbrokers
- Discount brokers
- Investment advisors (money managers)
- Financial planners
- Lawyers

Q: What advice can I expect to receive from an accountant?

A: Most often you will use the services of an *accountant* or *CPA (certified public accountant)* in filing your income tax. However, a good accountant will not only assist you in filing your income tax, but also give advice on how to save tax dollars. Many accountants offer other forms of financial advice to their clients, such as financial planning, estate planning, and reviewing of investments and investment plans offered to you by other advisors.

Most accountants receive a fee, based on an hourly rate, for their services; however, some may also receive commissions on investments selected by their clients.

Recently, some accountants have started selling investment products, primarily life insurance, mutual funds, and annuities. If your accountant is selling investment products, it would be wise to ask if he or she also receives a fee or commission on the sale of those products. If so, you should get a second opinion.

If you have a good relationship with your accountant, that individual would be in an excellent position to assist you in monitoring your investments for potential tax problems. Your accountant may also suggest areas of investment that you may have overlooked or warn you if you show interest in areas of investment that are not suitable for you.

If you want your accountant to assist in monitoring your investments, make certain that he or she periodically receives copies of your investment statements and other investment documents that may be appropriate.

Q: What advice can I expect to receive from a bank?

A: Historically, you went to your *bank* for checking accounts, savings accounts, certificates of deposit, home mortgages, automobile loans, personal loans, and education loans. In recent years, many banks have started offering investment and insurance products. In fact, many banks now have their own mutual funds as well as offering mutual funds and annuities from other vendors. Often the individual who services your checking account, certificates of deposits, and loans is also offering you investment products that are not insured. Many banks also now have brokerage subsidiaries that provide the same services as a brokerage firm.

 Note of Caution: When you go to your bank to open an account or seek investment advice, always ask about the insurance and risk involved in the instruments being offered. In the early 1990s, many individuals who purchased mutual funds or annuities at their bank mistakenly believed that they were acquiring safe and insured accounts. In fact, they had become investors in pools of stocks and bonds.

Q: What advice can I expect to receive from an insurance agent?

A: An *insurance agent* was traditionally someone who advised you on estate planning and sold you what he or she considered to be the appropriate insurance policies to accomplish your objectives. Insurance agents today are often also involved in financial planning and can advise on how the various forms of life insurance may fit into your plans.

Like other advisors, in recent years, many life insurance agents have begun offering investment products like mutual funds and annuities. This makes life more complicated for investors because they sometimes find that their insurance agents, like other advisors, may have a conflict of interest when they offer various investment opportunities.

Q: How are insurance agents compensated?

A: Most insurance agents receive a commission on the policy they sell you. The commission is generally a substantial part of the first year's premium, and the agent usually earns a trailing commission for a limited number of years after the sale of the policy as well.

In recent years, some insurance agents have been offering no-load life insurance policies. Agents offering no-load policies are usually compensated by fees rather than commissions. If your life insurance agent is charging you a fee, you should ask the question: "Are you also receiving commissions on this policy?"

As is the case with any professional offering you advice or investment opportunities, the professionalism of the advisor and the quality of the advice is more important than the commission.

Q: What advice can I expect from a stockbroker?

A: A *stockbroker* is an individual who is employed by or associated with a brokerage firm that is regulated by the National Association of Security Dealers (NASD) and often a member of the New York Stock Exchange. Stockbrokers are often referred to as registered representatives, financial consultants, investment brokers, or account executives. They can be either full-service brokers or discount brokers.

Q: What can I expect from a full-service broker?

A: A *full-service broker* is a stockbroker who works for or is associated with a brokerage firm that offers services other than simply executing your orders to buy or sell securities. Most full-service brokers will meet and talk often with clients to offer their advice about stocks, bonds, mutual funds, annuities, and other investment products such as options and commodities. They also provide services such as research reports, custodianship of securities, investment planning, financial planning, retirement planning, and estate planning. A full-service broker should assist you in structuring your portfolio of investments (stocks, bonds, and other investments) to accomplish your stated financial objectives. Many stockbrokers will specialize in one area, and stockbrokers differ in their philosophies. You would not want to seek the assistance of a stockbroker who specializes in low-priced speculative stocks if you are retired and seeking a conservative portfolio or wish to earn income. If you are looking to speculate, you would not want the services of a stockbroker who is very conservative and is seeking long-term investment accounts.

Q: How is a full-service stockbroker compensated?

A: Generally, a full-service stockbroker is paid by commissions; he or she receives a portion of the total commission on each transaction as compensation. Commissions often appear as an additional cost on your transaction confirmation. However, you may also see transaction prices quoted as *net*, especially with over-the-counter securities, bonds, mutual funds, annuities, and other investment packages. Even though no commission is shown on your confirmation, these transactions are usually *not* commission-free. In the case of bonds or over-the-counter stocks, the commission is often part of the "spread" between the buy and sell prices. In the case of underwritings (new issues), some mutual funds, annuities, and certain other investment products, the commission is paid by the distributor after it receives the money and only the net amount after commission is invested.

Example: If you invest $10,000 in a mutual fund that charges a 4 percent commission, the net amount that goes into the underlying investments is $9,600 ($10,000 minus $400). Often, your confirmation statement will not show the commission.

In recent years, many stockbrokers have started offering investment advisory services and are licensed as investment advisors. When a broker is acting as an investment advisor, a fee is usually paid to the firm, and the individual broker may receive part of the fee as compensation. He or she may also receive commissions on the trades made in the account. There is nothing wrong with this arrangement so long as you understand that you are paying for both investment advice and transaction execution.

Q: What advice can I expect from a discount broker?

A: A *discount broker* is a broker who offers no investment advice and very little service, but is simply an order taker. Discount brokers usually charge lower commissions than full-service brokers because they do not offer investment advice or the other services offered by a full-service brokerage firm.

Q: Who should use the services of a discount broker?

A: If you have the time and expertise to do your own research and make your own investment decisions without advice, you may be able to save on commissions by using a discount broker. However, if you are not expert in the investment field, you may be more comfortable seeking advice from a full-service broker. A full-service firm provides more services and may be more motivated to help you find investments that are likely to accomplish your financial goals.

In recent years, many discount brokerage firms have started to offer more services. If a discount broker offers these additional services, the commissions may not be as low (discounted) as you may expect.

 Note: Before you open an account with a discount broker, you should always ask for a commission schedule and a list of any fees that may be charged. Some discount brokers charge low commissions but have high minimum transaction charges or additional fees, making the savings less than you anticipated.

Q: What advice can I expect from an investment advisor?

A: Generally, rather than giving you advice on which you may (or may not) choose to act, an *investment advisor*, often referred to as a money manager, acts on a discretionary basis after determining your objectives and guidelines for the money being managed for you. Managing money on a discretionary basis means that the advisor does not call you for permission to make each trade. When you open an account with an investment advisor, you generally give the investment advisor the authority to make all investment decisions within the guidelines you have established.

An investment advisor is usually paid a fee for managing your money. The fee arrangement, which is usually based on total assets, generally ranges from $\frac{1}{2}$ percent to 2 percent of the total portfolio value under management. In some cases, the advisor's fee is also partially contingent on performance of the portfolio. The fee is usually deducted from the value of the account on a quarterly basis. In addition to this fee, you may be charged a commission on any purchases and sales that are ordered by the investment advisor. If your securities are held by a bank as custodian, you may also pay a custodian fee.

While many money managers are generalists and will work with clients with a wide range of objectives and risk tolerances, many others have a strong orientation toward one investment style. Before opening an account with a money manager, you should be sure that you are comfortable with the advisor's orientation.

Q: When should I consider using an investment advisor?

A: If you are not comfortable with the relationship you have with your broker or if you do not feel that you can manage your portfolio yourself even with your broker's advice, you may want to consider the services of an investment advisor. You may also turn to an investment advisor if you do not have the time to manage your investments either on your own or with the assistance of a broker.

Q: Do investment advisors have minimum amounts they will accept?

A: Generally, yes. There is no standard in the industry. Some advisors will accept accounts of as little as $100,000, whereas some of the more prominent investment advisors will only accept portfolios of $1 million or larger. When looking for an investment advisor, you should determine the minimums that are required before proceeding with interviews.

Remember: The fees you pay your investment advisor and any additional charges to your account, like custodian fees, reduce the performance of your account. For example, if you are paying a total of 2 percent to have your account managed and your net assets increase by 10 percent, your net performance will be 8 percent.

Q: What advice can I expect from a financial planner?

A: A *financial planner* will work with you to plan your financial affairs and investments so that you have the best possible opportunity to accomplish your long-term goals. Most financial planners will prepare extensive financial reports showing your assets and liabilities; your expected cash flow, which will include potential inheritances; and target needs for money in the future. Some of those needs may be education of children or grandchildren, care of a family member, or a comfortable retirement. The reports should include suggestions as to how to accumulate wealth by the time the assets and/or income will be needed. What is more important than the report, however, is the execution of the plan. It is imperative that every family have a plan for accomplishing its objectives. However, whether a family needs total financial planning by a financial planner depends on how complicated the sources of the family's wealth are and how competent and disciplined it is in carrying out a plan.

A good financial plan may recommend repositioning many of the assets and investments you currently own; you will not necessarily need additional investments or the purchase of additional life insurance.

Q: Are there professional financial planner designations?

A: Yes. There is a designation called the *Certified Financial Planner (CFP)*, which is obtained by completing a several-course program through the College of Financial Planning. Generally, an individual with a CFP designation is well educated and well prepared to assist you in completing a financial plan.

However, your accountant, lawyer, or broker is often qualified through experience and training to offer financial planning services. When you seek financial planning assistance, it is more important that you are confident that the person to whom you are talking can assist you in accomplishing your objectives than that you are dealing with someone with the designation "CFP."

Q: How is a financial planner compensated?

A: A financial planner is generally compensated by hourly fees, charges based on the percentage of assets under management, commissions, or a combination of the three. Before entering into any arrangement with a financial planner, you should investigate thoroughly the fees that he or she charges and determine whether you think they are reasonable for the objectives you intend to accomplish.

A potential problem that has developed through the years with some financial planners occurs when a financial planner charges both fees and commissions. Another way to state this is: Is a financial planner designing a plan to sell a specific product, or is he or she legitimately performing the duties of a financial planner and giving you solid financial advice to help you accomplish your objectives? If you want to use the services of a financial planner who is compensated in this way, you may be well advised to have him or her design your plan for a fee and then make your investments through another organization. This may not save money, but it would remove the possibility of conflict of interest.

Because of the potential conflicts in financial planning, you may want to have your financial plan reviewed by your accountant and other advisors before you implement it.

Q: Can you develop a financial plan without hiring a financial planner?

A: Yes. Often, a number of your advisors working together can develop a financial plan for you that may not be as comprehensive as the report of a financial planner, but just as effective. Many very successful investors have used the combined services of their other advisors to develop financial plans, having each advisor (accountant, lawyer, insurance agent, and broker) give input on his or her areas of expertise, then having these advisors critique one another's input. Many people have found that the advice they receive through a coordinated effort of their advisors results in well-thought-out and usually profitable solutions. If they are congenial, having all of your advisors in one room often leads to extremely well-thought-out and successful plans because everyone is hearing what everyone else is saying.

Q: What advice can I expect from a lawyer?

A: A *lawyer's* main business is generally to write your legal documents, such as wills and trust agreements, and to file legal documents with the courts. However, many lawyers will give their clients advice on how to improve their financial situation. Lawyers can be an important part of an advisory team, and it is often advisable to have them involved in large investment decisions. Any time you are signing a contract that has long-term implications, you may be well advised to let your lawyer look at the contract before you sign it.

 Note: Lawyers often specialize, just as other professionals do. Just because a lawyer is a friend or has drafted the deed in buying or selling real estate does not mean that that lawyer has expertise in financial planning, estate planning, or investments. When you need the services of a lawyer for financial planning or estate planning, or to address your investment opportunities or risks, you should seek the advice of a lawyer who specializes in such law. Lawyers who specialize in trusts, estates, and financial planning are usually referred to as "trust and estate lawyers."

Q: How do I find an advisor who is right for me?

A: Before you begin looking for an advisor, you must first identify the type of advice you are seeking. Are you looking for someone to advise you in investing a modest amount of money? Are you looking for someone to assist you in arranging your financial affairs (financial planning)? Are you looking for someone to assist you in identifying your insurance needs?

Once you identify the advice you are seeking, you can begin to search for the organization or individual who can assist you in accomplishing your goals.

In seeking a possible advisor, one of the best sources is your friends, neighbors, and relatives. Such referrals may lead you to an advisor with whom you can have an excellent relationship and who can assist you in accumulating wealth and accomplishing your goals. If you cannot get a good referral from someone you know, do not hesitate to call a brokerage firm, bank, or insurance company and ask to speak to someone. Do not be hesitant to ask for an interview. These organizations and individuals want your business as much as you want good advice.

Q: Once I have some names, what do I do?

A: Once you have some names—either from friends, relatives, coworkers, or from institutions you have called—set up interviews. Do not be afraid to ask these people hard questions concerning their philosophies and what approach they would have in assisting you in meeting your financial goals.

You should have interviews with each person you are considering. Remember, the advisor should want to establish a relationship with you as much as you want his or her advice. It does not matter how good the advisor's reputation is; if you do not feel comfortable with this individual, you should continue your search.

Similarly, once you have selected an advisor, if at any time you begin to feel uncomfortable or unable to communicate with that advisor, you should seek someone new. Trust, communication, and comfort are key elements in a successful relationship between you and any of your advisors.

Most importantly, you need to select someone whose philosophy is consistent with yours. If you are a conservative investor, looking to conserve capital, you do not want an advisor whose orientation is speculation. This individual would tend to place your money in high-risk investments. If you are a beginning investor, you will need to find someone who will be willing to take the time to explain to you all the risk factors in each investment as well as the profit opportunities.

 Note: In interviewing potential advisors, the most important factors are: Are you comfortable with the individual, and does his or her area of expertise match the advice you are seeking? If not, keep looking!

Q: What questions should I ask when interviewing a potential advisor?

A: Here are a series of topics you may want to cover during the interview process. Obviously, you would not be limited to these topics, but you should incorporate them into your interviews.

- *References:* Ask your potential advisor for the phone numbers of some of his or her long-term clients. Do not hesitate to call these clients and get their opinions as to the professionalism of the advisor. Asking a reference the following question could be very helpful: "Is the individual I am considering using as an advisor more interested in solving my problems or in selling me products or earning his or her fees?"

- *Organizations/memberships:* Ask the advisor which organizations he or she belongs to and how active he or she is in these organizations.

- *Education:* Ask about the educational background of your potential advisor.

- *Licenses:* Ask which licenses your potential advisor and firm have.

- *Business background:* Ask how long the potential advisor has been in the business and how many firms he or she has been associated with. Individuals who are constantly changing firms may be more concerned with their own compensation arrangements than with their clients.

- *Personnel:* If your potential advisor has people working with him or her with whom you may need to have contact, you should meet these people.

- *Compensation:* Ask how the advisor is compensated. Will he or she receive a commission, a fee, or both? If appropriate, you may want to ask for a commission and/or fee schedule.

Q: Is there someone I can call to verify information on a firm or individual from whom I may choose to seek advice?

A: Yes. The securities regulators in your state maintain files on most investment brokers, brokerage firms, and advisors. You can look up the telephone number of the securities regulator in your state and place a call to it. You can also call the North American Securities Administrator's Association (NASAA) in Washington, D.C. (202-737-0900). The state regulators or NASAA can usually tell you if an individual or organization has had regulatory problems.

Questions concerning a lawyer can be directed to your local bar association.

As for insurance advisors, you can call the insurance regulators in your state to see if an insurance company or individual has had regulatory difficulties.

Q: Once I've found an advisor or advisors with whom I am comfortable, what can I expect from them?

A: What you can expect from your advisor will depend on the type of advisor you have chosen. However, during the interview process, the advisor should have made clear to you how he or she operates and exactly what you can expect. If you have any questions about whether you can expect certain things from your advisors, such as keeping you informed about your investments, giving you reviews of your investments on a periodic basis, or monitoring your positions for possible needed changes, you should ask.

You should not expect too much from your advisors. If you are dealing with a broker or investment advisor, do not expect unrealistic returns in a short period of time. Do not expect lots of phone calls from your advisor unless he or she agrees to call frequently. Ask your advisor the best time to place calls to him or her.

Any time one of your advisors is not meeting your expectations, you should contact that advisor immediately and discuss the problem with him or her. If you are not satisfied with the answer, seek another advisor.

Q: Are there situations that should raise concern about an advisor?

A: Yes. Listed below are several situations that should raise concern about the advice you may be receiving:

- Beware of advisors who highlight only the profit potential or the positive side of the products they are offering. Always ask the risk of any investment or product that you are being offered. It is important that you understand the risks as well as the profit opportunities.

- If a proposed investment sounds odd, ask another advisor to look at it and give you an opinion before you invest in it.

- Always be wary of the word *guarantee*. There are few investments that are guaranteed. In the world of insurance and deposit accounts, make certain you understand what the word *guarantee* refers to. It may mean no more than a promise to pay. If the party guaranteeing is the sole organization or party on the other side of the contract, it may be only as good as the organization making the guarantee.

- If the investment suggested is not registered with the Securities and Exchange Commission (SEC) or the state securities office, ask your advisor why not. Generally, investments that are not registered with the SEC or state securities office are highly speculative and risky. If your advisor has an interest in the investment, you need to investigate what that interest is and whether it is consistent with your objectives. Is your advisor making money even if you do not make money?

- If an investment appears too good to be true, it often is.

- Always ask about the liquidity of proposed investments. If you cannot liquidate an investment with relative ease, you should consider the possible impact on accomplishing your objectives.

Q: If I have difficulties with my advisor, what should I do?

A: Most advisors are very hard-working and honorable people. They are trying to help you to manage your money and assets so as to accomplish your objectives. However, sometimes there may be misunderstandings even with excellent advisors. Your first action should be to contact your advisor for an explanation. Communication is the best antidote for misunderstandings.

Unfortunately, there are some unscrupulous advisors. If you begin to have doubts about your advisor, or the investments or products into which your advisor has placed your assets, you should first call the organization that employs the advisor and ask to talk to the manager. You should explain your problem or difficulty to the manager in detail, with copies of documentation.

If the manager does not fully answer your questions or satisfy your concerns, you should call or write to the compliance officer or president of the firm. He or she will usually respond to any problems or potential problems very quickly, or have a senior officer respond to you.

If you are still not satisfied after corresponding with senior management, or if the problem is not solved, you can always contact someone in authority at the regulator that oversees your advisor's industry. For stockbrokers, such regulators include the New York Stock Exchange, the Securities and Exchange Commission, and the National Association for Securities Dealers. The address of each is:

New York Stock Exchange
11 Wall Street
New York, NY 10005
Tel: (212) 656-3000

The National Association of Securities Dealers
1735 K Street, NW
Washington, DC 20006
Tel: (202) 973-7000

ADVISORS

The Securitiés and Exchange Commission
450 5th Street, NW
Washington, DC 20549
Tel: (202) 942-8088

If you have problems concerning a lawyer, you should contact your local bar association.

If you have problems with an insurance advisor or an insurance product, you should contact the state insurance regulator in the state where you reside.

Q: Can good records reduce my risk when working with an advisor?

A: It is important to keep all records (confirmations, statements, and all communications from your advisor) both for tax purposes and in order to have proper documentation if you ever have a problem with your advisor. You should also make checks payable to the firm or the organization where the money is being invested, not to your advisor, and you should write on the check what it is for, such as purchase of stock, bond, money fund, mutual fund, or life insurance.

Q: Is it important to clarify my status or authority when hiring an advisor?

A: Yes. It is very important that you and your advisor clearly understand your status or authority before you work together. This will dictate what kind of account you establish:

- Individual account
- Joint account: right of survivorship, tenants by the entirety, joint tenants in common
- Custodian account: guardian, child, incompetent
- Trust account
- Estate account
- Corporate account
- Delivery versus payment account (DVP)
- Discretionary account
- Investment club account

Q: What is an individual account?

A: As the name implies, an *individual account* is registered in only one name. It is your personal account, in which investment purchases and sales are made in your name only and of which you are the sole owner. Unless you have given discretion to another individual or firm, you are the only person who can authorize transactions in this type of account.

Q: What is a joint account?

A: A *joint account* is an account owned by two individuals—usually husband and wife, although a joint account may also be owned by a parent and child or by two friends. When a joint account is established with a brokerage firm, all securities are registered in both names. The signatures or authorization of both owners are required to enter into a transaction. This is in contrast to a bank account in joint name, where often either individual can be authorized to sign checks and transact business. When establishing a joint account at a bank, you should inquire as to the regulations that would apply to that account. Joint accounts may be owned:

- With right of survivorship
- As tenants by the entirety
- As joint tenants in common

Q: What does it mean to own securities with right of survivorship?

A: If you have a joint account with *right of survivorship*, this means that upon the death of either joint owner, the property or securities will become the sole property of the surviving owner.

Q: What does it mean to own securities as tenants by the entirety?

A: Ownership as *tenants by the entirety* is a form of joint ownership available only to husband and wife. As with right of survivorship, upon the death of either spouse, the survivor becomes the sole owner. However, with this type of ownership, the property or securities owned can also be divided equally while both individuals are alive.

ADVISORS

Q: What does it mean to own property or securities as joint tenants in common?

A: If you own securities or property with another individual as *joint tenants in common*, upon the death of one of the owners, the surviving joint owner does *not* automatically become the owner of the securities or property. Half the assets will pass under the decedent's will or in accordance with state law.

Note: Generally, when you own securities or property jointly, you will use the Social Security number or tax identification number of only one owner. When the Social Security number is used, any income or capital gains will be reported to the IRS under that tax identification number. If a security is owned jointly by a parent and child and the parent's Social Security number is used, the parent will be taxed on the income paid.

Q: Is there a form of joint ownership in which a joint owner does not own half the security?

A: Some states have passed laws that allow you to put a second name on a security or brokerage account, but retain sole ownership and control until you die. This is referred to as transfer on death (TOD).

The TOD form of registration allows you to name a beneficiary of your securities. While you are living, you can change the beneficiary (joint name) and exercise total control. If you change your mind as to the beneficiary, all you need to do is change the TOD registration.

Note of Caution: The TOD form of registration is not available in all states, and many transfer agents do *not* recognize it as a valid form of registration. If you are interested in TOD, contact your broker or advisor.

Q: What is a custodian account?

A: A *custodian account* is an account established by a parent or other guardian for a child who is under the age of eighteen or twenty-one. When you establish a custodian account, you should use the child's Social Security (tax identification) number so that any income or capital gains will be taxed to the child and not the custodian. If the child's earnings are above a certain level, they may be taxed at the parent's or guardian's tax rate. Generally, when a child reaches the age of eighteen, the custodian relationship ceases and the securities transfer into the child's name. In some states, that age limit can be extended to twenty-one.

Note: Generally, the custodian is the custodian under the UGTM (Uniform Gift to Minors Act), which means the minor will own the securities at age eighteen. Under the form UTTM (Uniform Transfer to Minors), the minor usually becomes the owner at age twenty-one.

Note of Caution: Always check with your advisors as to the proper way to register securities when using a custodian form of registration.

Q: Is there an alternative to using a custodian account so that the minor will not get the securities or cash at age eighteen or twenty-one?

A: Yes. As an alternative to using a custodian account with a minor, you may consider a trust. In the trust document, you can designate the ages at which you want all or a portion of the assets of the trust distributed to the beneficiary. When you establish a trust, you will have to name a trustee and spell out in the documents how the assets will be managed and at what time distributions will be made.

Note: If you want to consider a trust as an alternative to a custodian arrangement for transferring the ownership of securities or cash to a minor, you should consult a lawyer.

Note of Caution: Once assets or securities are transferred to a custodian account or a trust, you have made a gift. The assets or securities cannot revert to the giver at a later time.

Q: What is a trust account?

A: A *trust account* is an account that holds the assets of a trust. Many investors will have access to or be managers of a trust that they themselves have established or that was established by a will of a family member. The trust document, which is drafted by an attorney, controls how the assets in the trust account can be managed and what types of investments the trust can make. The trustees of the trust are the legal representatives who can transact business within the account. The document will usually specify whether one trustee can act or whether all trustees must agree to any transactions.

Q: What is an estate account?

A: An *estate account* is an account established to receive the assets of a decedent while the estate is being settled. The estate account is run by the executors or administrators, who are the estate's legal representatives. Once all taxes and debts of the estate have been paid, the executors or administrators of the estate will authorize distributions from the estate account to the decedent's heirs. Generally, only the executors or administrators of an estate can transact business in an estate account. There are forms that must be signed in order to transfer securities from a decedent's name to an estate account. If you are an executor or administrator of an estate, you should ask your advisor what forms are needed to transfer the securities.

Q: What is a corporate account?

A: A *corporate account* is an account established by a corporation. The corporation will generally own the securities in the account. Brokerage firms and anyone else doing business involving a corporation's securities will require a *corporate resolution*, which is a document authorized by the board of directors of the corporation that specifies which corporate officers can sign and transact business in the account. Generally, when securities in a corporate account are sold, cash cannot be distributed until the securities are completely transferred, which may be much later than the normal settlement date.

Q: What is a delivery versus payment (DVP) account?

A: A *delivery versus payment (DVP) account* is a type of account usually used by institutions or individuals with extremely large investment accounts. Delivery versus payment means that when securities are sold, they will be delivered to a specified

ADVISORS

bank or depository, which will make payment upon the delivery of the security. When securities are purchased, once the certificate is delivered to a specified bank or depository, payment will be made for the securities. Normal settlement dates do not usually apply in this type of account.

Q: What is a discretionary account?

A: A *discretionary account* is an investment account whose owner or joint owners have given an advisor the authority to place buy and sell orders. The advisor is often a broker or money manager. A discretionary account can have *limited* discretion, with the advisor able to place only buy and sell orders. The advisor cannot withdraw either cash or securities from the account. An account with *full* discretion gives the individual or individuals holding the discretion the ability to withdraw cash or securities as well as place buy and sell orders.

 Note of Caution: Any time you consider establishing a discretionary account, you should understand that the individual holding the discretion will be free to manage your assets without consulting or even informing you. With full discretion, he or she can even remove cash or securities from the account.

Q: What is an investment club account?

A: An *investment club* is a group of individuals who meet regularly and pool their money, time, knowledge, and efforts to discuss and invest in securities. Generally, the members of an investment club will have similar investment objectives. The primary goal of the members is to learn about investments and to exchange ideas. Making money from their investments is usually a secondary objective.

An *investment club account* is an account established by and for the benefit of an investment club. Any investment club establishing an account will have to file certain papers with the brokerage firm with which it will be transacting business.

ADVISORS

Q: How can I start an investment club?

A: If you are interested in starting an investment club with several of your friends, you should consider joining the National Association of Investment Clubs (NAIC). The NAIC is a nonprofit organization owned by its membership, and its purpose is to encourage the creation of investment clubs and to assist investment clubs in becoming successful operations. The NAIC's address is:

P.O. Box 220
Royal Oak, MI 48068
Tel: (810) 583-6242.

Q: What type of information might I get from the NAIC?

A: The NAIC has an investment club manual that is a "how to" book on organizing and maintaining an investment club. It will give you sample partnership agreements, tax information, record-keeping procedures, and security analysis techniques. The organization also publishes a monthly magazine, *Better Investing*.

Q: What are the basic types of accounts that I can establish with a broker to purchase and sell securities?

A: There are two basic types of accounts to buy and sell securities. They are:

● Cash account
● Margin account

Q: What is a cash account?

A: A *cash account* is the standard account opened at a brokerage firm. When you purchase a security in your cash account, you will receive a confirmation of the transaction showing the amount you owe. You have to deliver a check to the business in the exact amount of your purchase.

Note: Always make the check payable to the *firm* or *organization*, not the individual. If you make the check payable to the individual, there is a risk that your check may not be deposited to your investment account.

When you sell a security in a cash account, if the certificate is on deposit at the firm or has been delivered to the broker, you can have a check for the proceeds mailed to you on the settlement date or you can have the proceeds held in your account to be used for future purchases.

Q: What is a margin account?

A: A *margin account* is an account established at a brokerage firm in which you use the securities that are held in the account or that you are purchasing as collateral for a loan. The brokerage firm is making a loan to you. Generally, you can borrow 50 percent of the value of the stocks in your account from your brokerage firm. You will be charged interest on the outstanding loan, which will accrue on a daily basis at a stipulated rate as determined by the firm.

When you establish a margin account, you must sign a margin agreement. The margin agreement will include provisions allowing the firm to lend you money, charge you interest on the loan, and sell securities from the account if the value falls below a required level.

Short sales (see Chapter 5, page 93) usually take place in conjunction with a margin account.

Generally, you can borrow a higher percentage of the value of bonds than you can of common or preferred stocks.

When considering a margin account, you should discuss all the factors, including the risks, with your broker.

Q: Can I borrow from my broker when I am not purchasing securities?

A: Yes. A margin account is similar to a line of credit at a bank. Instead of going to a bank for a loan, many individuals use a margin account in order to get a quick loan, often at a lower rate, using their securities as collateral. You may want a margin account loan for a bridge loan when you are buying a house or for a short-term need of some other kind. Some individuals use margin accounts to pay education expenses and allow the dividends to reduce the loan balance.

Q: How do I repay a margin loan?

A: In most margin accounts, there is no repayment requirement, but a certain relationship between the loan balance and the value of the securities, called the *margin requirement*, must be maintained. If the value of the securities falls below the required level, either you will have to repay part of the loan or your broker will sell some of your securities and use the cash to reduce the loan balance. You should check with your broker as to the rules. Many people simply make monthly deposits to the account in order to repay the loan.

 Note: Not all securities can be purchased on margin. Listed securities and certain over-the-counter securities are approved for margin. In addition, the Federal Reserve Board maintains a list of other securities that are qualified for margin.

Q: How do I establish a margin account?

A: In order to establish a margin account, you ask your broker for a margin agreement. Once you have signed the form, you may either deposit securities in the margin account or transfer securities from your cash account. The securities will be placed in the margin account and become collateral for the loan. All securities in a margin account must be in street name (see page 381).

Q: What are the risks of a margin account?

A: The primary risk of using a margin account is that the value of the securities may decline, since if you sell or have to sell some of the securities, the loan must be repaid before any distributions can be made to you. If the value of the securities in your margin account declines to a certain point, your brokerage firm may require you to deposit additional cash or securities, or to sell some of your margined securities to reduce the margin loan balance. This is referred to as a *margin call*.

 Example: Suppose you have $4,000 that you wish to invest in IBM at $80. If you buy in your cash account, you can buy 50 shares. If IBM's price declines to $60 and you sell, you will net $3,000. You will have lost $1,000, or 25 percent of your investment, when the price of the stock declines 25 percent. Alternatively, if you deposit $4,000 with your broker and borrow $4,000, you can buy 100 shares of IBM at $80, for a cost of $8,000. Now if IBM's price declines to $60 and you sell, you will net $6,000, but you will still have to repay the broker $4,000, and so you will have lost 50 percent of your cash investment, or $2,000, on a 25 percent decline in the price of the stock.

In addition, if you borrow from your margin account to purchase a depreciable asset, such as an automobile, and do not make regular payments, you may find yourself with a loan and a greatly depreciated asset.

 Example: Suppose you borrowed $15,000 from a margin account and purchased an automobile. Five years later, the car may be worth $2,000, but if you have not paid the loan, it still must be repaid.

Q: How can my securities be registered?

A: If you purchase securities in a cash account and they are fully paid for, generally they are registered in your name and a certificate representing ownership is mailed to you. Some securities, particularly government bonds and certain municipal bonds, cannot be registered in the owner's name; they must be held in street name with your broker.

Q: What is street name?

A: *Street name* is the term used to describe registration of your securities in the name of the brokerage firm, which maintains custody of the certificates representing ownership.

Q: What are the advantages of having my securities held in street name?

A: When you have your securities held in street name, your broker is responsible for receiving all income—dividends and interest—and proceeds on sales or redemptions. In addition:

● You will receive a monthly statement showing the value of your securities.

- You can have all the income paid to you in one check on a regular basis. You will not have to receive and deposit multiple dividend and interest checks.
- You will receive only one tax statement instead of one for each security you own.
- The brokerage firm will be responsible for reorganization notices or calls.
- If you do not want income or sales proceeds mailed to you, they can be automatically invested in a money fund.
- Purchases can be settled from a money fund.
- Your ownership will be anonymous, since the issuer will not have your name on record.

Q: If I have a street name account, am I tied to a broker?

A: No. You can request that your securities owned in street name be registered and the certificates mailed to you.

Also, if you want your securities transferred to another brokerage firm, you can do so through the National Securities Clearing Corporation, an organization owned by the brokerage firms to assist in the transfer of clients' securities.

SUMMARY

Selecting the right advisor or advisors is perhaps the most important factor in achieving your financial goals. There is no one perfect advisor, but you should seek one whose philosophy is the same as yours and with whom you are comfortable.

This chapter should help you to identify the types of advisors you need and to know what to expect from your advisors. Be certain that you understand how your advisors are compensated.

Also, this chapter gives you information on the various forms of ownership and types of accounts in which you can execute transactions.

The more you know about what to expect from your advisors and about types of ownership and brokerage accounts and their rules, the better are your opportunities for a good relationship with your advisors.

MORE COMMONLY ASKED QUESTIONS

No written work is ever truly complete, and this book is no exception. After reviewing the questions and answers in the manuscript, we realized there were additional questions readers may want answered. Some of the questions related to items, philosophies, or concepts the reader is likely to encounter in newspapers, and on radio and television.

Though the questions and answers were not ideal to be included in earlier chapters, we realized their value and have included them in the appendix.

Q: What is a bull market?

A: A *bull market* is one in which stock prices are generally moving up.

Q: What is a bear market?

A: A *bear market* is one in which stock prices are generally moving down.

Q: What does it mean to say that I am bullish?

A: If you are *bullish*, you expect stock prices will generally be moving higher.

Q: What does it mean to say that I am bearish?

A: If you are *bearish*, you expect stock prices will generally be heading lower.

Q: What is a bullish event?

A: A *bullish event* is a general news item or an occurrence related to a company, such as earnings being higher than expected or the announcement of a new product, that may cause you to believe that stock prices in general or the price of a stock in which you are interested will head higher.

Q: What is a bearish event?

A: A *bearish event* is a general news item or an occurrence related to a company, such as earnings being lower than expected or an unfavorable economic report, that may cause you to believe that stock prices in general or the price of a stock in which you are interested will go lower.

Q: What is beta?

A: *Beta* is a statistic that measures the risk associated with a stock by measuring the volatility of the stock relative to the volatility of the market as a whole. If a stock has a beta of 1.0, its price movement should parallel that of the market on a percentage basis. If a stock has a beta of 1.2, when the stock market in general rises 1 percent, the stock should rise by 1.2 percent. Conversely, if the market declines 1 percent, the stock should decline by 1.2 percent. Stocks with higher betas are riskier because they are more vulnerable to market downturns.

Q: What is alpha?

A: *Alpha* is a statistic that measures your investment's risk adjusted performance. The market as a whole has an alpha of 0. A positive alpha indicates a better than average performance after adjusting for volatility. A negative alpha indicates performance has been worse than average.

Q: What is float?

A: *Float* is an estimate of the number of shares that are available for active trading. Generally, the more shares there are that are available for active trading, the more liquid the stock's trading market, and thus the less volatile the stock. As the float of a company's stock is reduced, the stock's price may become more volatile because its market is less liquid.

Q: Why do some corporations repurchase, or buy back, their own shares?

A: Corporations may buy back their own shares for a variety of reasons. Some of the reasons include:

- The board of directors regards the common stock as undervalued at the present price and believes that a repurchase program is a prudent use of excess cash.
- The board of directors decides to repurchase shares so it can use them to pay for future acquisitions.
- The board of directors repurchases the stock to reduce the stock's float and eliminate problem shareholders. This will often reduce the chance that the corporation will be acquired involuntarily.

Q: Do corporate repurchases affect the earnings per share of a corporation?

A: Corporate repurchases will reduce the number of shares outstanding, thereby leaving fewer shares to be divided into the earnings. As a result, earnings per share will usually increase.

Q: Will the repurchase and ultimate reduction in shares outstanding affect the price of the stock?

A: Generally, if the earnings per share increase, so will the price of the underlying stock. Also, a corporate repurchase program will often place a floor under the price of the stock because the corporation will buy the stock over a period of time and thus will stand ready as a steady buyer. This often reduces the downside risk.

Q: What is the January Effect?

A: The *January Effect* theory holds that stocks that are heavily sold in December, often because investors want to take tax losses, will bounce back in early January.

Q: How can investors take advantage of the January Effect?

A: In order to take advantage of the January Effect, many investors will search for stocks that have declined in late November and throughout December, and buy them before the end of the year. If these stocks were sold in order to take tax losses, they are likely to bounce back in January, thereby offering a potentially profitable trading opportunity.

Many brokerage firms will publish a list of January Effect stocks in late November and throughout December.

Q: What are LEAPS?

A: *LEAPS* are a form of long-term options. The name is an acronym for Long-term Equity AnticiPation Securities. Many LEAPS will carry as long as a two-year time horizon before expiration.

Like other options, LEAPS are available in both calls and puts.

Q: Why were LEAPS created?

A: Basically, LEAPS were created in order to reduce the need for an investor to make an accurate near-term assessment of which way a particular stock will move.

Q: Are there many LEAPS traded?

A: There are LEAPS traded on more than 100 well-known companies, as well as on indexes such as the Standard & Poor's 500 average and the Standard & Poor's 100 average.

Q: What is a REIT?

A: A *REIT* is a real estate investment trust. It is a pool of capital from many investors that is invested in real estate. Most REITs trade on one of the exchanges or in the over-the-counter market.

Q: Why should I consider investing in a REIT?

A: REITs offer investors an opportunity to own real estate through the purchase of marketable securities. Many REITs provide a good yield and have a record of increasing the dividend on a regular basis.

Q: Is there a tax advantage to owning REITs?

A: As long as a REIT pays out 95 percent of its taxable net income and meets other IRS qualifications, it pays no tax on its earnings. The REIT's income is passed through to the REIT investors and taxed at that time. Thus, there is no double taxation. In addition, for many REITs, a portion of the distributions is not subject to current income tax, but is considered a return of capital and is subject to special treatment. Any distribution considered a return of capital reduces the cost basis of your REIT holding.

Q: What is a limited partnership that trades on the exchanges or over-the-counter?

A: A *limited partnership* is a partnership in which the majority of the partners have limited liability (that is, they can lose no more than they invest), just as investors in a corporation do. Some businesses whose securities trade on the exchanges or on the over-the-counter market take the form of limited partnerships rather than corporations. In such cases, the investors are generally investing in units of the limited partnership, not shares.

Q: Are there advantages to investing in actively traded units of limited partnerships?

A: The advantage of investing in an actively traded limited partnership is that, unlike corporations, partnerships are not taxed on their income. This allows more income to be passed along to the investors. The investors must pay taxes, but the income would only be taxed once. Often a part of a limited partnership's distribution may be treated as a return of capital, and the unit owner may receive other tax benefits. (This is true of any limited partnership; however, if the units are actively traded, the risk that you will be unable to liquidate the investment is reduced.)

Q: How will I know my tax liability if I own units of an actively traded limited partnership?

A: The management of the limited partnership will send you a K-1 tax reporting form . However, the tax reporting for limited partnerships is very complex and you usually will not receive the form until late March or early April.

Q: What is market timing?

A: *Market timing* involves making short-term decisions on buying and selling stocks in an attempt to be invested when the market is going up and not invested when the market is declining.

Q: Have market timers been successful?

A: Throughout the years, there has been as much risk to being out of stocks as to being invested in stocks. The table below shows the performance of the stock market as measured by the S&P 500 from 1980 to 1989. It is obvious that market timers who are wrong on a few days have missed substantial opportunities.

Missing a Few Good Days Is Expensive

Period Invested 1980 – 1989	S&P 500 Annualized Returns
All 2,528 trading days	17.5%
Missing 10 best days	12.6%
Missing 20 best days	9.3%
Missing 30 best days	6.5%
Missing 40 best days	3.9%

Q: What does the term currency translation mean?

A: *Currency translation* is the conversion of amounts of money in one currency into another currency. For U.S. corporations, it refers to the conversion to dollars of corporate earnings of foreign subsidiaries that are repatriated, or brought back into the United States, to the parent corporation. If the value of the dollar has declined relative to the currency of the country in which the earnings occur, the foreign earnings will be equivalent to more dollars, and the translation will be positive for earnings per share. If the dollar has strengthened versus the currency of the country in which the earnings occur, the foreign earnings will be equivalent to fewer dollars, and the translation will be negative for earnings per share.

As domestic corporations expand their foreign operations in the future, currency translation effects will be an increasingly significant factor in the earnings per share of the stocks you hold.

Q: What is a wrap account?

A: A *wrap account* is an account for which both management fees and transaction costs are "wrapped" into one flat fee based on the account size.

Q: How does a wrap account work?

A: A broker will assist you in finding and hiring a professional money manager. You then pay the brokerage firm a flat fee, from which the money manager is paid.

Q: What are the advantages to establishing a wrap account?

A: There are basically two advantages to establishing a wrap account:

- The flat rate is intended to eliminate the temptation for your broker to enter into transactions primarily in order to generate commissions rather than to earn you a profit.
- You will be getting a professional investment manager, who may be a better stock picker than you or your broker.

Q: What are the disadvantages of a wrap account?

A: The biggest disadvantage of a wrap account is the flat fee. This will generally be between 1 and 3 percent, depending on the size of the assets and what is being offered by the various brokerage firms. The fee will reduce the net performance of your portfolio. For instance, if a wrap account earns 10 percent and the fee is 2 percent, your net total return will be 8 percent.

Q: What is the General Motors Bellwether theory?

A: The *General Motors Bellwether theory* holds that the price movement of General Motors' common stock can predict the future direction of the stock market. The theory holds that in a market uptrend, if four months pass without General Motors' stock price hitting a higher high, a market decline may be imminent.

In a market downtrend, when four months pass without General Motors' common stock trading to a lower low, you can conclude that the general market is about to reverse direction and rally.

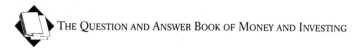
According to many analysts, the General Motors Bellwether theory has an accuracy rate of about 80 percent since the 1920s.

Q: What does the presidential election/stock market cycle indicate?

A: The presidential election/stock market cycle holds that there will be stock market gains in the last two years of a president's term. The reasoning is that a presidential election, which occurs every four years, has a significant impact on the economy and the stock market. Wars, recessions, and bear markets have had a tendency to begin in the first half of a president's term, whereas prosperous times and bull markets have occurred in the latter two years. Not coincidentally, an administration in office will usually do everything in its power to bolster the economy as the election nears so voters will be in a positive mood.

The presidential election theory has had a phenomenal record of accuracy for over 162 years. There has not been a down year in the third year of a presidential term since 1939.

Q: What is the Dow Theory?

A: The *Dow Theory* was originated by Charles Dow, the co-founder of Dow Jones & Company, publisher of the *Wall Street Journal*. The theory holds that the Dow Jones Industrial Average and the Dow Jones Transportation Average must move in the same direction to confirm a major trend in stock prices.

In theory, when the market is moving up, if either the Dow Jones Industrial Average or the Dow Jones Transportation Average makes a new high and the other fails to do so, this indicates the beginning of a market decline. Conversely, when the market is moving down, a new low in one average that is not confirmed by the other indicates the beginning of an uptrend.

Many Dow theorists will publish reports in which they interpret what the direction of the Dow Jones Industrial Average and the Dow Jones Transportation Average means for stock prices in general.

Q: What is the September reverse barometer?

A: September has always been believed to start a new business year following the summer vacation season. For many years it was held that stock prices during the final quarter of the year would continue in the same direction as in September. Since September of 1960, however, a transformation has occurred. September has become a reverse barometer. If stock prices decline or remain relatively flat in September, stock performance in the fourth quarter is generally positive. When stock prices increase in September, they generally decline in the fourth quarter.

Q: What is the Super Bowl theory?

A: The *Super Bowl theory* states that stock prices will increase for the year if the Super Bowl winner is or was a member of the original National Football League. Teams included in the original National Football League are those now in the National Football Conference plus the Pittsburgh Steelers and Cleveland Browns, which are now in the American Football Conference. Since its inception in 1967, the Super Bowl theory has had an 86 percent accuracy rate.

MORE COMMONLY ASKED QUESTIONS

Q: What is the "Dogs of the Dow" theory?

A: The *"Dogs of the Dow" theory* holds that if investors buy the ten stocks in the Dow Jones Industrial Average that have the highest dividend yields on December 31, during the ensuing year they will enjoy strong returns.

Statistics on the Dogs of the Dow theory show that following the practice has resulted in total returns almost twice that of the Dow Jones Industrial Average.

Q: What is inflation?

A: *Inflation* is an increase in the prices of products and services. There are a number of measures of inflation, of which the most commonly quoted is the Consumer Price Index (CPI).

Q: What is disinflation?

A: *Disinflation* is a decelerating rate of inflation, or a situation in which the rate of increase in prices is declining over time, although prices are still increasing.

Q: What is deflation?

A: *Deflation* is a situation in which the prices of goods and services are actually declining.

Q: How can I adjust my investments for inflation, disinflation, and deflation?

A: As with any other economic factor, significant price trends will affect the best allocation of your investments. Some common practices include the following:

- During periods of rapidly rising prices, investors want to own hard assets, such as gold, oil, silver, art, coins, or real estate, which historically have tended to rise in price at least enough to maintain their value in response to inflation. The same hard assets become less attractive investments in periods of *disinflation*.

- In periods of *disinflation*, highly capitalized stocks with a record of positive earnings growth and positive dividend increases have tended to be treated very well in the market.

- The best investment for periods of *deflation* would be cash or short-term government bonds. Because the dollar amount you will receive is fixed, assets hold their value as prices of other assets decline.

Q: What is a recession?

A: A *recession* is a temporary decline in economic activity following a period during which economic activity has been generally increasing. Most economists define a recession as two consecutive quarters of decline.

Q: What is a depression?

A: A *depression* is a prolonged period of substantial decline in economic activity. A depression will usually result in widespread unemployment, falling prices (deflation), and declining wages.

Q: What is stagflation?

A: *Stagflation* is a period in which sluggish economic growth is combined with inflation. It is a composite of four conflicting economic indicators. They are:

- A relatively high rate of inflation
- Slow real economic growth (usually less than 3 percent)
- High levels of unemployment (usually 6 percent or higher)
- High interest rates

Usually slow real growth and high unemployment do not occur at the same time as a high rate of inflation and high interest rates. In theory, slow economic growth leads to a decrease in inflation and lower interest rates along with increasing unemployment.

Q: How can I adjust my investments for stagflation?

A: For an investor, stagflation can be seen as the worst of all worlds. The weak economy will hurt traditional growth investments such as stocks, while the high inflation and rising interest rates will hurt conservative investments such as bonds. In such times, only very liquid investments such as cash or short-term government securities will preserve your capital and may be able to provide a return.

Q: What is taxflation?

A: *Taxflation* is a term that was coined by the late Peter Grace, President of W. R. Grace & Company, in the late 1970s. Taxflation refers to the combination of taxes and inflation. As taxable income is pushed higher by inflation, taxpayers are pushed into higher tax brackets. Mr. Grace was quoted as saying that "capital gains or tax rates, when the effect of the inflation over the years is recognized, border on confiscation."

Q: What is demand-side economics?

A: *Demand-side economics* is an economic theory that holds that the economy is best managed by concentrating on consumer demand. Demand-side economics uses the federal gov-

ernment's taxing and spending power as a means of managing the economy and stimulating investment and growth.

Q: What is supply-side economics?

A: *Supply-side economics* is an economic theory that holds that the economy is best managed by concentrating on producer supply factors. Supply-side economists advocate policies that encourage capital investment and increased business productivity as a means of creating employment, real income, and productivity.

Q: What is a financial supermarket?

A: A *financial supermarket* is an organization that claims to offer all of the financial and investment products that an investor needs. The intent is to offer investors "one-stop shopping" for all financial products. Many financial organizations would like to be considered financial supermarkets; they offer life and general insurance, stocks and bonds, real estate, individual retirement accounts (and other retirement plans), money market funds with debit cards or credit cards, certificates of deposit, and other bank-type services.

Q: What is the Securities Investors Protection Corporation (SIPC)?

A: The *Securities Investors Protection Corporation* is a nonprofit corporation created under the provisions of the Securities Investors Protection Act of 1970. The act provides insurance protection to customers of members in the event of the member's insolvency. Each customer's account is protected up to a maximum of $500,000, including $100,000 cash. Most brokerage firms are required by law to be members of SIPC.

Q: Does SIPC insure against losses caused by poor investment decisions?

A: No. SIPC insures investors against potential losses due to the insolvency of a member organization.

Q: What actions will SIPC take to protect a firm's customers?

A: SIPC will generally take one of three actions to protect clients of an insolvent brokerage firm or one that is having difficulty. The actions are:

- Ask the court to appoint an independent trustee to distribute securities to the customers or liquidate the firm.
- Ask to be appointed trustee to liquidate a troubled firm.
- Make direct payments and deliveries to clients without going to court.

Q: What is excess SIPC?

A: Many brokerage firms have purchased insurance from commercial insurance carriers to protect their customers above the limits offered by SIPC. This type of insurance is referred to as excess SIPC.

Q: How important is SIPC coverage to me?

A: You can look at SIPC coverage as similar to any financial firm's insurance, such as FDIC. Well-established brokerage firms usually do not go bankrupt; therefore, most likely you will never require your SIPC coverage. Nevertheless, it is important to make sure you are covered, and covered adequately. If the value of your securities is substantially above the SIPC limits or the limits offered by excess SIPC coverage, you may want to fully review your brokerage firm's insurance coverage or have your advisor review that coverage.

Q: What is the Women's Pension Act?

A: In late 1984, a law was enacted called the Retirement Equity Act. Originally, the law was referred to as the Women's Pension Act. The act gives spouses more influence on the disposition of retirement plan assets. If a married individual wants to name someone other than the spouse as the beneficiary of his or her retirement plan assets, the spouse must sign a consent agreement. The purpose of this law is to protect the rights of spouses.

The act includes many additional provisions, but the most important of these provisions provide for spouses' rights under a qualified retirement plan and allow "qualified domestic relations orders" to protect spouses' rights in case of divorce.

MORE COMMONLY ASKED QUESTIONS

Q: What are Pink Sheets?

A: Each business day, the National Quotations Bureau, Inc., publishes a list of securities being traded by over-the-counter market makers. The list includes the stocks of many small companies that are not included in the mainstream NASDAQ quotations. The quotes are published on long sheets of pink paper; hence the name "Pink Sheets." Your brokerage firm most likely subscribes to the publication.

Q: What are Yellow Sheets?

A: Each business day, the National Quotations Bureau, Inc., publishes a list of unlisted corporate bonds and market makers. The list is published on yellow paper; hence the name "Yellow Sheets." Your brokerage firm most likely subscribes to the publication.

Q: What is the Blue List?

A: The *Blue List* is a daily listing of municipal bond offerings, categorized by state and the name of the brokerage firm offering each bond. The list is printed on blue paper, hence its name. It is published by Standard & Poor's, and your brokerage firm most likely subscribes to the publication.

Q: What is churning?

A: *Churning* is excessive trading in an investor's account. Generally, an excessive amount of buy and sell activity is considered to be against the financial best interests of an investor. Churning is considered to be motivated more by the commissions earned than the client's profit, and thus is considered unethical.

Q: What is a private placement?

A: A *private placement* is a sale of securities to a few investors without the regulations and expense of a public offering. Generally, the number of investors in a private placement may not exceed thirty-five. In some instances, what are called "accredited investors" may be included above and beyond the thirty-five person limit.

Q: What is an accredited investor?

A: Generally, an *accredited investor* is defined as an institutional investor or an individual with a net worth of $1 million or more. Individuals with less net worth, but with an annual income of $200,000 or more, may also be accredited investors. An accredited investor is not counted as one of the limited number of participants in a private placement. Many private placement offerings will have an accredited investor form that spells out the rules for that particular investment and must be completed by any investor who wants to be considered an accredited investor.

Q: What is an insider?

A: An *insider* is an officer or director of a corporation or an individual who owns 10 percent or more of a corporation's stock. The term is also used to refer to someone who has inside information on a corporation that has not been released to the public or is not generally known by public investors.

Q: What is inside information?

A: *Inside information* is generally considered to be information that has not been publicized by a widely used means, and that will materially affect a corporation's stock price.

Q: What is a tombstone?

A: The term *tombstone* refers to a newspaper advertisement that appears after a public offering of securities. The advertisement publicizes the successful effort by the underwriters of the securities. It is called a tombstone because, like a real tombstone, it simply lists a name (the issuer), a date (the offering date), the event (the type of offering), and some related parties (the underwriters). For further details, the tombstone refers to the official offering document.

Q: What is Rule 144 stock?

A: Securities and Exchange *Rule 144* permits the owner of unregistered securities to make a public sale of the securities without a formal registration statement if certain conditions are met. The rule is extremely complex, and anyone who wants to sell stock that is considered Rule 144 stock should get legal advice. As a rule of thumb, Rule 144 sales must represent less than 1 percent of the outstanding stock of a corporation during any ninety-day period.

Q: What is Regulation T?

A: *Regulation T* is the Federal Reserve Board's rule that governs the amount and type of credit that a broker may extend to an investor to purchase, carry, or trade in securities.

Q: What is Regulation U?

A: *Regulation U* is the Federal Reserve Board's rule that governs the amount and type of credit a bank may offer to a customer to purchase, carry, or trade in corporate securities.

Q: What is hypothecation?

A: *Hypothecation* is the formalized pledge of securities, or other assets, as collateral for a loan while the owner retains ownership. For example, when an investor buys securities on margin, the securities are held by the broker as collateral until the loan is repaid.

Q: What is a block trade?

A: A *block trade* is the purchase or sale of an unusually large number of shares or bonds. A block trade in a stock usually involves 10,000 or more shares. A block trade in a bond generally involves a value greater than $200,000. Because of their size, block trades could affect the trading market for a stock or bond, particularly a smaller, less liquid issue.

Q: What is a hot issue?

A: A *hot issue* is a new issue of a security that rises in price as soon as the underwriting is over and active trading starts. If the price on the day of the offering rises enough for a seller to make a $\frac{1}{8}$-point profit or more, the issue is usually determined to be a hot issue.

An immediate rise in price indicates that demand for the new issue is strong, or "hot," and that perhaps the preset underwriting price was a bargain. If an issue is determined to be a hot issue, certain buyers could be restricted under "free-ride" regulations.

Q: What are free-ride regulations?

A: *Free-ride regulations* are regulations prohibiting employees of the issuing company or its underwriters, or family members of such people, from being assigned shares in a hot issue. They are intended to prevent insiders in a company or its underwriters from guaranteeing themselves profits if the company's underwriting is a hot issue. Such profits would constitute an unfair advantage, or "free ride," since the insiders could enjoy preferential treatment in obtaining shares at the underwriting price and selling them for a profit.

Q: What is a green shoe?

A: A *green shoe* is a provision in an underwriting agreement allowing the underwriter to purchase additional shares at the same price as the original offering. The provision gets its name from the company (the Green Shoe Co.) whose offering was the first one to include the provision. The green shoe provision becomes important if the offering is very popular, with demand exceeding the number of shares originally planned for the offering. It allows the underwriters to cover (purchase) shares sold short without the risk of having to cover at higher prices.

Q: What is a chartist?

A: A *chartist* is an analyst who makes buy/sell recommendations or decisions on the basis of the plotted price movements of a security rather than on fundamental analysis of the company issuing it. A chartist is also called a technical analyst.

Q: What is the hemline theory?

A: The *hemline theory* is a stock market forecasting theory that uses the trend of hemline fashions in women's dresses to predict the trend of stock prices. If hemlines are trending down, the theory indicates stock prices should trend downward. If hemlines are trending up, so should stock prices.

Q: What is meant by saying a stock's price "breaks resistance"?

A: The term resistance is used by technical analysts, who study the pattern of a stock's past price movements to make predictions about its future price movement. If a stock's price has shown a pattern of rising to a certain level, but not rising past that level, that price level is termed a *level of resistance*. The more times this pattern repeats, the stronger the resistance factor.

If the stock's price succeeds in rising above the resistance level, it is said to have "broken resistance," or "broken out." Technical analysts believe that breaking resistance indicates that further price appreciation may be imminent, since the stock had enough momentum to overcome significant past resistance.

Q: What is meant by saying a stock's price "breaks support"?

A: The term support is used by technical analysts, who study the pattern of a stock's past price movements to make predictions about its future price movement. If a stock's price has shown a pattern of declining to a certain level, but then rebounding as if that price level were a floor, that price level is termed a *level of support*. The more times this pattern repeats, the stronger the support factor.

If the stock's price decline carries it below the support level, it is said to have "broken support," or "broken down." Technical analysts believe that breaking support indicates that a further price decline may be imminent, since the stock had enough downward momentum to overcome a significant past pattern.

Q: What is meant by saying that a stock's price is "basing"?

A: The term *basing* is used by technical analysts, who study the pattern of a stock's price movement. If a stock's price declines, but then remains at a certain price level for a period of time, it is said to be basing. The longer the price holds at that level, the stronger the base it builds.

Technical analysts believe that a basing pattern indicates that a stock's price decline has finished, and the price may be poised for a subsequent rebound.

Q: How is a stock's trading volume an important indicator?

A: Technical analysts look at a stock's trading volume as an indicator of momentum in its price movement patterns. If a stock's price is rising, or falling, on heavy volume, it is logical to conclude that a lot of investors or some very large investors are contributing to the movement. Heavy volume may thus indicate that the pattern may have strong momentum and continue for some time.

Conversely, if a stock's price is rising, or falling, on decreasing volume, the investor interest in that movement may be thinning out. This may indicate that the pattern is losing momentum and may end soon.

MORE COMMONLY ASKED QUESTIONS

Q: Why do some people say one should never buy a closed-end fund at its original offering?

A: A closed-end fund is first made available through an initial public offering. An initial public offering generally requires hiring lawyers, accountants, investment bankers, and other professionals. Also, brokers will ultimately sell the fund's shares to investors and must be paid for their effort. The fees earned by these professionals can often amount to a noticeable percentage (say 7 percent) of the offering's proceeds.

Since a percentage of the price paid for each share is going for fees, the initial investor is paying more money than the shares will be worth. Many advisors say that this is, in effect, paying a premium for the fund's shares. If you believe that the fund's shares will generally trade at a price equal to (or below) the fund's net asset value per share, you would not want to pay such a premium for the shares.

Some closed-end fund shares, however, subsequently trade at a higher premium. If you believe this will be the case with a certain new fund, the public offering price may, in fact, be a lower-cost way of buying the shares.

Q: What is double taxation?

A: *Double taxation* refers to the fact that a corporation's earnings that are distributed as dividends are taxed twice: the company pays taxes on its earnings, and investors pay taxes on the dividends they receive.

Q: What is the conduit theory?

A: The *conduit theory* is the term for the IRS treatment of income received by certain qualified investment organizations, such as mutual funds, REITs, and limited partnerships. Generally, interest, dividends, capital gains, and other income are passed through to the investors without the mutual fund or partnership being subject to taxation. This avoids the disadvantage of double taxation.

Q: What is Subchapter M?

A: *Subchapter M* refers to the section of the IRS code that permits investment companies (mutual funds) and real estate investment trusts (REITs) to make distributions to shareholders that are taxable only to the shareholders and not to the mutual fund or REIT.

Q: What is a Subchapter S corporation?

A: A *Subchapter S* corporation is a small corporation that qualifies and chooses to be taxed as a partnership rather than a corporation. Under a Subchapter S election, all income would be taxable to the individual owners.

Q: What is the advantage of using appreciated securities to make charitable contributions?

A: If you are making a donation to a charity, you might consider giving appreciated securities instead of cash. If you keep the cash and contribute the securities, you will be able to deduct their full value for income tax purposes. Had you sold the securities and given the cash, the value of the gift would have been reduced by capital gains taxes.

- If you paid $1,000 for securities that now have a value of $10,000, and you make a gift of the securities, the cost of your tax-deductible gift is only $1,000.
- Extremely large gifts of appreciated assets may be subject to an alternative minimum tax (see your tax advisor).

Q: How do I identify my cost basis when selling stocks?

A: Your cost basis in shares of stock is the price you paid when you purchased them plus commissions. Identifying your cost basis may be straightforward if you simply bought the stock in one transaction. But if you bought shares at different prices, you will need to carefully identify which shares you are selling. You do this by instructing your broker which shares are being sold and receiving a written confirmation of the instructions. Your instructions should include the number of shares, purchase price, and date of purchase.

If distributions you have received are considered a return of capital, as some REIT distributions are, your cost basis is reduced by the amount of these distributions.

Q: How can I identify my cost basis when selling mutual fund shares?

A: Identifying the cost basis of mutual fund shares can be quite complicated, since your mutual fund holdings may consist of shares bought at many different dates and prices through new purchases or reinvestment of fund distributions. To assist investors, the Internal Revenue Service allows four different methods of identifying shares:

- Specific identification method
- FIFO (first in, first out) method
- Single category averaging method
- Double category averaging method

Q: How does the specific identification method work?

A: If your records are complete enough that you can identify the purchase date and cost for each share you are selling, you may make specific identification of these shares. As when selling common stocks, if you use the specific identification method, you must instruct the broker or agent exactly which shares you are selling and receive written confirmation for your records.

Q: How does the FIFO method work?

A: The *FIFO* method, which stands for first in, first out, assumes that the first shares you sell are the first shares you bought. If your investment generally rose in value during the time you owned it, the FIFO method will probably result in the greatest gain, and thus produce the highest taxes. Not coincidentally, the IRS requires you to use the FIFO method if your records cannot support another method.

Q: How does the single category averaging method work?

A: In the *single category averaging method*, the total cost of all your shares of the mutual fund is divided by the number of shares you hold to produce an average cost basis for use with all shares. If you elect to use this method, you must use it for all accounts in the same mutual fund, and you must notify the IRS of your election of this method by attaching a statement to your tax return. In determining long- or short-term holding status, the IRS assumes that the first shares you bought are the first shares you sell.

Q: How does the double category averaging method work?

A: In the *double category averaging method*, your mutual fund shares are divided into short-term shares and long-term shares, then the average cost for each category is calculated. You may specify which category of shares you are selling. This allows you to choose the short-term shares (they may have a smaller taxable gain) or the long-term shares (lower long-term capital gain's tax rates may reduce the tax bill).

You must instruct your broker or agent to confirm your choice of category in writing. After short-term shares have been held for longer than a year, they must be transferred into the long-term category.

Q: What is a paper loss?

A: The term *paper loss* refers to an unrealized loss in a security position. Paper losses become realized losses only when a security owned is sold or a short position is covered.

Q: What is a passive investment activity?

A: A *passive activity* is the conduct of any trade or business in which you do not materially participate. You are considered passive if you are not involved in the operations of the activity on a regular, continuous, and substantial basis. The most common examples of passive activity are rental of real estate and participation in limited partnerships.

Q: What is the significance of passive activity?

A: If you are involved in a *passive activity*, you may be in a disadvantageous tax situation. On one hand, any net income from your passive activity is taxable. But any net losses from your passive activity cannot be deducted from nonpassive income to reduce your taxes. In general, passive losses can be deducted only from passive income.

The restrictive rules on passive loss deductions are significant because the most common types of passive activities, such as real estate rental, tend to generate losses on a regular basis. You may consider passive losses to be a "wasted" deduction, since it is generally difficult to find an activity that generates passive income against which to deduct your passive losses. You may, however, accumulate nondeductible passive losses over an unlimited time and deduct them from passive income or from any gain you realize when selling the passive investment in the future. See your tax advisor for details on passive activities.

Q: What are grandfather provisions?

A: *Grandfather provisions* are provisions written into new laws or rules to prevent them from affecting people retroactively. They permit people who previously engaged in certain activities, functions, or investments to continue to qualify under the old laws or rules.

Q: What is phantom income from a limited partnership?

A: *Phantom income* arises when an investment generates taxable income without generating comparable cash income at the same time. As a common example, many limited partnerships generate very substantial tax-deductible losses, which save the investors money on their income taxes when the losses are declared. Many such partnerships also incurred heavy debt to finance their projects for the investors' benefit.

If such a partnership were to fail and be liquidated, however, any unpaid debts would count as taxable proceeds from the liquidation (limited partners cannot be held responsible for unpaid debts), and the limited partners' cost basis would have been reduced by the losses declared in the past. If the partner's taxable proceeds are higher than his or her reduced cost basis, the partner must report a taxable gain. Since the partner generally does not get any cash back from the failed partnership, he or she must pay taxes without receiving any cash income in return. This gives the "phantom income" its name.

MORE COMMONLY ASKED QUESTIONS

Q: Is it advantageous to make IRA contributions early each year?

A: Yes. If you make IRA contributions early each year, you may earn considerably more money over time. Many people wait to make their contributions until the end of the year. In fact, they often wait until the contribution deadline in April of the following year. If you were to make your contribution at the beginning of each year, your contribution would begin to benefit from the IRA's tax deferral much earlier.

If you assume that you make annual IRA contributions of $2,000 and earn 8 percent, an early-contribution policy would make an increasing difference in your retirement capital accumulation:

Contribution Date

Time to Retirement	January 1	April 15 Next Year
5 years	$12,672	$9,523
10 years	$31,291	$26,390
20 years	$98,846	$87,590
30 years	$244,692	$219,715

Q: Can my IRA continue compounding tax-deferred after my death?

A: Yes. If you do not need to substantially deplete your IRA during your retirement, you may want to keep the tax shelter intact as long as possible for your benefit and your heirs'. Your IRA does not necessarily have to terminate at your death. Your beneficiary can maintain the IRA and retain some of the benefits of tax deferral over his or her remaining lifetime. In some instances, the beneficiary must continue the yearly withdrawal schedule that began when you turned $70^1/_2$, but the remaining funds continue to compound tax-deferred.

Since the benefits of tax deferral are greater for longer periods, you may want to name a young beneficiary, such as a grandchild, and set the withdrawal schedule over your joint life expectancy. With this method, the schedule is spread over a much longer period and your heir will ultimately receive significantly more money. The rules are complex, so you should consult your tax advisor if you are considering this method.

 Note: The tax rules covering IRA distributions to beneficiaries are very complex. You should always consult a tax advisor about how the rules may affect your personal situation.

Q: What is a top-heavy retirement plan?

A: The rules governing retirement plans are designed to promote fair treatment of all employees in an organization. Among other goals, the rules discourage allocating a disproportionate share of a plan's benefits to the highest-paid employees. A top-heavy plan is one in which more than 60 percent of the accumulated value is dedicated to "key employees." The regulations restrict key employees' contributions in a top-heavy plan until their share falls below that level.

Q: What is a key employee?

A: A *key employee* is someone whose compensation or ownership could cause him or her to dominate a company's benefits from a retirement plan. The status is defined in a number of ways, including:

- An officer earning over $45,000
- One of the top ten shareholders
- An owner of more than 5 percent of the organization
- An owner of over 1 percent of the organization earning over $150,000

Q: How do I choose a trustee for a trust?

A: The most important decision when establishing any trust is choosing proper trustees to achieve the goals you have established. Individual trustees, such as family members or trusted advisors, should be close enough to you to know your intentions beyond what is written in the trust document. Their familiarity with your priorities and your heirs' needs should lead them to watch the trust's investments, keep fees down, and do as you intended.

A corporate trustee, such as a bank or trust company, should have the administrative, custodial, and investment capabilities to handle your trust's affairs on a day-to-day basis. Though such considerations may favor large institutions, a smaller corporate trustee may have less bureaucracy and the flexibility to tailor its fees to your trust's needs. Your estate planning advisor should assist you in selecting a trustee or co-trustees, as well as in writing the all-important rules for succession and removal of a trustee.

 Note: The terms of your trust document will control the powers, authority, and actions of the trustee or co-trustees.

Q: What is the Glass-Steagall Act?

A: The *Glass-Steagall Act* is a federal law, passed during the Depression of the 1930s, that prohibits commercial banks from owning brokerages. The law also prohibits commercial banks from owning, underwriting, or trading corporate securities for many of their accounts. In recent years, the provisions of the law have been diluted, and many commercial banks now own brokerage subsidiaries.

Q: What is a legal transfer?

A: A *legal transfer* is a brokerage industry term that refers to a transaction that requires formal legal documentation. Examples of a legal transfer would include transactions in a security registered in the name of a decedent or a corporation. When a security registered in a legal form is sold, payment cannot be made to the seller until the legal registration is removed from the security.

Q: Is Uniform Gift to Minors a legal form of registration?

A: No. Securities registered under the Uniform Gift to Minors Act can be sold without being reregistered. All that is required is the signature of the guardian.

Q: What is a stock power?

A: A *stock power* is a form the owner signs to sell or transfer a registered security. A stock power is a separate piece of paper that serves the same function as the transfer form on the reverse side of a security's certificate. Once a stock power is signed by the registered owner, witnessed and guaranteed by a member of the New York Stock Exchange or a commercial bank, and attached to the registered certificate, the security can be transferred to the new owner.

Q: Is a stock power different from a bond power?

A: Generally, no. Most stock powers will be phrased so that they can be either a stock or a bond power.

Q: What is arbitration?

A: *Arbitration* is a method of settling controversies or claims that is an alternative to seeking settlement through the courts. Each exchange and the National Association of Securities Dealers have provisions for an arbitration procedure for settling disputes between brokerage firms or between brokerage firms and investors. Many brokerage firms require their brokers and employees, and also investors who deal with them, to sign forms that require settlement of disputes through arbitration rather than through the courts.

Q: What is the Curb?

A: The *Curb* is the nickname for the American Stock Exchange. Prior to the 1920s, the American Stock Exchange conducted its business outdoors on the curb of Broad Street in New York City.

Q: What is the Nifty Fifty?

A: The term *Nifty Fifty* was used to describe the 50 stocks most preferred by institutional investors during the 1970s.

MORE COMMONLY ASKED QUESTIONS

Q: What is a penny stock?

A: *Penny stock* is a term used to describe a relatively low-priced speculative stock. The term usually refers to stocks that sell for less than $1 per share, although it can also be used to refer to stocks that sell for somewhat higher prices. Many brokerage firms have special rules and margin requirements for penny stocks.

Q: What is short interest?

A: *Short interest* is the total short position in a stock, or the number of shares that have been sold without delivering certificates and thus represent future buying of that stock.

Q: What is the significance of short interest?

A: Before the popularity of options, a large short interest position in a stock was considered to be bullish because it represented future buying power. With the popularity of options and program trading, short interest is no longer considered to be as bullish as in the past.

Q: What is a COD transaction?

A: COD (*cash on delivery*) is the common designation on buy orders for institutional or very large investors. In a COD transaction, the broker buys a security for an investor and will be paid when the security is delivered to the buyer's agent.

Q: What is a DVP transaction?

A: *DVP* (*delivery versus payment*) is the common designation on sell orders for institutional or very large investors. In a DVP transaction, the broker sells a security for an investor and will be given the certificate by the seller's agent when payment is made to the agent.

Q: What does "when distributed" mean?

A: The term *when distributed* means that a transaction to buy or sell a security is conditioned upon the underlying security being delivered. For example, if a corporation is spinning off a subsidiary, the shares of the subsidiary may be trading before the spin-off date, but delivery cannot be made and transactions completed until the corporation delivers certificates representing ownership in the subsidiary. Until that time, the shares of the subsidiary are said to be trading when distributed.

Q: What does "when issued" mean?

A: A *when issued* transaction is a purchase or sale that establishes the price, but not the settlement date. The settlement date will be set when the security is available for delivery.

Q: What is a due bill?

A: A *due bill* is the documentation for a specified number of shares or dollars that a seller must deliver to a buyer. A due bill arises when a transaction occurs so close to the settlement date that there is no time to get the buyer's name registered for payment. The due bill ensures that the buyer will receive the cash or distribution to which he or she is entitled.

Q: What is a Yankee bond?

A: *Yankee bond* is a brokerage industry term for a bond of a foreign issuer that is denominated in dollars and registered for sale in the United States.

Q: What is a straight bond?

A: A *straight bond* is any bond that is not convertible into another security.

Q: What is a baby bond?

A: A *baby bond* is a bond with a face value of less than the usual $1,000. Many baby bonds have a face value of $100 or $500.

Q: Do banks report deposits and withdrawals to the IRS?

A: Banks do not report deposits and withdrawals unless the amount is over $10,000 and in cash. Smaller transactions are not seen as significant enough, and noncash transactions, such as check payments and wire transfers, leave a paper record that can be traced.

The intent of the reporting requirement is to prevent major illegal activities from being hidden by using untraceable cash. In practice, most legitimate individuals and businesses would not carry out major transactions in cash, but would prefer to use checks and other methods to assist their record keeping.

CLOSING THOUGHTS

The authors of this book have used the question-and-answer format to give you straightforward answers to questions on money and investments and how they are used.

By using the question-and-answer format, the authors have taken the same approach to helping you learn about money and investing that was used in school and that you have continued to use throughout your life: You acquire knowledge by getting the answers to questions. We have attempted to ask the right questions and give you understandable answers.

The first chapters take you through investment opportunities, such as your money, stocks, bonds, mutual funds, and life insurance and annuities. These are the investment products you will use to accumulate wealth. Although you may never use some of the investment opportunities discussed, reading this book will give you a better understanding of their benefits (and risks). You can then determine which investments are appropriate for you given your personal situation.

The next chapters answer questions about the ways in which you can use the investments discussed in the earlier chapters to achieve your financial goals. They discuss such topics as retirement plans, retirement planning, estate planning, and advisors.

The book is designed to cover the information you will need throughout your entire financial life cycle. The majority of the questions and answers concern building wealth during your earlier years. However, once you have accumulated wealth and achieved your financial goals, you will want to ensure that your assets are distributed in accordance with your wishes. While this is something you may not like to think about, you should consider how you want the assets in your estate to be distributed and decide if you have an adequate amount of life insurance.

By reading this book, you have taken steps to learn about money and investments so that you can achieve your personal financial goals. Once you have had the satisfaction of obtaining the wealth you want, you can start thinking about how you will enjoy it. With financial independence, you can have a comfortable lifestyle during retirement, using the income from your investments rather than having to continue to work. You will have the opportunity to travel, play golf, fish, provide for children or grandchildren, support your favorite charity or community activities, or do whatever else you wish.

Hopefully, this material will assist you in working with your advisors. The goal of this book is not to make you an expert in all the financial areas you will be involved with during your financial life cycle. You should let your professional advisors do their job. However, this material will help you to better understand the advice you receive.

If you are a beginning investor or just starting your financial life cycle, you will probably want to read this book from cover to cover. If you are a seasoned investor, you will probably scan the questions and answers to see if you can pick up some new ideas. Regardless of your investment experience, the questions and answers will be a continuing resource as you hear about different investment opportunities and how they are used.

This book will probably not be the last investment book you will read. It is not an exhaustive discussion of investing. Rather, it is intended to present basic information in an easy-to-understand way. You can build on this knowledge by doing additional research or by working with your advisors. In doing so, you will be moving along the path to wealth accumulation and a comfortable financial life style.

INDEX

INDEX

D

E

F

INDEX

INDEX

INDEX

INDEX